China Since 1978

Studies on Contemporary Asia

China Since 1978

Reform, Modernisation and 'Socialism with Chinese Characteristics'

Colin Mackerras

Pradeep Taneja

Graham Young

Longman Cheshire

St. Martin's Press
New York

Longman Cheshire Pty Limited
Longman House
Kings Gardens
95 Coventry Street
Melbourne 3205 Australia

Offices in Sydney, Brisbane, Adelaide and Perth. Associated companies, branches and representatives throughout the world.

First published 1994

Designed by Lauren Statham, Alice Graphics
Set in 11/13 Plantin
Produced by Longman Cheshire Pty Limited
Printed in Singapore

First published in the United States of America 1993 by
Scholarly and Reference Division,
ST. MARTIN'S PRESS, INC.,
175 Fifth Avenue,
New York, N.Y. 10010

ISBN 0-312-10252-6 (Cl)
ISBN 0-312-10306-9 (PBK)

Library of Congress Cataloging-in-Publication Data

China since 1978 : reform, modernisation and 'socialism with Chinese characteristics' / Colin Mackerras, Pradeep Taneja, Graham Young.
p. cm.
Includes bibliographical references and index.
ISBN 0-312-10252-6. — ISBN 0-312-10306-9 (pbk.)
1. China—Politics and government—1976– 2. China—Economic policy-1976– 3. China—Economic conditions—1976– 4. China—Foreign relations—1976– I. Mackerras, Colin. II. Taneja. Pradeep. III. Young, Graham.
DS779.26.C473527 1993
951.05'8--dc20 93-24509
CIP

National Library of Australia
Cataloguing-in-Publication data

Mackerras, Colin, 1939-
China since 1978.

Bibliography.
Includes index.
ISBN 0 582 87106.9.
ISBN 0 582 80183 4 (pbk.).

1. China - Politics and government - 1976– . 2. China — Economic policy — 1976– . 3. China — Social conditions — 1976- . I. Taneja, Pradeep. II. Young, Graham. III. Title. (Series : Studies on contemporary Asia).

951.058

Contents

1 Introduction

THE aim of this book is to provide a simple and accessible account of the history of China from 1978 to 1992. The particular aspects of that history covered attempt to focus on the themes of reform and modernisation. Some of the policies most related to reform and modernisation, which have made the greatest contribution to them, are given special coverage.

Late in 1978 a series of intense debates took place within the Chinese leadership, culminating in the Third Plenary Session of the Eleventh Central Committee in December. Two closely related results of these debates and of the Third Plenum stand out as important. One was the establishment of reform policies, originally proposed several years earlier by Zhou Enlai. This primarily involved a thrust towards the modernisation of China's economy and society as the supreme official line of the Chinese Communist Party (CCP) and of the People's Republic of China (PRC). The other was the consolidation of the power of Deng Xiaoping, who had long advocated and pushed reform and modernisation for China. Deng's brand of reformed Marxism–Leninism with modernisation as its core is called 'socialism with Chinese characteristics'.

For Deng Xiaoping, modernisation meant more industrialisation, greater use of more advanced technology throughout society — including the countryside and the military — more rapid economic development and a higher standard of living for as many people as possible. It also meant a transformation of the people's attitudes, leading them to want to move away from the stereotypes of the Cultural Revolution period and from the bonds of the traditional feudal past, and towards a society more open to the outside world. One part of Deng's 'modern' China was a formal legal system before which everyone would be equal. On the other hand, at no time did Deng Xiaoping envisage that a more modern society guided by 'socialism with Chinese characteristics' would result in a threat to — let alone the overthrow of — the CCP, or of the formal abandonment of Marxism–Leninism as the ideological basis of China. Modernisation meant democracy in the sense that people would be freer to learn new ways and ideas and discard the 'mass line' of the Maoist era, but it certainly did not mean the Western style in which rival parties would compete for political power. It is unlikely that in 1978 Deng Xiaoping and his followers ever seriously confronted the possibility that China would break up as it modernised, but for them modernisation most certainly meant a strengthening of national unity, not a weakening.

This book is designed not as an academic monograph, but as a textbook. The main target readership is university or college students. However, since the coverage is quite broad and general, the authors hope that journalists, business people or general readers wishing to gain an understanding of China since 1978, under the leadership of Deng Xiaoping, may find it interesting and suitable for their purposes.

The three authors of this book belong to different disciplines: history, political economy and political science. In that sense this book is genuinely multidisciplinary. Within that framework, the authors have sought to describe, analyse and interpret the development of the human condition in the contemporary period in one part of the world: China. The book is descriptive in that it seeks to convey the kind of accurate information which the authors think necessary for a good basic understanding of Chinese history from the late 1970s to the early 1990s. It is analytical and interpretative in its division and arrangement of material, in the selection of information, and in the significance which the authors attach to particular events or other facts.

The particular aspects of development selected for treatment in this book are dictated by three related but separate factors. These are the actual and potential needs of the university and college students for whom the book is mainly designed; the social trends operating in the countries where it is likely to be most useful; and the scales of importance adopted by the three authors.

The control of population growth and conservation of the environment are extremely pressing issues throughout the world in the 1990s. Natural and social scientists are among those groups of people who have for years been aware of the magnitude of the problems posed by population increases and environmental despoliation. In the case of population, governments have tried to find solutions for some time. Population size looms as a recognised and enormous problem in China, and the government has been at the forefront of world authorities in its preparedness to take action. As far as the environment is concerned, governments were, until the late 1980s, generally slower to recognise the urgency for solutions. The Chinese government has never placed the same priority on the environment that it has accorded to curbing population increases. Nevertheless, trends in the West and the authors' own values have convinced them of the need to include a chapter on the environment in a book on contemporary Chinese history.

There is no special message in this book. All three authors recognise both the immense problems which the Chinese leaders have faced in the era of reform and their achievements — both their successes and failures; both their good and bad actions. All authors were and remain appalled at the Beijing massacre of June 1989, and see it as a very black mark on the period of reform. On the other hand, none sees it as a reason for negating everything China, or indeed Deng Xiaoping, has accomplished since 1978.

All authors know the Chinese language and have lived in and travelled widely in China during the period with which this book is concerned. Clearly each has relied to some extent on his personal experiences and on the information and insights he has gathered in China. All follow the Chinese media and read works in Chinese on their topics of special interest, and have used them in preparing this book. In addition, the extensive and excellent research which has been carried out in the West since the late 1970s has proved an invaluable reservoir of information. The analytical bibliography at the end of the book attempts to draw attention to some of the best works relevant to the topics of the chapters in this book, as well as to giving the reader some idea of where to look further for insights and information.

This is a genuinely joint work in the sense that each author has studied carefully and critiqued what the others have written with a view to avoiding excessive overlap and securing some coherence and integration in the book as a whole. However, one or other of the authors has undertaken the basic writing of each chapter. Colin Mackerras has written Chapters 1–5, 11, 13, 14, 15, 16 and 18; Pradeep Taneja Chapters 6–8, 12 and 17; and Graham Young Chapters 9 and 10.

We acknowledge gratefully comments and criticisms from others, in particular Professors David Goodman of Murdoch University and Peter Lisowski of the University of Tasmania. However, each author remains responsible for the points of view expressed in his own chapters, as well as for any mistakes which might have survived the extensive checking and criticism to which the text has been subjected.

2 Historical Background

THREE personalities have dominated China's politics since the Chinese Communist Party (CCP) came to power on 1 October 1949 and established the People's Republic of China (PRC). They are Mao Zedong, Zhou Enlai and Deng Xiaoping.

Mao Zedong was the Chairman of the CCP without a break from March 1943 until his death on 9 September 1976. In addition, he was President of the PRC from 1949 until 1959, this being the most senior state (as opposed to Party) position. Zhou Enlai was Premier of the PRC government from its establishment until his death on 8 January 1976. He was also Minister of Foreign Affairs from 1949 to 1958 and dominated China's foreign relations throughout the whole period until his death.

Alone among the three, the career of Deng Xiaoping spans the whole period of the CCP's and PRC's history so far (1992). He had already occupied major CCP and state positions from 1949 to the beginning of the Cultural Revolution in 1966, particularly First Secretary of the CCP Central Committee's Secretariat from 1956. At that time, Deng was subordinate both to Mao and Zhou and his career suffered interruptions through defeat in power struggles. By far the most serious hiatus was during the Cultural Revolution, when for several years he was publicly humiliated and excoriated as 'the Number 2 person in authority taking the capitalist road'. Deng's period of greatest power was from the end of 1978 onwards — in other words, the period of focus of this book.

Among the many other personalities who played a prominent role in PRC history, there was one in particular who competed with Mao and Zhou in the period 1949–66. Liu Shaoqi occupied senior CCP and state posts during that period, including replacing Mao Zedong as the President of the PRC in 1959. During the Cultural Revolution, Mao Zedong had him humiliated as 'the Number 1 Party person in authority taking the capitalist road'. Less fortunate than Deng Xiaoping, he died in prison in 1969 after having been expelled from the Party and dismissed from all posts the year before.

These four men were all dedicated Marxist–Leninists. Yet even such brief biograpical treatments show that in general terms they were associated with particular types of policies. Mao Zedong was the architect of the ultra-radical Cultural Revolution, with its passionate anti-bureaucratism; Zhou Enlai was the diplomat who helped moderate Mao's worst excesses; while Deng Xiaoping and Liu Shaoqi were much more interested in using Marxism–Leninism for economic growth and social progress than for egalitarian revolution.

The introductory period, 1949–66

The early to mid-1950s were a period of consolidation of CCP rule. Given the appalling state of the economy and the disintegration of society in the late 1940s following a century or so of turbulence, civil war and foreign occupation, the early period of CCP rule was a reasonably creditable one. The economy recovered and the people were generally enthusiastic about their new rulers. China was strongly supported by the Soviet Union, at that time an extremely powerful socialist state.

Certainly there were problems. The Chinese faced implacable opposition from abroad, especially from the United States, and the internal opposition did not simply give up because it had lost power. Many of the CCP's main reforms, such as land reform, turned out to be very violent affairs, and many people were killed in the process of revolution.

But the fact is that the CCP did succeed in effecting a major transfer of power which destroyed the richest classes, such as the landlords and comprador bourgeoisie, redistributed land and much other property to the poorer classes, and carried out some much-needed reforms such as eliminating the worst excesses of oppression against women and the minority nationalities. The new regime succeeded in reuniting the country under a single government more effectively than any other since the late years of the Qing dynasty (1644–1911). The CCP's political and economic order was clearly one which worked reasonably well and brought major political, economic and social benefits to the Chinese people.

Mao Zedong was a revolutionary who wanted much more than a stable economy and society for China. At least from the late 1950s he appeared bent on changing the nature of the Chinese people altogether, to make them more co-operative and more anxious to 'serve the people', rather than being concerned about individualistic or family interests. In 1958 he engineered two major related social experiments. One was the Great Leap Forward, the other the people's communes. Both relied on the masses to raise production and thrust China forward to a new and supposedly higher level of socialism. In the countryside, the people's communes pushed peasants into large co-operative groups in which land was collectively owned and worked, and the private economy dwindled. The experiments were disastrous failures and resulted not in a leap forward, but instead a severe downturn in the economy, including a famine so catastrophic that China's overall population showed an actual decline in both 1960 and 1961.

The country recovered somewhat during the 1960s. The Great Leap Forward was discontinued. The people's communes survived, but they were changed in nature to some extent to allow for larger private plots of land and a much greater degree of private life and production in general. Mao postponed but did not cancel his attempt to take China on to a radical socialist path. The very clear opposition which his Great Leap Forward policies had aroused both within the CCP and society as a whole did not deflect him from his course. No sooner did the economy begin to recover than he began measures for a new and larger attempt at radicalisation. In 1962 he began to re-emphasise the importance of class struggle in a Marxist–Leninist state.

For Mao, class and class struggle became an absolute obsession. He became convinced that the bourgeoisie was still plotting a comeback, and even that senior members of the CCP were bourgeois elements in disguise. These he dubbed as 'revisionists'. In the meantime, he became convinced that the Soviet Union was taking a revisionist road which was destroying the gains of the revolution there. He decided that, although the economic base had undergone revolution in China, it was necessary to carry out yet another revolution — this time in the superstructure of Chinese society: its culture. He planned that this revolution would transform the superstructure of Chinese society into a proletarian culture.

Most of the senior leaders believed that these radical notions were both fatally flawed and harmful. They saw no need at all for another revolution in the superstructure of Chinese society, and were certain that a cultural revolution such as the one Mao envisaged would have devastating effects on China's economy and its social stability. They also saw that they themselves were under direct and serious threat from this revolution. Consequently, most of them opposed it. Determined to get his way, Mao appealed to the youth of the country, especially the students, among whom his notions found intense support.

The Cultural Revolution

In August 1966, Mao pushed through the Central Committee a decision in favour of undertaking a cultural revolution. The document recording this decision describes it as 'a great revolution that touches people to their very souls and constitutes a new stage in the development of the socialist revolution in our country, a stage which is both broader and deeper'.[1] Immediately afterwards, Mao held several gigantic rallies in Tiananmen Square in the centre of the PRC capital, Beijing, at which he gave his blessing to the Red Guards, or young people who were to be responsible for carrying out this revolution.

The main two leaders whom Mao designated as revisionists opposing his revolution were Liu Shaoqi and Deng Xiaoping. His chosen deputy was Lin Biao, who had been appointed as Minister of National Defence and thus a leader of the People's Liberation Army (PLA) in 1959. Lin called himself an ardent supporter of Mao and the radical notions which underlay the Cultural Revolution. He pushed an excessive, even grotesque, personality cult for Mao and organised the publication of *Quotations from Chairman Mao Zedong (Mao Zhuxi yulu)*, usually called simply 'the little red book'. By the end of 1966, over 350 million copies of this book had been published. Mao's wife Jiang Qing also gave very strong assistance to his aims in the Cultural Revolution, not only through playing a major political role but also through carrying out a very radical but desperately unpopular revolution in the arts, especially the Peking opera.

Another supporter of the Cultural Revolution was Zhou Enlai. Unlike Lin Biao or Jiang Qing, however, he was keen to prevent the excesses which it involved and was a moderating influence throughout. What he really thought about it remains unclear, but he was quite certainly determined not to quarrel with Mao.

The young Red Guards took their job and Mao's notions extremely seriously and appeared to believe in them passionately. Mao's recipe for revolution was, however, extremely misguided. Attempts to destroy the old culture included the public humiliation of any individuals associated with it, the banning of most old-fashioned, traditional or Western art, and the suppression of virtually all forms of religious practice, which involved the closing and ransacking of churches and temples.

The Cultural Revolution was designed as a seizure of power by the masses from all persons in authority perceived as taking the capitalist road. Not surprisingly, those so accused disagreed with the charge, thinking of themselves as honest people who had devoted their lives to the revolution. They resisted pressures from young persons shouting Maoist slogans and carrying banners to yield up their power to 'true revolutionaries'. The Maoists themselves split into factions, each claiming to be more revolutionary than the others. Despite Zhou Enlai's efforts to prevent it, violence broke out often, with all-out civil war occurring in quite a few locations.

One important specific instance was in Wuhan, capital of the central Chinese province of Hubei, in July and August 1967. The regional military commander, Chen Zaidao, led a large faction hostile to the Cultural Revolution, which was supported by local Red Guard groups. After an attempt by Zhou Enlai to mediate between them failed, war broke out, lasting nearly three weeks. Although Chen Zaidao was defeated and dismissed, the incident threatened a return to warlordism, which the centre could ill afford to tolerate. In 1968, serious localised civil wars costing many lives broke out in several parts of China, including Sichuan and Guangxi.

One of the aims of the revolution was to create a new and supposedly more revolutionary and egalitarian mass system of administration. The model selected was the 'revolutionary committee', a tripartite alliance among the masses, the army and the revolutionary cadres. At the provincial level the first of these was set up in Heilongjiang, in China's extreme north-east, in January 1967. In September 1968 the last two were established in Tibet and Xinjiang, both autonomous regions of minority nationalities in the far west. All units at almost all levels of society, whether government or not, were encouraged to establish a revolutionary committee, including communes, factories, educational institutions, commercial enterprises and art troupes.

In October 1968, the Central Committee expelled Liu Shaoqi from the Party and dismissed him from all his posts. He was imprisoned and died in November 1969, although this fate was kept a total secret at the time. Mao later contrived to have even the post of President of the PRC abolished, arguing that it had been poisoned by one occupant, the revisionist Liu, and was unnecessary in his new revolutionary order. Neither of the two PRC Constitutions influenced by the Cultural Revolution, those of 1975 and 1978, includes provisions for the post of President.

In a formal sense, Mao had been victorious in the Cultural Revolution. He had brought about the downfall of his main enemies and the institution of his central policies. But in fact the new political order was extremely fragile and rent by dissension. China had paid dearly for Mao's victory. The education system had closed down universities for several years while people argued about how best to implement a revolution in education. To maintain his revolutionary clique in power and to keep the people's revolutionary spirit alive, Mao felt it was necessary to orchestrate a series of ideological campaigns in favour of his particular line. Most people found them not only a waste of time and tedious in the extreme, but also harmful to production as well as to national unity and stability.

The worst case of a split within the CCP was between Mao and Lin Biao. In 1969 the CCP Constitution adopted by the Ninth Party Congress had specified Lin as 'Chairman Mao Tsetung's [Zedong's] comrade-in-arms and successor'.[2] However, in 1971 Lin turned against Mao, conspiring to assassinate him and seize power. The plan failed, so Lin fled towards the Soviet Union on an aircraft which crashed in Mongolia, killing all on board. At least that is the theory which, after a long silence, the Chinese authorities first revealed late in July 1972 through the Chinese Embassy in Algiers and later embellished at some length, especially at the trial of the gang of four in 1980 (see Chapter 3). A document purporting to be the text of Lin Biao's plot was published in the Taiwan press on 13 April 1972 and, although it has never been published in the PRC, it has often been cited there as genuine. According to this document, Lin had become very disillusioned by Mao's behaviour during the Cultural Revolution, coming to the conclusion that he was 'the biggest feudal despot in Chinese history'. Mao and his followers had 'turned China's state machine into a kind of meat grinder for mutual slaughter and strife' and 'made the Party and the whole country's political life into a patriarchal life of the feudal, dictatorial and autocratic type'.[3]

There are several alternative explanations of what happened. One theory, put forward by a man writing under the pen-name of Yao Ming-le and claiming to be based on inside information, argues that Mao invited Lin Biao to a banquet after finding out through Zhou Enlai that Lin was plotting against him, and then had him blown up. Meanwhile a separate anti-Mao plot was being hatched by Lin Biao's son Lin Liguo. It was he who fled on the plane which crashed in Mongolia.[4] Yet another theory alleges that it was Mao's wife Jiang Qing who eliminated Lin Biao because of the threat he posed to her own ambition to rule China. According to this version of events, which originated from a Soviet-run clandestine radio station in 1986, agents of the gang of four murdered Lin Biao and his family and later staged the plane crash, having loaded their bodies on board. A Soviet account based on the reminiscences of the Chinese Ambassador in Mongolia at the time of Lin's death, Xu Wenyi, and of Mongolian eyewitnesses, argues that Lin Biao, his wife Ye Qun and son Lin Liguo were definitely on board a Chinese airliner which crashed over Mongolia in mid-September 1973.[5] In 1990, two Mongolian officials confirmed that they had indeed found a crashed aircraft from China, but there was no evidence that Lin Biao was on board.[6] The Soviet story would support the official Chinese version, while the 1990 Mongolian account would disprove it and go some way towards clearing Jiang Qing, as well as lending some credence to Yao Ming-le's story. The whole episode has the air of a spy-thriller and we may never know what really happened. On two important points, however, all accounts agree: there was major dissension and plotting in the Chinese leadership, and Lin Biao died as a result.

Soon after Lin Biao was out of the way, Mao launched a campaign against him, linking him with China's sage of ancient times, Confucius. This was the Campaign to Criticise Lin Biao and Confucius, which began in 1973 and reached the proportions of a mass movement in the early months of 1974. The Chinese people to whom Lin Biao had so recently been presented as Mao's close comrade-in-arms and successor were now asked to excoriate him as a traitor and would-be assassin. It is hardly surprising that there was much confusion in their minds and that the Lin Biao affair had the effect of seriously weakening the notion of the Cultural Revolution.

The events of 1976

The year 1976 turned out to be a dramatic one in PRC history. It began with the death of Zhou Enlai and an outpouring of grief in his memory. It was widely assumed that his successor as Premier would be Deng Xiaoping, who had returned to prominence in 1973 after his disgrace during the early years of the Cultural Revolution. However, Mao launched another of his campaigns — his last, as it turned out — against Deng Xiaoping. Instead, it was the comparative non-entity Hua Guofeng who assumed the role of Acting Premier in February 1976.

On 5 April a massive demonstration of mourning for Zhou Enlai in Tiananmen Square in central Beijing turned to violence, with some deaths and destruction of property. The radical faction led by Jiang Qing immediately leapt in to declare this Tiananmen Incident 'a counter-revolutionary political incident'. Hua Guofeng, who at this stage had thrown in his lot with the radicals, was appointed as Deputy Chairman of the CCP under Mao and confirmed as Premier on 7 April.

One of the features of Mao Zedong's last years was the series of foreign visiting leaders wanting to see the aged revolutionary while they still had the chance. All such meetings were ritually photographed and displayed to the people, each one showing Mao weaker and sicker than the previous one. At last, on 15 June 1976, a government spokesman announced that Mao was now too busy with his work to see distinguished foreign visitors — in other words, he was too ill.

On 28 July, nature stepped into the mounting political crisis with a gigantic earthquake in the coal city of Tangshan in Hebei province, close enough to Beijing to be felt there. There were many casualties, including deaths running into hundreds of thousands. Hua Guofeng led a delegation to visit the earthquake-stricken city. The radicals tried to make political capital out of the disaster for their campaign against the unfortunate Deng Xiaoping and issued divisive, even idiotic, statements such as the following:

> The broad masses of the people in the earthquake-stricken areas were deeply moved by the fact that Chairman Mao and the Party Central Committee had sent the delegation to visit them . . . Under the impetus of the struggle to criticise Teng Hsiao-ping [Deng Xiaoping] and beat back the Right deviationist attempt to reverse correct ver-

dicts and taking class struggle as the key link, they pledged to work hard and self-reliantly and fight in unity so as to restore production and rebuild their homes as soon as possible. They expressed the determination to fear no sacrifice and surmount every difficulty to win victory.[7]

Apart from the economic effects of so large an earthquake in a major coal-producing area in a country where energy is based on coal, earthquakes are traditionally taken as signs of dynastic change in China. With Mao clearly near death, no amount of revolutionary sloganeering was going to persuade the Chinese people that this earthquake was other than a sign of the pending end of an era. Duly Mao Zedong died on 9 September. There was mourning, of course, though probably less deeply felt than for Zhou Enlai only a few months earlier. There was relief that at last the aged tyrant had gone. But above all there was apprehension over who would take control next.

Hua Guofeng's visit to Tangshan had a significant effect on his political ideas, even though this was not obvious at the time. It convinced him that the endless campaigns simply could not go on, and that what China needed above all was stability. Jiang Qing was unrepentant. She was ambitious to take over the Party Chairmanship to replace Mao. Relations between her and Hua Guofeng deteriorated, with open arguments erupting at major CCP meetings.

It was Hua Guofeng who emerged victorious in this power struggle. On 6 October he had four of the leaders of the radical faction, headed by Jiang Qing, placed under house arrest, an event known as 'the smashing of the gang of four'. He then immediately had himself declared the CCP Chairman in succession to Mao. At a mass rally on 24 October 1976 he had Beijing's First Party Secretary, Wu De, announce that on 30 April Mao had designated Hua Guofeng as his successor by writing the six characters *ni ban shi, wo fang xin*, 'with you in charge, I'm at ease'.[8] At the same rally, a major campaign against the 'gang of four' was launched.[9]

In a major speech on 25 December, Hua Guofeng made reference to a 'grand plan' he claimed Mao Zedong had 'mapped out' and Zhou Enlai had reiterated in January 1975. Its aim was to strengthen China's economy and specifically 'to accomplish the comprehensive modernisation of agriculture, industry, national defence and science and technology and bring our national economy to the front ranks in the world before the end of the century'.[10]

The successor interregnum

Hua Guofeng had achieved the nation's highest positions. Nevertheless, he faced the daunting task of establishing his own legitimacy and authority in the shadow of the two giants (at that stage) of PRC history: CCP Chairman Mao Zedong and Premier Zhou Enlai. Hua had gained enormous kudos from his overthrow of the gang of four, but this was hardly equivalent to proving himself able to govern the country effectively, especially given the very difficult situation in which it found itself.

Hua's basic policy was to continue overall support for the policies of the Cultural Revolution and for Chairman Mao, but to denounce the gang of four for their wild exaggerations in pushing his ideas too far and hence seriously undermining their effectiveness. The gang of four may have looked like leftists, but in fact they were counter-revolutionary rightists, and would have brought the country to a total civil war had they remained in power. Hua's appeal continued to be to Chairman Mao's authority.

Hua saw his task as righting the excesses of the gang of four. In the economic field, his policy was summed up by the term 'four modernisations', those of agriculture, industry, national defence and science and technology to which he had referred in his 25 December speech. In other fields China entered a period which was somewhat less tense and more optimistic than the preceding years had been, and one in which it was possible to blame all ills on the catch-all scapegoat the 'gang of four'.

In leadership terms, Hua's major problem was what to do about Deng Xiaoping. With the fall of the gang of four, the anti-Deng campaign began to wither, and died not long afterwards. Hua might well fear that Deng Xiaoping could become a rival if he returned to power. But his influence and stature were already so great that Hua could hardly prevent his rehabilitation forever. In July 1977, the Party Central Committee decided to restore Deng Xiaoping to all his posts, including Deputy Chairman of the CCP and Vice-Premier of the State Council. It also confirmed Hua Guofeng as CCP Chairman.

The appointments were the prelude to the Eleventh National Congress of the CCP, which took place from 12–18 August 1977. Hua's report continued to stress his preoccupation with the evils of the gang of four, but also reiterated how necessary and desirable he believed the Cultural Revolution to have been. Since class struggle continued to exist and would become very sharp at times, there would obviously need to be many more political revolutions in the future 'in the nature of the Cultural Revolution'. However, Hua also cited Mao's authority to show the need for stability at present and declared that 'the smashing of the "gang of four" marks the triumphant conclusion of our first Great Proletarian Cultural Revolution, which lasted eleven years'.[11] For the first time, the Cultural Revolution was declared to be over.

Over the year and a half following the Eleventh Congress, the political order which the Cultural Revolution had destroyed revived at an accelerating pace. During 1978 there were major meetings not only of the National People's Congress, which had indeed convened once during the Cultural Revolution years, but also of many major organisations which had been dormant and which had apparently been destroyed. The meetings included one of the national committee of the Chinese National Federation of Literature and Art Circles from 27 May–5 June, the Fourth National Women's Congress from 8–17 September, the Ninth National Congress of Chinese Trade Unions and the Tenth National Congress of the Communist Youth League of China, the last two in October 1978.

The Fifth National People's Congress, the first session of which met from 24 February–5 March 1978, confirmed Hua Guofeng in his role as Premier. It also adopted a new PRC Constitution. Although it continued the rhetoric of the Cultural Revolution, there were some significant changes which suggested that some ideas not only of the gang of four but even of Mao were beginning to be downgraded. One was the status of revolutionary committees, the organs of administrative power introduced as a result of the Cultural Revolution. Under the 1978 Constitution these remained only as governmental organisations, a category which includes provinces, counties and communes. But in non-governmental units such as factories, educational institutions and cultural organisations they were replaced by directors, executives and other such people. The Cultural Revolution's notion of mass participation was thus largely conceded as having failed and as being inappropriate to the new order.

Intellectuals were at the forefront of pushing for a much more rapid retreat from the Cultural Revolution and for a greater emphasis on modernisation. Many believed that the vitriolic and persistent condemnation of the gang of four was inconsistent with the continuing praise heaped on Chairman Mao, who apparently could still do no wrong. On 19 November 1978 a fourteen-page poster appeared on a wall in central Beijing, suggesting that Mao was to blame for supporting the gang of four and orchestrating the campaign against Deng Xiaoping in 1976. The movement focusing round this 'democracy wall' was of enormous value to Deng Xiaoping and was probably masterminded by him. However, he was quite happy to turn against it once it had fulfilled his purpose. The showdown over China's future climaxed at the famous Third Plenum of the Eleventh Central Committee.

Conclusion

The first 29 years of the PRC, from late 1949 to late 1978, changed the country irrevocably. The individual who dominated the period can be accounted one of the great leaders of the twentieth century, but even so he left a mixed legacy, most of it controversial. Mao had come to be like a god to the Chinese, terrible but wonderful, powerful and fearful but generally beneficial to the people as a whole. It was a truly spectacular event when the poster containing open criticism of the Chairman appeared on the 'democracy wall' at the very end of the period discussed in this chapter.

The revolution had swept away much of the dross of China's past, and China had made some progress towards modern industry. The standard of living of most Chinese was considerably higher in 1978 than it had been in 1949. But the continuities with the past were also substantial, in particular the weakness of the individual before the oppressive power of the state. Some of China's main characteristics were more pronounced than ever, especially its gigantic population and enormous peasantry.

To be sure, China had needed a revolution. But there are costs to revolution and even the best things can be overdone. Might not China have been better off if Mao had died in 1966 or earlier instead of in 1976? China would be paying the price of the Cultural Revolution for years to come.

Notes

1 'Decision of the Central Committee of the Chinese Communist Party Concerning the Great Proletarian Cultural Revolution', in K.H. Fan, *The Chinese Cultural Revolution, Selected Documents*, Grove Press, New York, 1968, p. 162.

2 The Constitution of the Communist Party of China adopted by the Ninth Party Congress on 14 April 1969 is contained in full in 'Quarterly Chronicle and Documentation', *China Quarterly*, no. 39, July–September 1969, pp. 164–68, among many other places.

[3] See the 'Outline of Project 571' in Michael Y.M. Kau (ed.), *The Lin Piao Affair: Power Politics and Military Coup*, International Arts and Sciences Press, White Plains, NY, 1975, pp. 83, 84.

[4] See Yao Ming-le, *The Conspiracy and Murder of Mao's Heir*, Knopf, New York; Collins, London, 1983.

[5] See Victor Vlasov, 'The Last Days of Lin Biao', *Far Eastern Affairs*, no. 6, 1990, pp. 150–59. *Far Eastern Affairs* was published by the Soviet Academy of Sciences' Institute of the Far East in Moscow.

[6] See Robert Delfs in *Far Eastern Economic Review*, vol. 148, no. 19, 10 May 1990, p. 14.

[7] New China news dispatch of 4 August 1976, in *Peking Review*, vol. 19, nos 32–3, 9 August 1976, p. 7.

[8] Wu De's Speech at the Celebration Rally in the Capital, *Peking Review*, vol. 19, no. 44, 29 October 1976, p. 12.

[9] The four were Jiang Qing, Zhang Chunqiao, Yao Wenyuan and Wang Hongwen.

[10] Hua Guofeng, 'Speech at the Second National Conference on Learning from Tachai [Dazhai] in Agriculture', *Peking Review*, vol. 20, no. 1, 1 January 1977, p. 42.

[11] Hua Guofeng, 'Political Report to the 11th National Congress of the Communist Party of China', *Peking Review*, vol. 20, no. 35, 26 August 1977, pp. 38–39.

3 Political History I: Two Third Plenums and the Interim, 1978–84

THE Third Plenum of the Eleventh Central Committee, from 18 to 22 December 1978, introduced the policies of reform under the leadership of Deng Xiaoping. The first half-decade from the end of 1978 on was the period of reform *par excellence* in China. In policy terms changes were introduced in the economy in the direction of market socialism and free enterprise in the countryside. The Cultural Revolution was totally negated and China seemed able to throw out all the Maoist propaganda which had been so deleterious to the Chinese revolution as a whole. The legal system, which had been all but destroyed as a result of the Cultural Revolution, made tentative steps towards revival. Economic and social freedoms of various sorts became permissable. In leadership terms, Deng Xiaoping appeared able to solve any struggles in the top power echelons of the Party or state with reasonable ease.

The policy changes were reflected in practical realities. The economy boomed and the standard of living rose everywhere, especially in the countryside. There were problems, of course. The revived law system did not prevent the worsening of corruption, and crime began to assume worrying proportions. Quite quickly there were signs that the intelligentsia were losing enthusiasm for socialism, and some were even turning their backs on it. But in general things appeared to be going well.

The Third Plenum of the Twelfth Central Committee met in October 1984. Its task was to extend the economic reforms in the countryside to the cities by loosening up state controls over prices and management. It thus introduced a new and important stage in reform, but one which turned out to be rather less successful than the first.

The Third Plenum of the Eleventh Central Committee

The Third Plenum was the climax of a series of major high-level meetings which had taken place behind the scenes as demonstrators wrote up posters on the 'democracy wall' in the centre of Beijing. It formalised decisions reached in those meetings about the future policy of the CCP and its leadership. One writer has called it 'the fulcrum, which he [Deng] had sought for nearly two decades, with which he could move the Chinese nation dramatically on to a new track in its search for identity'.[1]

For some time, Deng Xiaoping had been critical of the slow pace of modernisation under Hua Guofeng. He also pushed for a much more radical rejection of the Cultural Revolution than Hua Guofeng appeared willing to countenance. The Third Plenum showed very clearly that Deng Xiaoping was getting his way over these matters. It was the single most important point in his phoenix-like rise to ascendancy. Although Hua Guofeng remained in the position of Chinese Communist Party (CCP) Chairman and Premier of the State Council, his influence was sharply on the wane from then on, and his disappearance as a major power-holder was only a matter of time.

The main decision of the Third Plenum was to push modernisation far more strongly than had been done over the previous years:

> Now is an appropriate time to take the decision to close the large-scale nationwide mass movement to expose and criticize Lin Biao and the 'gang of four' and to shift the emphasis of our Party's work and the attention of the people of the whole country to socialist modernization . . . Socialist modernization is therefore a profound and extensive revolution. There is still in our country today a small handful of counter-revolutionary elements and criminals who hate our socialist modernization and try to undermine it. We must not relax our class struggle against them, nor can we weaken the dictatorship of the proletariat. But as Comrade Mao Tsetung [Zedong] pointed out, the large-scale turbulent class struggles of a mass character have in the main come to an end.[2]

This statement signalled not only the end of the campaign against the gang of four, but, at least for several years, any other campaigns that seemed remotely similar to the sort of ideological movements which had characterised the last years of Mao Zedong. In particular, the lid was opened on criticism of the Cultural Revolution. The Plenum suggested that the Cultural Revolution should 'be viewed historically, scientifically and in a down-to-earth way' and that its shortcomings and mistakes 'should be summed up at the appropriate time'.[3] In fact, Deng Xiaoping had no time at all for the Cultural Revolution — not surprising considering how deeply he had suffered as a result of it — and his intention was to move to discredit it altogether in due course.

Other major policy decisions of the Third Plenum pointed in the same direction of a new deal for China and against the policies of Mao's last years. The Tiananmen Incident of April 1976 was reinterpreted. Whereas the power-holders of the time, mainly Mao and the gang of four, had castigated it as a 'counter-revolutionary political incident', the Third Plenum described it simply as the unfolding of a 'great revolutionary mass movement'.[4]

Nowhere was the hand of Deng Xiaoping more clearly visible than in this 'reversal of verdicts'. What had followed immediately on the Tiananmen Incident of 1976 was the confirmation of Hua Guofeng as Premier and a major acceleration of the mass campaign of criticism against Deng Xiaoping. In other words, Hua had done very nicely out of the Tiananmen Incident, whereas for Deng had come only humiliation and bitterness. Hua must have been extremely uneasy about the Third Plenum's view of the Incident, no matter how strong his public endorsement of it may have been.

Hua was right to worry. He was deposed as Premier at the Third Session of the Fifth National People's Congress in September 1980 and as Party Chairman at the Sixth Plenum of the Eleventh Central Committee, which met from 27–29 June 1981. Zhao Ziyang replaced him as Premier, and Hu Yaobang as CCP Chairman. Both were strong supporters of Deng Xiaoping and his reformist policies, and equally strong critics of the Cultural Revolution. In particular, Hu Yaobang had served under Deng Xiaoping as early as the period of the war against Japan. He had been head of the Chinese Youth League in Beijing from 1952 until the League was destroyed, and Hu himself purged, in 1966 at the onset of the Cultural Revolution.

The Third Plenum ushered in extensive changes in more or less all major spheres of life. Apart from the legal system and the economy, these included ideology, education, literature and the arts, the minority nationalities and religion. Some of them are discussed in other chapters of this book.

Although Deng Xiaoping is rightly regarded as the prime leader of the reforms in China, he was at all times absolutely insistent that China should remain socialist. It was he who formulated the terminology, or jargon, around which the debate over the speed and nature of socialist modernisation was joined. It was he who summed up the new ideology appropriate to the period of reform in the phrase 'socialism with Chinese characteristics'. It was he who first specified the requirement that the Chinese people must 'uphold the four cardinal principles' but at all costs oppose 'bourgeois liberalisation'. In a major speech given on 30 March 1979, at a forum on the principles for the CCP's theoretical work, he had declared these four as 'the basic prerequisite for achieving modernisation' and enunciated them as follows:

- We must keep to the socialist road.
- We must uphold the dictatorship of the proletariat.
- We must uphold the leadership of the Communist Party.
- We must uphold Marxism-Leninism and Mao Zedong Thought.[5]

Putting the matter in very stark terms, Deng later declared that 'the essence of the four cardinal principles is to uphold Communist Party leadership'. In other words, he perceived the third of the four principles, the one affirming the Leninist notion that the Party must on no account relinquish its monopoly on power, as the most important (see Chapter 9). On the other hand, 'the keystone of bourgeois liberalisation is opposition to Party leadership'.[6] Although Deng had thus laid down the parameters of discussion long before the Third Plenum of the Twelfth Central Committee, it was not until the mid-1980s that upholding the cardinal principles and opposing bourgeois liberalisation came to dominate both the public media and the concerns of CCP conservatives in China.

Reform and the negation of the Cultural Revolution

The political history of China in the wake of Third Plenum can be viewed either as a trend in favour of reform or as being against the whole idea of the Cultural Revolution. Of course, the two themes are actually two sides of the same coin. The trend against the Cultural Revolution strengthened through a series of moves which reached a climax in the policy reached at the Sixth Plenum of the Eleventh Central Committee.

An early sign of how the reform meant the negation of the Cultural Revolution was the complete abolition of the revolutionary committees at the Second Session of the Fifth National People's

Congress in mid-1979. Early in 1978, these institutions, which were among the 'new-born things of the Cultural Revolution', had been downgraded to make them applicable only to organisations with governmental functions. But among the new laws of the Second Session were two governing the local people's congresses of the PRC, the organs which replaced the local revolutionary committees. Moreover, the senior governmental positions at various levels were changed accordingly. So, for instance, the most senior governmental position at province level had been the chairman of the provincial revolutionary committee, but was now the provincial governor.

Immediately freedom in society increased and religion began to be tolerated again. Early in 1979 the PRC's first national conference on the study of religion was held in Kunming, Yunnan province. Later in the year, Chinese Muslims went on a pilgrimage to Mecca for the first time since 1964. The arts blossomed and became incomparably more varied and interesting. Traditional drama, which had been totally banned during the Cultural Revolution, came back quickly and prolifically.

Late in February 1980, several further steps were taken by the Fifth Plenum of the Eleventh Central Committee in the discrediting of the Cultural Revolution. Four leaders with known sympathies for the Cultural Revolution and for Hua Guofeng were dismissed, including Wang Dongxing, who had actually managed the arrest of the gang of four on the night of 6 October 1976. At the same time, the very symbol of opposition to Mao during the Cultural Revolution, Liu Shaoqi, was rehabilitated posthumously. The decision of October 1968 to expel Liu Shaoqi from the CCP and to dismiss him from all posts both inside and outside the CCP, which had been taken at Mao's behest, was not only reversed but condemned as the 'biggest frame-up our Party has ever known in its history'.[7] In connection with Liu's rehabilitation, his death in prison in November 1969 was for the first time announced, over a decade after the event, and a memorial service was held in his honour. Official pronouncements were careful to blame Lin Biao, the gang of four and so on for Liu's death, but his rehabilitation was certainly a major slap in the face for Mao's memory and for the Cultural Revolution.

In August 1980, Deng Xiaoping gave a major speech to the Politburo on his vision of political reform. Naturally he blamed the Cultural Revolution, Lin Biao and the gang of four for the fact that China's political system had suffered so severely and become so very undemocratic and feudal. Part of his argument for this position was that Lin Biao and the gang of four had contrived to persecute so many good cadres that virtually everybody, including the young, had become too cowed to express an opinion or to take any administrative initiative. He was speaking from bitter experience and his position gained very widespread support. Attempts were made to implement his ideas over the next few years — some fairly successfully, but others much less so.

Deng wanted a major separation of the roles and powers of the Party and the government. He believed there was too great a concentration of power, with too many senior leaders holding too many posts both in the Party and the government. He called for tighter rules on the retirement of old cadres and a major infusion of young blood into the CCP and government at all levels, affirming his faith in the youth against attacks that they 'may be too inexperienced and not equal to the tasks'.[8] He attacked bureaucracy and patriarchal ways throughout society, denouncing the old way of thinking which had demanded subservience to old age. Deng's stated ideal was that China should 'practise people's democracy to the full . . . and develop a political situation marked by stability, unity and liveliness'.[9] Deng was probably quite genuine in this belief. After all, what he had in mind was not Western-style democracy, but a kind which would preserve his 'four cardinal principles', especially Party leadership, and conform to 'socialism with Chinese characteristics'. He may not have bargained either for the direction which the process of democracy would take or for the extent to which he would be unable to control it.

From 20 November to 29 December 1980, a specially formed court held a trial of sixteen persons involved in the Cultural Revolution. Of the sixteen, ten were living, among whom the gang of four were the most important. Six were dead, including Lin Biao. Some legal implications of the trial are considered in Chapter 11. The trial also had very considerable political significance, especially regarding the negation of the Cultural Revolution: the ten years of the Cultural Revolution (1966–76) were on trial as much as ten living people. Lin Biao's relations with Mao were brought up again and much new information was revealed, aimed at supporting the thesis that indeed Lin had wickedly attempted to assassinate the Chairman and died in an air crash during flight after his plan had failed. The main charge against the living defendants was of framing and persecuting CCP and state leaders as well as large numbers of cadres and ordinary people. For the first time, specific figures of the number of sufferers were issued: in twelve major cases mentioned in the indictment, 729 511 cadres and ordinary people were framed and persecuted, while 34 800 were persecuted to death.[10] Jiang Qing did not just give in to her accusers, she fought back and on 12 December was actually dismissed from the court for disrupting it by interrupting the judges and prosecutors and abusing a witness.

The climax of the move to discredit the Cultural Revolution came with the Sixth Plenum in June 1981. The Plenum issued a long document called 'On Questions of Party History', which analysed and assessed the history of the CCP from its beginnings until the aftermath of the Third Plenum, including reference to various ideological issues (discussed at greater length in Chapter 9) and to the career and status of Mao Zedong. The Plenum adopted the view that the CCP had done very well until the late 1950s, when things began to go wrong due to 'left' influence. The Great Leap Forward was basically a mistake caused by the impatience of Mao and other leaders for quick results. But the main barbs of the document were reserved for the Cultural Revolution itself, which it portrayed as a total disaster without any relieving features:

> The 'cultural revolution', which lasted from May 1966 to October 1976, was responsible for the most severe setback and the heaviest losses suffered by the Party, the state and the people since the founding of the People's Republic. It was initiated and led by Comrade Mao Zedong . . . The history of the 'cultural revolution' has proved that Comrade Mao Zedong's principal theses for initiating this revolution conformed neither to Marxism–Leninism nor to Chinese reality. They represent an entirely erroneous appraisal of the prevailing class relations and political situation in the Party and state . . .
>
> Practice has shown that the 'cultural revolution' did not in fact constitute a revolution or social progress in any sense, nor could it possibly have done so. It was we and not the enemy at all who were thrown into disorder by the 'cultural revolution'.[11]

So the social analysis which underlay the Cultural Revolution was utterly inaccurate, and the results were catastrophic and entirely harmful both to China and the CCP. As far as the Cultural Revolution was concerned, the new leadership had swung a full semi-circle since the days when Mao Zedong was trying to preserve it as the acme of human achievement and development.

The Sixth Plenum went on to analyse the Third Plenum, claiming that it 'marked a crucial turning point of far-reaching significance in the history' of the CCP since 1949.[12] It alleged that Hua Guofeng had made quite serious mistakes during his tenure of power, mainly in being far too slow to renounce the Cultural Revolution altogether. That confirmed Deng's victory in his ideological battle with Hua Guofeng at the time of the Third Plenum.

The status of Mao Zedong

The main personality involved in the deliberations over the Cultural Revolution was, of course, Mao Zedong. It had been obvious that the immense power wielded by the 'gang of four' was due to Mao's backing. Indeed, should not one rather speak of a 'gang of five', with Mao being the fifth but most important member? During the trial of 1980, Jiang Qing defended herself against all charges by arguing that everything she had done was on orders from Mao. She told her judges that their purpose was 'to make me stink, and through me to make Chairman Mao stink, so as to revise the development of Marxism–Leninism and the immense contributions Chairman Mao made'.[13]

Mao Zedong was the major absentee not only from the 'gang of four' but also from the list of sixteen living or dead criminals of the Cultural Revolution tried late in 1980. The negation of the Cultural Revolution, and especially the trial of the sixteen, could not possibly avoid affecting the status of Mao Zedong. In particular, one question inevitably bulked large: If sixteen leaders of the Cultural Revolution, including virtually all the luminaries of the period, were criminals, why was Mao Zedong still regarded as a great revolutionary leader? Was not he the biggest criminal of them all?

Deng Xiaoping repeatedly insisted that while Mao had made serious mistakes in his later years, his reputation should remain fundamentally intact. After all, as Deng told a foreign journalist in August 1980, 'for most of his life, Chairman Mao did very good things. Many times he saved the Party and the state from crises.' But towards the end of his life he began to go wrong. He lost touch with reality and began to go 'counter to the style of work he himself had advocated'.[14] However, because of his major earlier contributions he could not be compared in any way with criminals like Jiang Qing. Naturally the line was echoed by the official press,[15] but that did not ease concern among many ordinary people. The argument that Mao had made major contributions beforehand did not really absolve him for wrongdoings during the Cultural Revolution. If there was one point on which Deng Xiaoping and Jiang Qing could agree, it was that Mao was primarily responsible for the Cultural Revolution and it was he who was giving the orders at that time. For Deng Xiaoping, it was one thing to denounce the Cultural Revolution and virtually all its proponents. But to downgrade Mao Zedong himself past a certain point was more or less tantamount to downgrading the CCP and the People's Republic, and that was something Deng Xiaoping could not possibly do.

Deng himself made this point clear when on 22 June 1981, a few days before the Sixth Plenum was to convene, he told a preparatory meeting that 'certain recent remarks about some of Comrade Mao Zedong's mistakes' had gone too far. He asked that the excesses should be corrected 'so that, generally speaking, the assessment will conform to reality and enhance the image of the country and the Party as a whole'.[16] His reference to China's and the CCP's image is very revealing: whether good or bad, Mao's role in the history of the CCP was just too towering to allow him to be fully discredited. The 'limits of criticism' of Mao were dictated by the need to preserve the authority of the CCP.[17]

The Sixth Plenum did duly criticise the actions of Mao in his later years. It attacked not only the mistakes he had made during the Cultural Revolution, but also the fact that he had allowed or encouraged such a disaster to occur in the first place. It charged him with arrogance and other faults. At the same time, it reaffirmed that 'Comrade Mao Zedong was a great Marxist and a great proletarian revolutionary, strategist and theorist', whose 'contributions to the Chinese revolution far outweigh his mistakes' and whose 'merits are primary and his errors secondary'(see Chapter 9).[18]

The aftermath of the Sixth Plenum

The Sixth Plenum was like a kind of purging of the Chinese system. People could think: 'Now we've admitted the mistake we made, let's forget about the Cultural Revolution and get on with reforming the system and building socialism.' In the years following the Sixth Plenum the Cultural Revolution did not dominate Chinese politics in the same way it had in the previous period.

Nevertheless, China was confronted with a problem of confidence, especially among young people.The Chinese people had been told, 'believe in radical revolution' and then soon afterwards told, 'radical revolution is nonsense and harmful; believe in reform'. Many were left feeling confused and deceived. The new reformed order encouraged them to get rich, and that is precisely what they did as far as they could. But the implication was that their order of priorities had changed. Whereas love of country and the people and loyalty to the Party had been primary, the top of the priority list was now self and family, with the people and the country, let alone the Party, a long way down the list. The Party found itself faced with a 'crisis of faith'.[19] Even more serious, the new attitudes and values produced by reform, coupled with the greater freedom, paved the way for a growth in the extent of corruption. This had been one of the reasons for the establishment in December 1978 of the Central Commission for Discipline Inspection.

When the Twelfth National Congress of the CCP met in 1982 it endorsed the conclusions of the Sixth Plenum and took several further measures to reform the system, as well as confronting such problems as the crisis of faith and corruption. The two main changes in the Party system were, firstly, the abolition of the post of CCP Chairman and, secondly, the establishment of a new Central Advisory Commission. The first of these measures flowed directly from the criticism of the excessive power the single figure of Mao Zedong had been able to wield, especially during the Cultural Revolution. Hu Yaobang was appointed General Secretary of the CCP, which from this time on was the most senior formal position within the Party.

The Central Advisory Commission is supposed to act as assistant and consultant to the Central Committee, and thus contribute to sharing power. However, the first person to be appointed to chair it was none other than Deng Xiaoping, who also remained Chairman of the Central Committee's Military Commission. The effect of the Twelfth Congress was actually to *increase* Deng's power, even though he showed no aspirations to the job of General Secretary.

In his report to the Congress, Hu Yaobang raised the issue of of 'socialist spiritual civilisation', presented as a kind of recipe to counter the crisis of faith and the growing corruption. 'While working for a high level of material civilisation,' he said, 'we must strive to build a high level of socialist spiritual civilisation. This is a strategic principle for building socialism.'[20] The two aspects of this socialist spiritual civilisation were cultural and ideological, with each permeating the other. The people should accept a working-class world outlook, communist ideals, beliefs and moral values, including a collectivism corresponding to a system of socialist public ownership — in other words, precisely all the things which appeared to be deteriorating quicker than ever under the impact of reform. Hu also echoed Deng Xiaoping's demand for a socialist democracy and an improvement in the the CCP's system of democratic centralism. He attacked the corruption which he recognised as very destructive of inner-Party life, claiming it was getting worse: 'Undemocratic practices and patriarchal ways have still not been eradicated in many organisations,' he said. While claiming that discipline inspection committees at all levels had made some progress, he also acknowledged that they had met 'considerable, and in some cases shocking, obstruction in their work'.[21] Clearly the route towards the 'socialist spiritual civilisation' would not be an easy one.

At the end of 1982, the National People's Congress adopted the PRC's fourth constitution. It made quite a few changes from the constitutions of 1975 and 1978. One point in particular stands out in importance in administrative terms and yet again separates the China of the 1980s from that of the Cultural Revolution period. The post of President of the PRC, which Mao had abolished because his arch-enemy Liu Shaoqi had occupied it, was now brought back. It was supremely ironical that only a few months after the Twelfth Party Congress had removed the Party chairmanship, a post to which Mao himself had lent such lustre for so long, the state Constitution should restore the post which he had acted to eliminate. In 1983, Li Xiannian was appointed to fill this newly revived position.

Despite the rejection of the Cultural Revolution and the mainly successful implementation of reform, no resolution appeared imminent for the tensions within the Party and society as a whole. In October 1983, the Second Plenum of the Twelfth Central Committee decided to undertake another ideological campaign, the closest to the Maoist style of campaign since the Third Plenum of 1978. The target was 'spiritual pollution'. The campaign represented a minor shift against an over-hasty pace of reform, conservatives being motivated by the worsening of such problems as crime and corruption. But it did not represent an attempt to go back on reform.

The Second Plenum decided to 'consolidate the Party'. This meant 'an overall rectification of Party style and a consolidation of Party organisations over a period of three years'. Blame for the rather poor situation was put on 'the corrosive influence of decadent bourgeois ideology and remnant feudal ideas'.[22] Decadent bourgeois ideology meant ideas from abroad, especially the West, while feudal ideas represented thinking left over from the past, especially China's Confucian traditional attitudes. What was *not* blamed was the process of reform.

Some people were expelled from the Party and the CCP did indeed go through a formal process of 'consolidation' over three years. However, the effects on the CCP and society were actually rather less than spectacular. It is true that intellectuals and artists, among others, experienced some serious tension in the late months of 1983, with the banning of a limited number of dramas and other works of art and fears of a renewed purge. However, by the beginning of 1984, the influence of the campaign had waned to the extent that many people were no longer taking it seriously and few were still worried about it.

If the campaign against 'spiritual pollution' signified a minor trend towards slowing down the pace of reform, the Third Plenum of the Twelfth Central Committee, in October 1984, suggested a swing back in the opposite direction. The decision of the Third Plenum focused mainly on the economy, concerning such matters as the price system (see Chapter 7). However, issues such as management policy in urban units were closely involved. Directors were given greater powers to hire and fire, disposing of the old idea that workers in a socialist society could never be sacked. The idea of absolute egalitarianism was roundly condemned, simply because it prevented people from working hard and showing initiative. The widening gaps between rich and poor were of slighter concern than this disincentive. Just as reform really derived its origins from the Third Plenum of the Eleventh Central Committee in 1978, the pace and extent of reform clearly took a very substantial step forward through the Third Plenum of the Twelfth Central Committee some six years later.

Conclusion

Change had been extraordinarily rapid in China between these two Third Plenums. Yet, despite the incipient modernisation throughout society, the development was uneven. Already economic modernisation was beginning to outstrip reform, its political partner. Although some aspects of society were becoming distinctly 'modern', there were others in which the trend appeared to be in precisely the opposite direction — towards the reinstatement of very ancient traditions. The reference which the Second Plenum of the Twelfth Central Committee made to the corrosive influence of feudal ideas must be taken seriously. The lifting of restraints had allowed back all kinds of traditional ideas and customs, including not only neutral or beautiful ones such as religious worship or traditional dramas and festivals, but also some less worthy, like superstitions, patriarchal domination of the young and of women, and ill-treatment of mothers failing to bear sons.

Many in the West noted the return of market mechanisms and free enterprise with enormous enthusiasm. Here was a communist party which seemed to be making genuine progress towards something which, if not really capitalism, was at least beginning to look like it. Although the situation changed greatly in the following period, it is doubtful that, as of 1984, many in the top Chinese leadership were seriously worried that the reforms could lead to capitalism. The leading role of the CCP had not yet been seriously challenged. The state ownership of the major enterprises was still perfectly secure. The reforms could genuinely be identified as quite consistent with 'socialism with Chinese characteristics', which represented at least one interpretation of Marxism–Leninism. The new leadership could, and did, argue that it was not they, but the late Mao, who had departed from Marxism–Leninism.

The trouble was that the logic of reform implied the acceleration of change in a system which could not readily handle the shock. The policies of the Third Plenum of the Eleventh Central Committee led directly on to those of the Third Plenum of the Twelfth Central Committee. And the second of these two Third Plenums unleashed forces with very serious long-term implications, specifically the gathering pace of inflation. The reforms increasingly took on their own momentum. Deng Xiaoping had accused Mao of arrogance and becoming divorced from reality. Perhaps he was himself suffering from the same weaknesses if he thought he could keep the situation on an even keel indefinitely.

Notes

1 David Bonavia, *Deng*, Longman, Hong Kong, 1989, p. 168.

2 'Communiqué of the Third Plenary Session of the 11th Central Committee of The Communist Party of China', *Peking Review*, vol. 21, no. 52, 29 December 1978, pp. 10–11.

3 ibid., p. 15.

4 ibid., p. 13.

5 Deng Xiaoping, 'Uphold the Four Cardinal Principles', *Selected Works of Deng Xiaoping 1975–1982*, Foreign Languages Press, Beijing, 1984, p. 172.

6 Deng Xiaoping, 'Concerning Problems on the Ideological Front', *Selected Works of Deng Xiaoping*, p. 369. The comment was made during a talk Deng had with leaders of the central propaganda departments on 17 July 1981.

7 'Communiqué of the Fifth Plenary Session of the 11th Central Committee of the Communist Party of China', p. 9.

[8] Deng Xiaoping, 'On the Reform of the System of Party and State Leadership', *Selected Works of Deng Xiaoping*, p. 307.

[9] ibid., p. 304.

[10] *Beijing Review*, vol. 23, no. 48, 1 December 1980, p. 19.

[11] 'On Questions of Party History — Resolution on Certain Questions in the History of Our Party Since the Founding of the People's Republic of China', *Beijing Review*, vol. 24, no. 27, 6 July 1981, pp. 20–21.

[12] ibid., p. 26.

[13] Quoted in Craig Dietrich, *People's China, A Brief History*, Oxford University Press, New York, 1986, p. 268.

[14] Deng Xiaoping, 'Answers to the Italian Journalist Oriana Fallaci', *Selected Works of Deng Xiaoping*, pp. 326–27.

[15] For example, in *Renmin ribao*, 22 December 1980, p. 5, which argued that Mao's actions, even in his last years, were crucially different from those of the gang of four in their nature, methods and aims.

[16] Deng Xiaoping, 'Remarks on Successive Drafts of the "Resolution on Certain Questions in the History of our Party since the Founding of the People's Republic of China" ', *Selected Works of Deng Xiaoping*, p. 295.

[17] See also John Gittings, *China Changes Face, The Road From Revolution 1949–1989*, Oxford University Press, Oxford, New York, 1990, p. 183.

[18] 'On Questions of Party History', p. 29.

[19] See Dietrich, *People's China*, p. 281.

[20] Hu Yaobang, 'Create a New Situation in All Fields of Socialist Modernization', *Beijing Review*, vol. 25, no. 37, 13 September 1982, p. 21.

[21] ibid., pp. 34–35.

[22] 'The Decision of the Central Committee of the Communist Party of China on Party Consolidation', *Beijing Review*, vol. 26, no. 42, 17 October 1983, p. 1.

4 POLITICAL HISTORY II
The Worsening of Reform Problems
1984–89

THE period following the Third Plenum of the Twelfth Central Committee late in 1984 until the eve of the student protests beginning in April 1989 saw a sharpening debate over reform. It was not that CCP leaders were in any doubt that they *should* reform and modernise. By that time very few indeed were actually prepared to oppose reform or modernisation altogether. But intensive debate raged over the nature, scope and speed of reform and modernisation.

On one side were those who feared that over-hasty and excessive reform and modernisation would lead China to capitalism. They saw the market forces gathering momentum, corruption increasing and feeding upon the processes of reform and modernisation, and levels of inflation rising. If these trends continued unchecked, they believed that the legitimacy and even power of the CCP itself would come under threat. Just how far could a communist party reform in a free-market direction and still call itself communist? If its validity were undermined, would not its power also be in danger?

On the other side stood those who emphasised the rise in the standard of living produced by reform and modernisation. 'To get rich was glorious' they argued. Their view was that the greater political and social freedom engendered by market forces should be encouraged and expanded. According to this faction, only through continuing the trend towards openness to the outside world could these favourable trends develop and blossom. They also thought that the harmful results of reform and modernisation could be controlled and could never lead to a threat to CCP power.

It was the old guard, the faction often called the 'conservatives', which favoured slow and cautious reform. This faction included men such as Peng Zhen and Chen Yun, who had very long revolutionary careers which included humiliation during the Cultural Revolution. They were very enthusiastic about the denunciation of the Cultural Revolution, but they were less keen on anything which could undermine their vision of socialist values. The group advocating faster and more radical reform was headed by Hu Yaobang and Zhao Ziyang, who late in 1984 occupied the positions of CCP Secretary-General and Premier of the State Council — in other words, the most senior positions in the Party and the government — respectively.

Hovering over these factions was the architect of reform, Deng Xiaoping. Nobody hated the Cultural Revolution more than he; few had suffered more from it. But correspondingly he had devoted his entire life to the CCP and invested more effort and influence than any other living person in the establishment and development of the PRC. It was he who had put the radical reformers, Hu and Zhao, into their positions of power. But at the same time he reserved the right of veto over actions or decisions he saw as going too far or too fast along the road of reform. In particular, he was at all times much more enthusiastic about reform in the economic sphere than in the political one, and was never convinced that the two needed to be in harmony with each other. His ability to side with the conservative wing of the CCP in political matters but with the radical reformers in the economic sphere was probably a major reason why his influence remained so strong.

Political reform

The ideas which Deng Xiaoping had advocated in August 1980 had been implemented with rather limited success in the early 1980s (see Chapter 3). One of them was the abolition of lifelong tenure of senior office and the related issue of old age. As reform gathered momentum, pressures grew stronger for older leaders to retire in favour of the next generation. On 16 September 1985, the Fourth Plenum of the Twelfth CCP Central Committee accepted the resignations of 64 of its members, representing 18 per cent of the total, on the grounds of old age. Ironically, these did not include Deng Xiaoping or Chen Yun. There followed a national conference of the CCP, which featured the theme of promoting younger and better educated people to the senior leadership. Immediately afterwards, another Plenum, the Fifth, elected some younger and better educated members to the Politburo. They included several radical reformers, such as Hu Qili, but also Li Peng, who was later to distinguish himself as being on the 'cautious' wing of the reformers.

In 1986, discussion on issues of political reform widened among the intelligentsia and in the media. They included reduction of bureaucratic practices and the control of corruption, which was gathering momentum at an alarming rate. Just as important was the whole issue of democracy and elections. Deng Xiaoping had argued in 1980 that power should not be concentrated in few hands, yet that was precisely what people saw happening around them. Elections held at local levels may have resulted in some veteran CCP people losing their grip on power, but on the other hand they did not go far in giving ordinary people any real say in the affairs that mattered most to them.

One writer has observed of 1986: 'it seemed that significant elements in the Party leadership were willing to countenance a reduction in the Party's power'.[1] One such element was undoubtedly Hu Qili, who told CCP members attending the National People's Congress in March that reform would 'inevitably lead to a readjustment of the powers and interests of various social strata' and 'affect the relationship between various interests',[2] probably meaning that Party members could expect to lose some degree of their influence to experts and technocrats. Shortly afterwards, the Central Committee's main daily newspaper ran a front-page editorial which called for the enhancement of 'democratic supervision of cadres by the masses', a trend which was necessary to solve such problems as 'the abuse of power for private purposes and bureaucratism'.[3]

The CCP was supposed to exercise leadership, with executives at all levels implementing its decisions. The power of experts and managers was meant to have increased at the expense of CCP members. But in fact CCP leaders and members were apt to use their power to interfere in all kinds of matters which, in the view of technical experts or managers, were simply not their business. Of course, the dividing line between leadership and technical implementation of decisions is a fine one, but it is not surprising that many CCP members were reluctant to give up power in the interests of a rather hazy vision of political reform, especially since it was obvious to all that what really counted for the top leadership was economic reform. It was also clear that Deng Xiaoping had never been in any doubt that the CCP's leadership was paramount (see also Chapters 9 and 10).

The Sixth Plenum of the Twelfth Central Committee met late in September 1986. It was in many respects a victory for the radical reformers. It laid emphasis on democracy, legality and freedom in the arts, as well as on economic reform. But there was also much in the Plenum's communiqué which should have given pause to anybody expecting any progress towards anything remotely resembling the Western concept of democracy. For a start, it is from this time that obsession with the 'four cardinal principles' gathered momentum. As mentioned in Chapter 3, Deng Xiaoping had articulated these principles very clearly in 1979, just after the beginning of the reform period. The Plenum expressed itself in strong terms in support of the main principle: the leadership of the CCP. The antithesis of the 'four cardinal principles' was attacked in strong terms: 'Bourgeois liberalisation, which means negating the socialist system in favour of capitalism, is in total contradiction to the people's interests and to the historical trend, and it is therefore firmly opposed by the masses.'[4] While the Plenum criticised regarding Marxism as a 'rigid dogma', it also attacked those who would 'negate its basic tenets, view it as an outmoded theory and blindly worship bourgeois philosophies and social doctrines'.[5]

Student demonstrations and the reaction

It appears that 'negating its basic tenets' in favour of ideas from the West, and especially the United States, was precisely what many among the intelligentsia and students were doing. Western political, intellectual and other influences were strong among students in the mid-1980s. What they admired about the West was the spirit of democracy, freedom and innovation, and the ability to get rid of old-fashioned notions in favour of new ones. Many were quite reluctant to hear of any weaknesses in Western society; and were correspondingly critical of their own. They admired also the capitalist economies of East Asia and believed China should learn from them. Other than Japan, places held up for admiration included South Korea, Taiwan and even the Philippines, where 'people power' had just raised Corazon Aquino as President over the disgraced dictator Ferdinand Marcos.

In November and especially December 1986, major student demonstrations took place in many cities. One of the main centres of the demonstrations in the early stages was Hefei, the capital of

Anhui province. There the Vice-President of the Chinese University of Science and Technology, Fang Lizhi, was already known for his radical and open views, critical of Marxism and the CCP order in China. Fang Lizhi went on a tour in November and encouraged students to participate in politics, calling them a progressive force for democratisation. On 4 December he gave a speech at his own university, in which he told the students that 'democracy is not granted from the top, it is won by individuals'.[6] The following day, several thousand students marched through the streets of Hefei demanding democracy and denouncing the Chinese government as a feudal dictatorship.

From 19–21 December, several tens of thousands of students demonstrated in Shanghai, China's largest city. They were warned that permission would be required for further marches. Although demonstrations did continue after this in defiance of the warning, they were on a much smaller scale. The students of Beijing then took the cue until on 26 December a municipal government order banned any demonstrations without police approval. Nobody was surprised that such approval was not forthcoming. On New Year's Day, in open defiance of the ban, students held demonstrations in Tiananmen Square in the centre of Beijing, including a public ceremonial burning of the *People's Daily* newspaper.

The city with the largest numbers of demonstrators was Shanghai, where at one point some 50 000 had taken to the streets. Besides Hefei and Beijing, other cities affected were Wuhan, Shenzhen, Kunming, Nanjing, Suzhou, Tianjin, Chongqing, Xi'an and Guangzhou. They were by far the largest demonstrations in China since the days of the Cultural Revolution. Considering that the students had a great deal to lose in career terms by taking part, they showed a good deal of courage. They knew perfectly well that dossiers were being kept on their activities. At the same time, they must also have known that the government would react if it were pushed hard enough. The concepts of freedom and democracy needed much more careful working out than the students were able to give them. They tended to be rather blind in following Western, and especially American, notions, without fully appreciating the vastly different economic levels and historical experiences which separated China from these models.

The government could see the enormous damage the demonstrations were doing to its authority. Yet at first its reaction was very mild. There were a few arrests, and the government asserted that these were not in fact students at all, but miscreants who were taking advantage of the demonstrations to commit acts against China's constitution. One writer claims that the demonstration in Tiananmen Square on New Year's Day 1987 was the last straw, driving the government to a stronger reaction with serious political ramifications.[7]

A strong press campaign began which bore the hallmarks of Deng Xiaoping's views on Party leadership. On 6 January 1987, the *People's Daily* ran an editorial denouncing 'bourgeois liberalisation'. It argued that there was no basis for turmoil because the CCP was united and its line had popular support. It blamed the occurrence of the student demonstrations on 'the weakness of some comrades in fighting the spread of bourgeois liberalisation over the last few years' and called for adherence to the 'four cardinal principles'. In particular, it demanded the strengthening of Party leadership in ideology, theory, literature and art, and education. Six days later the same newspaper attacked the idea of 'complete Westernisation', arguing that this theory simply meant abandoning socialism in China in favour of capitalism. This was a typical example of 'bourgeois liberalisation'.

These articles presaged a purge in the leadership. That 'some comrades' who had been weak in opposing 'bourgeois liberalisation' meant primarily Hu Yaobang became obvious on 16 January when he resigned as CCP General Secretary, having made a self-criticism of his mistakes while he held that office. Zhao Ziyang replaced him in the post in an acting capacity. The next day Fang Lizhi was expelled from the CCP for 'bourgeois liberalisation'. He was among several prominent intellectuals, journalists and writers to suffer the same fate at about this time.

The student demonstrations had thus achieved precisely the opposite effect from the one intended and a conservative backlash appeared inevitable. Sensitive to this fear, Zhao Ziyang took the occasion of a Spring Festival gathering in Beijing to assure the world that China was not in the throes of another campaign. He said opposition to 'bourgeois liberalisation' would be confined to the Party and the cities and there would be absolutely no going back on reform or on opening to the outside world. Whether there was actually a campaign depends on how one defines such a term. But public pressures against 'bourgeois liberalisation' did not actually last very long.

The Thirteenth Congress of the CCP

This became fairly clear when the Thirteenth Congress of the CCP took place late in 1987. Zhao Ziyang's report placed a major focus on the economy and, although it mentioned 'bourgeois liberalisation', it did not give that concept any emphasis. In ideological terms, Zhao's main contribution to the Thirteenth Congress, and indeed to 'socialism with Chinese characteristics', was the notion that China was in 'the initial stage of socialism', a notion which is explored in much more detail in Chapter 9.

In political terms, Zhao's report was notable for its enthusiasm for reform, for the harsh words it had to say about bureaucracy, and for its advocacy of a further split between the functions of the Party and those of the government. Of course, he supported the leadership of the CCP, suggesting that the separation of Party and government would actually strengthen the former's leadership and improve its methods. On the other hand, however, he was very clear that CCP leaders at the grass-roots level should restrict themselves to political work and refrain from interfering in day-to-day management:

> In enterprises, Party organisations should supervise the work and ensure that it is accomplished. Instead of attempting to provide centralized leadership, they should support the directors and managers in their assumption of overall leadership. In institutions, Party organisations should play the same role once a system is introduced under which administrative heads assume full responsibility.[8]

Zhao was also insistent that Party Commissions for Discipline Inspection should restrict themselves to fostering a sense of discipline and refrain from concerning themselves with breaches of the law. The implication of this was extremely significant. As one writer puts it, 'the General Secretary would look to the government and not to the party to apply sanctions against errant party members — a dramatic departure from current practice'.[9] It was clear that in fact Zhao was willing to countenance a further sacrifice of real power by the Party to the government.

The Thirteenth Congress and the First Plenum of the Thirteenth Central Committee which followed it brought about substantial changes in the central CCP leadership. The most important was that Deng Xiaoping resigned even from the Central Committee itself, although he retained the crucially important post of Chairman of the Central Committee's Military Affairs Commission. He was among quite a few of the older generation to retire, making the average age of the new Central Committee, at 55.2, nearly four years younger than the previous average. Zhao Ziyang was confirmed as General Secretary and Li Peng and Hu Qili were put on the Standing Committee of the Politburo, thus becoming two of the most powerful men in China.

Two signs appeared to indicate an enhanced sense of reform and democracy within the CCP. One was that Hu Yaobang was retained on the Politburo, with no attempt being made to humiliate him for his earlier errors of 'bourgeois liberalisation'. The other was that the elections held for membership of the Central Committee were more open than ever before. Moreover, in contrast to previous Congresses, the slate contained more names than people to be elected so that voters were given a real choice. That the change showed a genuine move towards democracy was suggested by the fact that the list of those who failed to be elected included Deng Liqun, who had taken a lead in the campaign against 'bourgeois liberalisation' earlier in the year.

Since Zhao Ziyang had been both Premier of the State Council and Acting General Secretary of the CCP since the beginning of 1987, his confirmation as General Secretary suggested he should step down as Premier. Late in November 1987, he was replaced as Premier in an acting capacity by Li Peng, a younger man who had risen to membership of the Politburo in 1985 and to its Standing Committee at the First Plenum of the Thirteenth Central Committee. Li was a Soviet-trained engineer with a background suited to controlling a centralised economy.

The aftermath of the Thirteenth Congress

The First Session of the Seventh National People's Congress met in March and April 1988. It confirmed Li Peng as Premier and appointed Yang Shangkun as President of the PRC. Born in 1907, Yang was definitely a member of the old guard, with conservative political views to match. He was a senior military leader, a member of the Eighth, Eleventh, Twelfth and Thirteenth Central Committees, and was elected to the Politburo in November 1987.

Three factors dominated Chinese politics in the period following the Thirteenth Congress until the early months of 1989. The first was Zhao Ziyang's implementation of his liberal approach to reform, accelerating corruption and inflation. Hovering over these, and related to them, was a rising unease in the conservative wings of the leadership that Zhao's policies ran the risk of creating instability. The third factor was a growing tension between Zhao and Li Peng. Deng Xiaoping, having retired from the Central Committee, was not taking a notably active role in politics at the time.

However, he maintained his right of veto, continued to oppose 'bourgeois liberalisation' and told United States President George Bush, at a meeting on 26 February 1989, that 'the need for stability overrides all other problems in China',[10] a comment which appeared to place him, at least for the time being, in the conservative wing of politics.

By the early months of 1988 the liberalist reformism of Zhao Ziyang was again politically in the ascendant. One Western writer observed that 'suddenly' there were 'no more warnings of the dangers of bourgeois liberalisation, nor exhortations to adhere to the key conservative doctrinal tenets' of Deng Xiaoping's four cardinal principles.[11] It was as if the upsets of early 1987 had never happened.

Zhao Ziyang described the liberation of ideas as the central point of the Thirteenth CCP Congress. An editorial in the *Workers' Daily* stated that 'intellectual freedom is everyone's naturally-given right, the most basic and minimal of all human freedoms'.[12] Zhao Ziyang successfully accelerated his efforts to put his radical reformist supporters in positions of authority everywhere he could.

Freedom in the arts expanded to the extent where, from 22 December 1988, there was a two-week exhibition of paintings of nudes in Beijing. It was the first time such an exhibition had been held in the PRC and would have been inconceivable even a couple of years before. There were occasional student demonstrations — one took place early in June 1988 in Beijing over the death of a postgraduate student murdered near Beijing University and was followed by wall posters demanding press freedom, higher priority for education and a better legal system, among other things. On the whole, however, the most significant action in the student movement was taking place behind the scenes.

Corruption was nothing new to the late 1980s and has been mentioned several times in this book. But for all his best preventive efforts, it appeared to thrive on the radical reform policies of Zhao Ziyang. In mid-July 1987, the leadership decided to re-establish the Ministry of Supervision, which dated originally from the early 1950s but was abolished later in that decade, in a desperate but unsuccessful bid to curb corruption. People everywhere worried about the ability of power-holders to use their *guanxi* (relationship) networks to get benefits for themselves and their families. Naturally those affected furiously resented seeing less well qualified persons getting better jobs through corrupt connections (see also Chapter 11).[13]

Between late 1987 and early 1989 it was in the field of the economy that the conservative Premier Li Peng was most successful in asserting his views against Zhao Ziyang, particularly with regard to the fight against inflation. In a news conference held on 13 April 1988, just after the First Session of the Seventh National People's Congress, Li Peng stated that 'the main thing is that China must continue with its reforms and open policy and stabilise the economy'.[14] By the last phrase, he meant the control of inflation. Despite this, down to the summer of 1988, much discussion took place on price reform and the decontrol of prices. In August there was panic buying in most of China's major cities when rumours spread that all price controls would be removed on 1 September. Although the government weathered this crisis by postponing decisions on price reform, inflation was not solved and continued generally upwards throughout 1988 and into 1989. Although all government leaders were naturally worried about this, it was apparently a higher priority for Li Peng than for Zhao Ziyang. Economists in Hong Kong were predicting by the autumn of 1988 that Zhao Ziyang and his advisers were facing declining power and influence, even dismissal, because of the inflation and other aspects of the economic malaise over which they had presided.

Tibet

Among various other problems afflicting the Chinese government in the second half of the 1980s was unrest in Tibet. In 1951 an agreement had been reached between the central Chinese and the local Tibetan government under which Tibet would become a part of the PRC, but retain its own social system and autonomy. However, in March 1959 a major rebellion was launched against the Chinese; it was put down quickly but with much bloodshed. The Tibetan spiritual and temporal leader, the Dalai Lama, fled to India, where he set up a kind of government-in-exile. The net effect of the rebellion was that both sides went back on the 1951 agreement. In other words, the rebels had wanted total independence, but the Chinese reaction was to abolish the old Tibetan system and impose Chinese socialism on the Tibetans. The Cultural Revolution period saw much destruction of Tibetan culture, including major monasteries, and savage religious persecution.

In the early 1980s the government had taken several major actions suggesting that the policy of autonomy for areas inhabited by minority nationalities would be strengthened and given real teeth. These included the incorporation of several major articles into the 1982 Constitution, including one that the government head of all nationality areas must belong to the relevant minority. The head of the Tibetan Autonomous Region must thus be a Tibetan. In 1984 the National People's Congress adopted the PRC Law on Regional Autonomy for Minority Nationalities.

In September and October 1987, serious demonstrations flared in the Tibetan capital Lhasa, led by monks demanding total independence for Tibet. The Chinese authorities reacted harshly, many monks being arrested or beaten by police and some people being killed. Further disturbances took place in the following months, not only in Lhasa but in other Tibetan areas of China.

March 1989 represented the thirtieth anniversary of the major rebellion against Chinese rule which had resulted in the Dalai Lama taking refuge in India. When even more serious disturbances than in 1987 and 1988 broke out in commemoration of this event, China's reaction was to declare martial law and send in the people's armed police to suppress the independence movement once and for all. The action was probably brutal; there was certainly shooting and people were killed, although the number remains very unclear. However, inquiries in Lhasa in August and September 1990 among Tibetans and Han of various classes produced absolutely no confirmation of a report purporting to emanate from a defector in the Tibetan government that over 400 had been killed in a massacre similar to that in Beijing. Martial law was not lifted until the end of April 1990.

The Chinese and Tibetans both blamed each other for the disasters from 1987 to 1989. The Tibetans accused the Chinese of breaches of human rights and sent out messages calling for international support for their cause. The Chinese blamed separatists trying to split the motherland and repeatedly declared that Tibet was part of China. In addition, the Chinese blamed American and other overseas interference (see Chapter 16). Tibetans in exile and their supporters were making no secret of their delight about the disturbances and the harsh Chinese reaction. They believed all along that the softer policy of the early 1980s had been false; now they felt the true face of Chinese rule was being exposed.

The eruption of troubles in Tibet was related to the general decline taking place in China as a whole in the late 1980s. Economic problems were not being solved properly. In September 1988, the central government announced the establishment of a research centre to find ways of improving conditions among the minority nationalities. In so doing, it revealed appalling living standards among the minorities. According to the government account, people in the minority nationality areas 'still do not have enough food or clothes. Some 10 million have difficulties in finding enough housing and clean water to drink.'[15] This report refers to minority nationality areas in general, not just Tibet. However, although Tibet was economically a great deal better off than it had been under the dalai lamas, it was still notable for being among China's poorer nationality regions.

Just as elsewhere in China, corruption was causing serious problems for the people. Tibetans who saw themselves bypassed by Han people for good jobs blamed the corruption and injustices of the system for their failure. Since many of the senior cadres were Han Chinese, not Tibetans, corruption merely exacerbated the already bad relations between Han and Tibetans and intensified the widespread feeling among Tibetans that the Han were overlords in a country where they had no right to be in the first place.

Conclusion

When the Third Plenum of the Twelfth Central Committee introduced market reforms into the cities in 1984, the advocates of reform had every reason to be confident and the people to be optimistic. But by 1989, reform was faltering and optimism had to a large extent given way to pessimism. The Party and government realised that there would be disadvantages in reform, and that corruption and inflation, among other things, would present themselves as serious problems. But they could not find ways to solve these problems without undermining reform itself, and this they were not prepared to do. The various factions within the CCP and government could not agree on precisely which problems should take priority and on how a whole package could be found which would point the way to the future without undermining the achievements made in the earlier stages of the People's Republic. The Thirteenth Congress tried to address the problems, but its aftermath showed that the consensus it appeared to have forged was only temporary.

In the late 1970s and 1980s the Party told the people that they had in effect been deceived by Mao and his revolutionary vision, and they must change radically to a course which had a good chance of bringing modernisation and a higher standard of living to China. In 1984 the new direction appeared to be bringing excellent results and the problems were only in their early stages of development. But by the early months of 1989, the extent of success seemed much more limited. At the same time the problems had magnified greatly. Corruption was more rampant than ever and inflation was getting out of control. In Tibet the prospects for real autonomy had turned very sour. The problems associated with reform definitely worsened in the second half-decade of the 1980s.

The basic reason was a more or less insoluble dilemma. The very process of reform bred values among the people which were inimical to the sharing which is so essential to socialism. It raised expectations which could not properly be met. Openness to the outside world made the Chinese people, and especially the intelligentsia, acutely aware of how backward their country really was. Forgetting the desperate conditions from which the CCP had originally extracted the Chinese people, many even began to blame the revolution itself for China's backwardness and poverty. A crisis may not have been inevitable, but the ingredients were certainly in place for one.

Notes

1 Tony Saich, 'Reforming the Political Structure', in Robert Benewick and Paul Wingrove (eds), *Reforming the Revolution, China in Transition*, Macmillan, Houndmills and London, 1988, p. 29.

2 Robert Delfs, 'Back in the Saddle', *Far Eastern Economic Review*, vol. 132, no. 22, 29 May 1986, pp. 43–44.

3 *Renmin ribao (People's Daily)*, 8 May 1986, p. 1.

4 'Resolution of the Central Committee of the Communist Party of China on the Guiding Principles for Building a Socialist Society with an Advanced Culture and Ideology', *Beijing Review*, vol. 29, no. 40, 6 October 1986, p. v.

5 ibid., p. vii.

6 *Beijing Review*, vol. 30, no. 8, 23 February 1987, pp. 17–18.

7 Robin Munro, 'Political Reform, Student Demonstrations and the Conservative Backlash', in Benewick and Wingrove (eds), *Reforming the Revolution*, p. 71.

8 ibid., p. xvi.

9 Michel Oksenberg, 'China's 13th Party Congress', *Problems of Communism*, vol. 36, no. 6, November–December 1987, pp. 12–13.

10 *Beijing Review*, vol. 32, no 29, 17–23 July 1989, p. 18.

11 Robert Delfs, in *Far Eastern Economic Review*, vol. 139, no. 12, 24 March 1988, p. 49.

12 ibid.

13 On corruption in the CCP, see also Colin Mackerras, 'The Political Situation in China in 1989', in Colin Mackerras, Kevin Bucknall and Russell Trood, *The Beijing Tragedy: Implications for China and Australia*, Australia–Asia Papers No. 51, Centre for the Study of Australia–Asia Relations, Griffith University, Brisbane, 1989, pp. 3–5.

14 *Beijing Review*, vol. 31, no. 17, 25 April–1 May 1988, p. 12.

15 Cheng Hong, in *China Daily*, 10 September 1988, p. 3.

5

Political History III
Crisis to Recovery 1989–92

FROM April to June 1989 further student demonstrations took place over most of China. The demonstrations were far bigger than those of 1986, in Beijing climaxing in the massacre of 3–4 June. This was followed by a period of tension in Beijing and other major cities, but there was no major unrest and political stability was quicker to return than most in the West had expected.

The student demonstrations brought on an extremely sharp struggle within the leadership, in which the main loser was CCP General Secretary Zhao Ziyang. During the period following the Beijing massacre, the new General Secretary, Jiang Zemin, and the other victors struggled to have their leadership accepted by the people at large. They were given a major boost in their endeavours by the holding of the eleventh Asian Games in Beijing from 22 September to 7 October 1990. At the beginning of 1992, Deng Xiaoping came out of retirement to reassert his influence. However, most Chinese remained apprehensive about the kind of leadership which might take over after his death.

In policy terms the crisis showed an unprecedented degree of liberalism and toleration of dissent, followed by its direct antithesis when the crackdown occurred. Even then, the policies of reform were never in serious danger. The aftermath of the massacre certainly saw the more cautious proponents in control, but the screws began to be loosened from about the middle of 1990, with an acceleration of reform early in 1992 on the reappearance of Deng

Xiaoping. Rapid economic reform was the line confirmed at the Fourteenth National Congress of the CCP late in 1992. However, there was (as usual) no corresponding emphasis placed on political reform.

The student demonstrations

Hu Yaobang died on 15 April 1989. His dismissal from the post of General Secretary of the CCP early in 1987, for 'bourgeois liberalisation', had made him into a hero figure in the minds of the students — the symbol of the kinds of reforms they wanted. Hu's death sparked off a wave of student demonstrations which grew more and more complex as time went on, and gathered their own momentum in a way which none of the student or government leaders could control.

While strongly in support of reform, students had for some time been increasingly dissatisfied with certain aspects of Deng Xiaoping's regime. They resented the corruption which allowed more and more CCP bureaucrats to grab the benefits of reform for themselves and their families at the expense of everybody else. Students saw jobs which they felt ought to go to themselves, as the most highly educated and qualified people, being allocated to those with lesser ability but better connections.

Inflation was another cause of serious worry for the students and intellectuals. It affected professional people on fixed incomes much more seriously than it did peasants or free business people, whose incomes were better able to expand in line with inflation. Moonlighting became a more or less essential part of life for professionals, who experienced great difficulty in making ends meet from their incomes (see Chapter 7).

The students were also very unhappy with the pace of political reform, which they thought was much too slow and ought to be accelerated to accord with the speed and extent of economic reform. They regarded the kinds of political reforms being undertaken by Gorbachev in the Soviet Union as appropriate also for China. Moreover, many Chinese students had studied in, or had friends who were studying in, Western countries or Japan, where conditions were incomparably better than in China. Western, and especially American, political and social influence had become very extensive by the mid-1980s and continued to expand as the decade progressed. Most Chinese students believed that China needed far more freedom and democracy than it enjoyed — or than Deng Xiaoping seemed willing to grant.

As early as 26 April 1989, Deng Xiaoping had put forward his view on the student demonstrations through a major editorial published in the official *People's Daily*. His opinion was that the demonstrations constituted a 'turmoil', which was a challenge and even a threat to the Party and the people. This view enraged the students, who added a demand that this 26 April editorial should be retracted and an apology issued to their list of other demands. Of course, Deng Xiaoping had no intention of acceding to such a demand. The students' reaction was to demand the resignation of those leaders they perceived as being most hostile to them, particularly Deng Xiaoping and Li Peng.

The CCP leaders repeatedly said that they were fully supportive of attempts to curb corruption and inflation, just as the students were demanding, but the idea that students should dictate the method to be used, and should hold a knife at the government's throat through massive demonstrations, was absolute anathema to Deng and his supporters. As for issues of freedom and democracy, the government continued to advocate a gradualist approach and was not prepared to tolerate what it saw as a sudden collapse of authority just because the students appeared to be getting so much popular support.

The students demanded dialogue with the government. But the terms of this dialogue were not acceptable to the government leaders, in particular Deng Xiaoping or Li Peng. Firstly, the students required to be represented by their newly founded independent association, whereas the government was prepared to talk only to its own CCP-founded and dependent body. Secondly, the students wanted a public, televised dialogue, in which selected government leaders were both willing and able to make on-the-spot decisions in response to the student demands. They wanted to debate policy on equal terms with senior government leaders. This the government was not prepared to concede.

Although Fang Lizhi continued to exercise great influence on the student body, he did not take a prominent lead in the student movement of 1989. One of the leading dissidents was political scientist Yan Jiaqi, a member of the Chinese Academy of Social Sciences and advisor to Zhao Ziyang. On 17 May he and several others drafted the 'May 17 Proclamation' which called Deng Xiaoping 'a dictator' and claimed that the government had 'lost its sense of responsibility and humanity' and could no longer 'be accepted as the government of the republic'.[1] Other leading dissidents included Hou Dejian, a noted Taiwanese pop singer who had defected to the PRC in 1983, and literary critic Liu Xiaobo, who returned from overseas in April 1989 especially to take an active role. Among student leaders to emerge from the movement were Wuerkaixi, a young man of the Uygur nationality, and Chai Ling, both from the Beijing Normal University, as well as Wang Dan, from the prestigious Beijing University.

The seventieth anniversary of the great May Fourth Movement of 1919, which had contributed to the development of a new, freer and more youth-oriented culture in China, was the occasion for further massive demonstrations, not only in Beijing but in many other cities as well. The demonstrations continued over the following days, attracting participants in the hundreds of thousands in Beijing and several other cities. Portraits of Mao Zedong appeared in the Square. The government forbade the demonstrations, but made no attempt to clamp down on them at this stage. Popular support for the students and their demands was obvious in Beijing and elsewhere, with individuals waving enthusiastically and even contributing money to the students.

Among those who used the occasion of the May Fourth anniversary to comment on the student demonstrations was a group of intellectuals, including some quite well known figures such as Yan Jiaqi. On the crucial issue of democracy, they came down in full support of the students and in opposition to the government position:

> We cannot accept the absurd view that democracy must be delayed because the quality of the Chinese nation is too low . . . Democracy, freedom, human rights and rule by law . . . are the pre-requisites of building socialism. We are opposed to taking 'Chinese national conditions' as a pretext for refusing to accept them.[2]

For these intellectuals, democracy and freedom were the essential basis of socialism, not its enemy. Such views put them on a collision course with Deng Xiaoping and his followers. The irony and tragedy are that neither the students nor their intellectual backers put forward a clear notion of precisely what form democracy, freedom and human rights should take if not the well-tried model of the rich and industrialised West, especially the United States.

On 13 May 1989, the student movement reached a new and much more serious stage, when thousands of students occupied the Tiananmen Square in the centre of Beijing and announced that they intended to stay there until their demands were met. As a sign of their seriousness, some of them went on a hunger strike. Gorbachev made a much-heralded visit to Beijing and Shanghai just after the occupation of the square began, and the students, who had not been fully aware of just how historically significant his presence was, were able to take advantage of the presence of a large corps of the world press, especially from the West and Japan. Many Western journalists joined in the demonstrations enthusiastically, giving the students all the favourable publicity they wanted, including interviews in English and round-the-clock attention.

From the beginning, the various members of the government were divided about the best way to react to the student demonstrations. CCP General Secretary Zhao Ziyang was very much more sympathetic to them than Deng Xiaoping or Li Peng. The week following the occupation of the square and the beginning of the hunger strike saw a sharpening of the struggle within the leadership. Both Zhao and Li actually visited the student hunger strikers in hospital, with Zhao showing much more feeling for them than Li.

On the evening of 18 May, immediately after Gorbachev had left China, Li Peng and several other leaders did in fact hold a public televised debate with some student leaders, including Wuerkaixi and Wang Dan. The debate produced nothing in the way of compromise. Li Peng was interested in only one thing: getting the students to end their hunger strike. The students, on the other hand, wanted discussion of their demands. Li Peng's manner to the students was decidedly condescending. Wuerkaixi behaved to Li Peng rather as a haughty teacher might to a recalcitrant schoolboy. By the end of the television show, the two sides could agree on only one point: no 'dialogue' had taken place.

Early the following morning, 19 May, Zhao Ziyang appeared in Tiananmen Square to talk to the students. He implored them to call off the hunger strike and made it perfectly plain to them that they were not making his battle with Li Peng any easier by their activities. He knew that he was losing the power struggle against Li Peng and that Deng Xiaoping had come down very decisively against him. As of mid-1993, this was Zhao's last political appearance.[3]

Within a few hours of Zhao's talks with the students, Li Peng declared martial law in parts of Beijing. Troops of the 38th Army of the PLA began to move into Tiananmen Square with the aim of clearing it of students. However, the students put up barricades and many tried to persuade the troops to their side. The net result was a victory for the students, in the sense that nobody was injured in the fight and the square remained under student occupation. The soldiers of the 38th Army were simply not prepared at this stage to push martial law to the point of bloodshed, and may have been under orders not to shoot. The students called off their hunger strike.

Deng Xiaoping's reaction was to test out opinion from among the military throughout China and in the senior echelons of the CCP and the government. Most of the military commanders sided with Deng and Li for a tough line against the students. Of the five members of the Standing Committee of the Politburo, only Hu Qili was prepared to support Zhao Ziyang, an opinion which was to cost him his job. On 25 May, Li Peng went on television to announce that he was fully in control of the government and would enforce martial law. The demonstrations persisted, but many of the students from Beijing in the square began to go home, being replaced by those from outside the capital, including Hong Kong.

Just how spontaneous the protests were is a matter of debate. However, the likelihood is that demonstrations of such size and persistence required support from within the top leadership of the CCP, at least initially. This can only have come from Zhao Ziyang and his advisers. On the other hand, the demonstrations obviously had developed their own momentum, and it may be that by the time of Gorbachev's visit in the middle of May nobody was really able to control them. The possibility that they were to some extent taken over by people with more opportunistic motives than a concern for democracy cannot be overlooked.

The Beijing massacre

At the end of May some students of the Central Fine Arts Academy put up a statue in Tiananmen Square. They called it 'the Goddess of Democracy', but it bore a striking resemblance to the Statue of Liberty in New York. This was a crassly stupid action because it gave Li Peng and others precisely the weapon they needed to convince the leadership that American influence, money and interference were behind the student movement. Four known dissidents, including Hou Dejian and Liu Xiaobo, began another hunger strike in Tiananmen Square. Demonstrations began again, although on a very much smaller scale than before. Most of the demonstrators at this stage came from outside Beijing. On the night of 2–3 June, small quantities of arms were distributed to various groups throughout the city. Deng Xiaoping had been convinced right from the beginning that a small number of 'evil' people were taking advantage of the students for their own purposes. He interpreted the renewed activity early in June as a cue that a counter-revolutionary rebellion was brewing, aimed at overthrowing the

CCP and the PRC, and replacing them with an American-style government.

During the night of 3–4 June, troops of the 27th Army of the PLA moved into Tiananmen Square with the aim of enforcing martial law and clearing the square of demonstrators. According to a message intercepted by a Western communications satellite, they were under orders from the top to retaliate when they met with violence. There was certainly some violence against some soldiers armed only with tear-gas.[4] Whether it was started by the enraged crowd or troops remains unclear, but as the night proceeded, armed forces asserted themselves more forcefully, ignoring student barricades and pleas and fighting their way with tanks and guns along the main boulevard of Beijing leading to Tiananmen Square. It is true that they did indeed succeed in clearing the square of demonstrators, and in suppressing the student movement, but at the cost of a massacre which cast a permanent blight over the reputation of Deng Xiaoping and those leaders seen as involved.

Primary responsibility must certainly rest with Deng Xiaoping. He was the Chairman of both the state and the CCP Military Commissions. His authority was high enough that no major decision, let alone one involving a military action right in the centre of the nation's capital, could possibly have taken place without his approval. Another leader to whom major blame was allocated was Yang Shangkun, the President of the PRC. Not only did he occupy the top state position, but was also very senior in the military. Moreover, the man who actually led the troops into the square, Yang Baibing, was a very close relation of his. Of course, Li Peng also became an object of hate and contempt among large numbers of Chinese.

The casualties from the fighting in Beijing and the massacre on the night of 3–4 June 1989 have been variously reported. On 30 June 1989, Chen Xitong, the Mayor of Beijing, issued a report stating that only about 200 civilians, including 36 students, and several dozen soldiers, armed police and public security officers had been killed, with about 3000 civilians and more than 6000 troops and police injured.[5] Foreign reports put the number of people killed at a very much higher figure, ranging as high as 10 000.[6] In August 1989, Amnesty International published an account claiming a casualty figure of at least 1000 killed and several thousand injured.[7] The issue is a complex one, which has aroused heated feelings. A reliable and universally accepted figure may never be known and must certainly await future research. It is beyond the scope of this chapter to examine the question properly, but a Chinese medical contact estimated the number killed, based on direct experience at the hospital nearest to the most affected parts of Beijing, at over 1000.[8]

Even now this event is often referred to as the 'Tiananmen massacre'. But in fact the main battles and killing took place not in the square itself, but along the main boulevard which at one point passes through it. Chen Xitong's government report, which was confirmed by contacts in Beijing, suggested that in fact the great majority of the students in the square itself were warned of the danger and given time to escape unharmed.[9] An excellent account by Robin Munro of the American human rights organisation Asiawatch agrees that, contrary to many Western reports at the time, there was no slaughter of students in the Tiananmen Square itself. He describes what he saw in the square at a time between 4.30 and 5.00 a.m. on 4 June. Hou Dejian had just made a speech asking the students to leave the square and they had taken a vote deciding on that action:

> For an agonizing minute, it seemed as if the students might not comply with the decision to leave. Then, slowly, they began to stand up and descend from the monument [in the centre of the square]. As the first group filed past us [Munro himself and journalist Richard Nations], heading toward the open southeast corner of the square, we burst into spontaneous applause. Many in the ten-deep column, each contingent following the banners of its college, had tears rolling down their cheeks. All looked shaken; many were trembling or unsteady on their feet. But all looked proud and unbeaten. One group shouted, 'Down with the Communist Party!' — the first time I had ever heard this openly said in China.[10]

On 9 June, Deng Xiaoping congratulated and thanked the troops and their leaders for putting down a counter-revolutionary rebellion. His argument was that the 'turmoil' had changed into a 'rebellion' at the beginning of June. Deng stated his belief that 'what we faced was not just some ordinary people who were misguided, but also a rebellious clique and a large number of the dregs of society'. He continued that 'the key point is that they wanted to overthrow our state and the Party'.[11] This was not a case of murdering unarmed students, but of protecting the CCP against almost certain overthrow.

What Deng Xiaoping and his main followers feared most was organised dissent and unrest among the working class. For them resistance to the CCP following the model of Poland's Solidarity was much more threatening than the students or intellectual backers.[12] Already Solidarity had gone far towards undermining communist power in Poland. The collapse of communist power in parts of Eastern Europe later in 1989 gave the CCP leaders ammunition in defence of their position, because it suggested that indeed there was a real possibility of the CCP's overthrow.

The evidence for the view that a counter-revolutionary rebellion occurred does, however, seem to be insufficient. Some anti-government forces may indeed have obtained arms early in June 1989, but not on a scale which would enable a successful rebellion against the CCP to be carried out. The students certainly wanted the resignation of Deng Xiaoping and Li Peng, but at no stage did substantial numbers of them call for the overthrow of the CCP. Munro's comment that he never heard anybody publicly call for the overthrow of the CCP until the morning of 4 June is very revealing. There was support for the students among the working class, but by June the students had become hopelessly factionalised and there is no evidence of a leadership or organisation based either on students or workers, let alone a union between the two, which was coherent or strong enough to be called a counter-revolutionary rebellion. The demonstrations were designed as protest, not a revolution. Unlike the communist parties of Poland or other countries of Eastern and Central Europe, which were installed by Soviet troops at the end of World War II, the CCP came to power through a long revolution which had a good deal of support among the masses. It did not depend on the Soviet or any other foreign army either for its establishment or for its long-term hold on power. Indeed, for most of the period from 1949 to 1989, the Soviet government treated it much more with hostility than support.

On the other hand, even had there been no specifically organised rebellion against the rule of the CCP in China, might not the student movement have led quite quickly to the CCP's overthrow had it not been suppressed? When one considers that virtually every other communist party in the world, even including that of the Soviet Union itself, was overthrown in the two to three years following the Beijing massacre, it is difficult to avoid the suspicion that the Chinese student movement might have been at the forefront of a kind of *Zeitgeist* hostile to Marxist–Leninist parties of all kinds and in all places. This argument gathers force in the light of the fact that the method of overthrow in virtually all cases has centred on massive demonstrations of protest against the ruling communist power.

Extensive conversations with ordinary people of various walks of life throughout China from late 1989 to early 1992 suggested that opinion was divided over the student demonstrations, about whether there was actually a counter-revolutionary rebellion in Beijing, and over the government's reaction. In Beijing itself, most people — especially the intellectuals — doubted very much that there was ever an attempt to overthrow the CCP, and that such an eventuality was ever possible. They therefore considered the government's reaction not only unnecessary but monstrous, even though many may indeed have wanted stability and accepted that the CCP would control China for quite a few years yet. Outside Beijing, opinion is much less clearly sympathetic to the students. A rural cadre outside Guiyang at the end of 1990, when asked what the peasants thought of the Beijing events, replied simply: 'People here want stability, they don't understand what the students were talking about.' The peasants and other ordinary people said they did not understand what the students were demanding: they worshipped Deng Xiaoping and his reform policies and opposed anything which could possibly endanger them. Such people accepted the government line that bad elements had used the students for their own ends, which included a rebellion against the CCP. Certainly there were middle-aged people who were convinced that the government action was necessary and who continued to support Deng Xiaoping. Young city-dwellers may have been much less enthusiastic about Deng and much less sure about any rebellion. However, the view expressed by the rural cadre outside Guiyang appeared to be very widespread indeed throughout the whole country in the early 1990s. Few people wanted instability. What they wanted was to get on with economic growth and modernisation.

Looking back over the period April to June 1989, the student demand which people remember most clearly was not the quest for democracy or freedom, but an end to corruption. From 1990–92 the issue of corruption was raised in numerous conversations held both with people who supported the students and those who opposed them. Naturally enough, everybody wanted an end to corruption, but to the supporters of Deng Xiaoping it was never clear how massive and persistent demonstrations would solve such a problem.

The aftermath of the Beijing massacre

On the same day as the massacre in Beijing, a similar event occurred in Chengdu, the capital of Sichuan. Although the scale was very much smaller than in Beijing, the incident involved the destruction of many of the government buildings in the centre of the city.

During a visit to Chengdu in August 1990, it was found that, although the buildings had been completely restored, the student movement had enjoyed quite a bit of support in the city. In Shanghai, a confrontation between the municipal authorities headed by Jiang Zemin and the students threatened to result in a massacre, but fortunately it was averted. Although huge areas of the country were quite unconcerned and knew only the government version of what had happened, enormous numbers of students throughout the country were outraged by the government's suppression of the student movement.

In Beijing itself, the situation was extremely tense for a few days after the massacre. It even looked as if civil war could break out, with the potential for the country to collapse into chaos. There were reports that the 27th and 38th Armies were facing each other in Beijing. However, no civil war broke out. Although economic control over some parts of the country was loosened, with some provinces adopting policies and practices to suit their own needs rather than those of the central government, any danger that the country would fall apart was very quickly shown to be quite unrealistic.

This is not to say that things soon returned to normal. The massacre was followed by a serious crackdown in Beijing and Shanghai. Quite a few people, mainly workers, were hastily put in front of courts controlled by the government and summarily executed for taking part in the rebellion.

Some of the main leaders of the movement were arrested and imprisoned. (The results of the trials of the leaders of the movement are discussed in Chapter 11.) Others of the leaders of the student movement were luckier or played their cards more carefully. Yan Jiaqi and Wuerkaixi got out of China immediately and continued their activities against the Chinese government from outside China, becoming respectively the Chairman and Vice-Chairman of the Federation for Democracy in China when it was set up in Paris in September 1989. Hou Dejian took refuge in the Australian Embassy in Beijing, but later was allowed to live as a rich dissident in Beijing; in May 1990 he announced he would petition for the release of political prisoners as a result of which he was expelled to Taiwan. Chai Ling escaped with her husband ten months after the massacre. Fang Lizhi took refuge in the American Embassy in Beijing despite a Chinese government call for his arrest and trial by the courts. However, a year later the Chinese authorities allowed him to leave the country for Britain, from there moving to the United States to take up a senior academic post. In general, those who fled abroad were members of Zhao Ziyang's think-tank and entourage, while those not associated with this group remained in China.

On 24 June 1989, the 13th CCP Central Committee held its Fourth Plenum, at which it adopted Deng Xiaoping's view of the events which had just shaken Beijing, declaring that a counter-revolutionary rebellion had been quelled. The Plenum formally dismissed Zhao Ziyang from his post as General Secretary of the CCP, but continued to refer to him as 'Comrade' and did not expel him from the CCP itself. It predicted that deliberations would continue concerning his case, suggesting that the possibility of accusing him of assisting the rebellion was still open.

The main problem facing the Fourth Plenum was who should replace Zhao as General Secretary. The man who got the job was Jiang Zemin, the Shanghai boss who had succeeded in solving the student problem in China's largest city. A suave pro-reformist, Jiang was nevertheless a surprise choice because at the time he was not a member of the Politburo, let alone its Standing Committee. Deng Xiaoping expressed his view that, whereas Mao Zedong had dominated the first generation of CCP leaders and he himself the second, Jiang Zemin had the ability to lead the third. Li Peng must certainly have been disappointed to see Jiang get the top job over his head. What this implied was that, while Li Peng got the odium of the massacre, somebody else got the main reward. Of course, Li Peng retained the job of Premier of the State Council and kept his place on the Standing Committee of the Politburo.

Apart from Zhao's replacement by Jiang, other changes were made in the composition of the Standing Committee of the Politburo, which contained China's most powerful leaders. Hu Qili was expelled and two others added, namely Li Ruihuan and Song Ping. Li had been Mayor of Tianjin and enjoyed a reputation for great intelligence and political skill. The composition of the Standing Committee was thus Jiang Zemin, Li Peng, Qiao Shi, Yao Yilin, Li Ruihuan and Song Ping.

In November 1989 the Fifth Plenum agreed to Deng Xiaoping's request to retire from his position as Chairman of the Military Commission of the CCP. To show that this was not a dismissal, it issued a statement lavishing enormous praise on his contribution to the CCP and to China, describing him as 'an acknowledged outstanding leader of the Chinese people' and the 'chief architect' of the achievements of the reform period.[13] Jiang Zemin replaced him as Chairman, Yang Shangkun retained his position on the Commission and Yang Baibing, who had led the troops into the square, was appointed to join it. A few months later Deng Xiaoping also retired from his position as the Chairman of the State Military Commission. Although this was the last of his official positions, most people believed that he retained some power and continued to be consulted on major matters. He almost certainly still held a power of veto on important appointments and other major issues.

In the wake of the crackdown on the student movement, there was another campaign against 'bourgeois liberalisation', defined in the same way as in the first half of 1987. At the same time, there was a movement against corruption and against the 'six evils', which included narcotics, prostitution, pornography, gambling and the buying and selling of women. The campaign against corruption and these 'six evils' continued throughout 1990 and following years. The government claimed major successes on both fronts, but corruption remained a major issue within society. Although curbed, pornography, gambling, narcotics and prostitution are still very much alive in China. As for the most serious of all the 'six evils', the buying and selling of women, arrests of offenders continued, including 400 people in Shaanxi province in mid-1992; their crime was to have sold women for wives, maids or concubines.

In January 1990, martial law was lifted in Beijing. Expectations continued in the West that the student movement would return to prominence, especially during May and June 1990, the first anniversary of the movement's high tide and suppression. However, although a very few people did demonstrate anti-government feelings in Tiananmen Square to mark the first anniversary of the massacre, they were promptly arrested and produced no impact. The student movement remained dormant, with no sign of major revival.

The Asian Games and their aftermath

The 1990 Asian Games in Beijing were a major political and social event for China. They dominated the television and news coverage there, and the government planned to use them to boost morale and confidence in the wake of the disasters of 1989. In terms of gold and other medals, China did extremely well, far better than any other country. On the other hand, although many came from abroad to watch the Games, the number of visitors was somewhat lower than the government had expected and been prepared for.

In general, the Chinese people were extremely enthusiastic about the Games. Enormous numbers of people watched the events on television, especially the opening and closing sessions, even during working hours. Most regarded the ceremonies at the beginning and end of the Games as exceedingly spectacular and magnificent. The Games certainly produced a significant and positive effect on the morale of the Chinese people, particularly outside Beijing. Even people who expressed anti-government views seemed to be very proud of the Games. On the other hand, in Beijing itself, many people were quite cynical about them. Some thought they were a waste of money and a political trick to win support for an unpopular government. Others expressed disappointment that not nearly as many foreigners attended as had been expected, in particular from the West. 'It wasn't as good for business as we thought it would be' was a refrain heard quite frequently. 'Tickets were too expensive, and ordinary people couldn't go' was another.

One important political aspect of the Games was Deng Xiaoping's failure to appear in public during them, even briefly. This led some to suggest that he was ill, and others that he really had retired. The political figures who dominated the opening and closing ceremonies were Jiang Zemin and Li Peng, and it is quite possible that Deng was quite happy to see them take the limelight. There was no danger of his falling from favour, at least until after his death, and he had nothing to gain from appearing in public during the Games.

One of the main implications of the Asian Games was that China wished to convince the world of its intention to continue and even expand the policies of reform and the open door. One of many illustrative examples came when the Singaporean leader Lee Kuan Yew visited Beijing in October 1990, not long after Singapore and China established diplomatic relations and shortly before Lee retired. Jiang Zemin and Yang Shangkun both assured him that China would 'step up the process of reform and opening up to the outside world'.[14] The only major changes in the leadership to occur in 1990 and 1991 were the promotion of Zhu Rongji and Zou Jiahua to Vice-Premiers on 8 April 1991. Zhu Rongji is noted for his support for reform, although Zou's enthusiasm is less obvious. Hu Qili, who had lost his position on the Standing Committee of the Politburo for siding with Zhao Ziyang against Deng Xiaoping and Li Peng over the student movement in 1989, returned again to favour, although not to a senior position in the leadership. In 1991 he was apponted a deputy minister in the central government and in October 1992, just after the Fourteenth CCP Congress, he was restored to the Politburo.

Two striking intellectual trends strengthened in China following the failure of the 1989 student movement, persisting into 1992. One was a return to tradition. Interest in Confucianism, traditional arts and sports gathered even further momentum than in preceding years. More and more people took up the traditional exercises known as *qigong*, believing that they could lengthen their life-span and renew their vigor. On the other hand, admiration for the radical and arch-anti-Confucian Mao Zedong also made a comeback. Quite a few books were published about him and gained a wide readership. Taxi-drivers delighted in hanging portraits of Mao on their inside rear-vision mirrors. The common thread in these two apparently contradictory trends was nationalism. It should be emphasised that the renewal of interest in Mao was not equivalent to support for the Cultural Revolution. Mao was more a symbol of patriotism and anti-corruption, with the idea that, though he may have been a tyrant in his last years, he was nevertheless one of the great leaders of the twentieth century and really did change China, so the people should be proud of him as a historical figure. Since 1993 marked the centenary of his birth, it was natural that it should see an upsurge of memorabilia about Mao.

The reappearance of Deng Xiaoping

At the time of the Spring Festival, early in February 1992, Deng Xiaoping briefly came out from retirement to inspect the special economic zones in Guangdong and to attend a Spring Festival celebration party in Shanghai. On 23 February, a front-page editorial of the *People's Daily* declared capitalism 'a beneficial supplement to the socialist economy'. With Deng's strong support, the Politburo issued a statement the next month declaring the left wing a greater danger to socialism than the right and calling for the policies of reform to last at least a century. Deng's intervention had once again strengthened the forces of reform within the leadership. A reshuffle began to get rid of some of the most conservative elements within the leadership.

When the next meeting of the National People's Congress convened in March, Premier Li Peng's report came under some strong criticism. One sign that he was losing favour was an attack on the major Three Gorges Dam Project on the Yangzi River, which he had long been pushing for its hydroelectric and other economic advantages. Although the National People's Congress passed it in the end, the vote in favour only just exceeded the necessary two-thirds majority, with substantial numbers either abstaining or voting against (see Chapter 12). It was unprecedented for a premier to come under open opposition in the National People's Congress. In addition to showing feeling about Li Peng, it also suggested a far greater freedom of debate within the National People's Congress and the beginnings of a loosening up of the system generally (see Chapter 10).

At the same time, the National People's Congress session most certainly should not be taken as a sign that Western-style democracy was in the offing. Along with the 'central task of economic development' and persistence in reform and opening to the outside word, official media continued their emphasis on Deng's 'four cardinal principles', especially CCP leadership. On 27 April 1992, a full-page article in the *People's Daily* quoted Deng Xiaoping as saying that 'once the factors of turmoil reappear in the future, we will, if required, not hesitate to use any means to eliminate them as soon as possible'. Since he added that 'we can use martial law or measures harsher and stricter', it was quite clear that he would even be prepared to repeat the sending in of the army to ensure that the CCP remained in power. The CCP's willingness to adopt capitalist methods did not signal the slightest intention of resigning its monopoly on power.

Deng's reappearance marked a significant shift in the direction of economic modernisation and growth, but a much slighter one in the area of political reform. Political leaders saw it as very much in their interests to take his ideas to heart and emphasise them accordingly. When Jiang Zeming gave a press conference on 1 April 1992, just before departing for a visit to Japan, he noted that the Party and people were studying Deng's 'recent important speeches' made during his trip to south China in January and February. He gave Deng the credit for the policies of reform and opening to the outside world and referred to 'his theory of building socialism with Chinese characteristics'.[15] In policy terms, 'socialism with Chinese characteristics' is synonymous with reform, modernisation, opening to the outside world, economic growth and a rising standard of living.

The Fourteenth Congress of the CCP in October 1992 confirmed the reformist line and Deng Xiaoping's influence. During the Congress the *People's Daily* even referred to his reformist ideas as a 'magic weapon'. The Congress confirmed the rise of the reformist Zhu Rongji by appointing him to the Standing Committee of the Politburo. Li Peng had done his best to associate himself with the reformist line through speeches he had made in the wake of the March 1992 meeting of the National People's Congress and kept his position in the Standing Committee of the Politburo. The Congress's failure to promote Yang Baibing to the Politburo suggests that the PLA's political influence has failed to increase and it is likely that Deng Xiaoping took a formal decision both to try to curb it from too strong a degree of dominance and to have reformers promoted to leading positions at the expense of conservative followers of Yang Baibing. On the other hand, the reformist pressures did not go so far as to rehabilitate Zhao Ziyang. On the eve of the Fourteenth Congress, the Ninth Plenum of the 13th Central Committee decided against any such move by reconfirming the overall verdict of the Fourth Plenum in June 1989. It also decided to end the investigation of Zhao's case which the Fourth Plentum had begun, foreclosing any possibility that he might be put on trial.

Conclusion

By late 1992, the situation had eased greatly in Beijing and most other cities. As a whole the country was stable and economic progress was rapid. The ideas of reform were considerably stronger than at any time since the crisis of June 1989, and the worst fears of the Chinese intelligentsia and foreigners of a return to the days of the stereotypical hard line in terms of ideology had not materialised. There were, of course, restrictions on discussion and publishing, but the extent of freedom was still incomparably greater than it had been before 1978. Many people had learned to live with the existing level of corruption, and inflation had been brought under control, at least temporarily.

Yet people remained apprehensive. Deng Xiaoping's death could not fail to bring on a period of uncertainty and instability. The aged Yang Shangkun and his military colleagues retained a high degree of power. How would the army react to the deaths of the old-generation leaders? Conversations held from late 1990 to late 1992 suggested that while nobody expected civil war, many realised it was a possibility. Few were quite as confident as Deng Xiaoping that Jiang Zemin would remain the third-generation leader following Mao Zedong and Deng himself. As is usual when a major political figure leaves the scene, people worried that things would get worse, but hoped and expected that a new leader would emerge who would usher in a better period. People were divided over whether the student movement would or should re-emerge, or whether, if it did, it would lead to a better result than in 1989. The really consistent feeling found among ordinary Chinese people late 1990 to late 1992 was a desire for a peaceful transition to a post-Deng leadership which would continue the policies of reform and opening to the outside world. Very few expected the post-Deng regime to be led by other than the CCP, but virtually nobody wanted a return to the radical policies which characterised the late years of Mao Zedong.

Notes

1 See Geremie Barmé and Linda Jaivin (eds), *New Ghosts, Old Dreams, Chinese Rebel Voices*, Times Books, Random House, New York, 1992, p. 62.

2 Quoted from 'Quarterly Chronicle and Documentation', *China Quarterly*, no. 119, September 1989, p. 675.

3 On one occasion in September 1990, Zhao Ziyang was seen by Japanese diplomats and employees playing golf at the Beijing International Gold Club near the Ming Tombs outside Beijing. See *Asiaweek*, vol. 16, no. 38, 21 September 1990, p. 23.

4 See Philippa Tristram, 'Tiananmen Revisited', *London Review of Books*, 19 November 1992, p. 7.

5 Chen Xitong, *Report on Checking the Turmoil and Quelling the Counter-Revolutionary Rebellion*, New Star Publishers, Beijing, 1989, pp. 46–47.

6 See David Humphries in *The Age*, 8 June 1989, p. 1.

7 See John Hoffmann and Robert Darroch, 'We Got It Wrong', *The Independent Monthly*, vol. 1, no. 3, 6 September 1989, pp. 10–11.

8 Tristram, 'Tiananmen Revisited', p. 7 states that 1000 is 'the number generally used today', adding that very few of the dead were *known* to be students.

9 Chen, *Report*, pp. 47–48.

10 Robin Munro, 'Who Died in Beijing, and Why', *The Nation*, vol. 250, no. 23, 11 June 1990, pp. 819–20.

11 *Beijing Review*, vol. 32, no. 28, 10–16 July 1989, p. 14.

12 See, for instance, Munro, 'Who Died in Beijing and Why', p. 812.

13 'Communiqué of the Fifth Plenary Session of the 13th CPC Central Committee', *Beijing Review*, vol. 32, no. 47, 20–26 November 1989, pp. 17–18.

14 Zhang Ping, in *China Daily*, 18 October 1990, p. 1.

15 *Beijing Review*, vol. 35, no. 14, 6-12 April 1992, p. 6.

6 Rural Economic Reform

IN the earlier stages of his political career, Deng Xiaoping supported the introduction of at least some elements of market forces in China's centrally planned economy. During the Cultural Revolution, radical leftists within the CCP branded him as a 'capitalist roader', and one reason he was purged was his advocacy of market forces. With his consolidation of power in the late 1970s, the way was open for Deng to implement his ideas in economic management. As events would show, his enthusiasm for the introduction of market forces was greater than ever.

The immediate post-Mao leadership embarked on a massive economic development program under the banner of the 'four modernisations', with the stated goal of transforming China into a 'powerful, modern, socialist country by the end of this century'. The basis for the program was the Ten-Year Plan (1976–85), belatedly promulgated by Mao's successor, Hua Guofeng, in February 1978. The plan envisaged imports of technology at a scale unprecedented in the history of the PRC. After the initial euphoria in which thousands of contracts were signed, it became clear that neither China's economic infrastructure nor its foreign exchange reserves could sustain the pressures of this program. In February 1979, therefore, the Chinese authorities temporarily suspended US$2.6 billion worth of contracts with Japanese firms and put many other projects on hold.[1] This was dictated in part by the excessively ambitious nature of the plan and in part by the great emphasis it placed on the development of heavy industry to the neglect of agriculture and light industry. The main forces behind the policy shift were Deng Xiaoping and the senior Party leader Chen Yun, who became a cautious supporter of Deng's economic policies. Deng and his pro-market followers advocated a more balanced approach to economic development, rejecting the 'quick fix' modernisation implied in Hua Guofeng's proposals. The revised approach to modernisation was to be guided by the principle of 'seeking truth from facts', a slogan borrowed from Mao Zedong's 1940 essay 'On New Democracy'.

Since the watershed December 1978 plenum of the Eleventh Central Committee of the CCP, the new strategy of development has focused on reform of the economic system. Deng and his advisers believed that China could not become a modern industrial country merely by importing foreign technology. Rather, they advocated two major changes in the economic system: the transfer of decision-making powers to the producers, and the introduction, to varying degrees, of the laws of the market. Reform of the economic system has since continued in these directions, although not without serious setbacks.

While all sectors of the Chinese economy have been affected by the reform policies, changes in the rural sector have been the most far-reaching. The rural population has obviously been most directly affected, although urban Chinese have also enjoyed the benefits of rural policy changes in the form of improved supply, better quality and greater variety of agricultural products. Rural economic policy changes can be divided into two stages: 1978–84 and 1985–89. From 1989 to 1992, there appears to have been a re-evaluation of past reforms, resulting in the slowing down of some of the more radical initiatives. Overall, however, rural reforms have marked a significant departure from the economic policies of the Great Leap Forward and Cultural Revolution periods.

Background

Immediately after its rise to power in 1949, the Chinese Communist Party launched an ambitious program of redistribution of land, known as the Land Reform, which was completed in 1952. This was followed by a policy to promote collective agricultural production. Initially it was envisaged that collectivisation would be accomplished in several stages, beginning with elementary collectives (mutual-aid teams) and progressing to agricultural co-operatives, over a period of fifteen years. But the process of collectivisation was rushed through and declared completed by 1957. The breakneck speed is evident from the fact that, whereas only 2 per cent of peasant households were in agricultural co-operatives in 1954, the figure had shot up to 96 per cent by 1956.[2] On average, each co-operative included about 160 households and covered an area of 140 to 160 hectares. In the first few years of collectivisation, there was a steady increase in agricultural production. But as the collectivisation drive went into high gear in the summer of 1955, the growth rate of agricultural production dropped.

As if unaware of the problems associated with rapid collectivisation, the Chinese leadership decided in 1958 to transform the agricultural co-operatives into 'people's communes', making them the basic units of social organisation, not only for agriculture but also for rural industry, commerce, education and government. This coincided with the launching of the Great Leap Forward. The creation of communes was motivated by the desire of the Party leadership to achieve the highest level of collectivisation, thereby attempting to fast-track the transition from socialism to communism. Towards this objective, many communes established community dining halls to distribute food according to the Marxist principle of 'to each according to need'. Coupled with natural calamities, this high level of collectivisation resulted in a sharp decline in agricultural production.

Consequently, several adjustments were made to the commune system between 1960 and 1962 in order to correct the excesses in collectivisation. Changes included the introduction of a three-tiered system of management and production in which the production team (consisting of 30 to 50 peasant households) became the basic unit of production. The people's communes were divided into 'production brigades', which functioned as middle-tier rural entities supervising and supporting the work of production teams. While the commune exercised control over heavy agricultural machinery and medium-scale irrigation facilities, the production brigade was in charge of the medium-size machinery and small-scale irrigation facilities, leaving the production team in control of draught animals and light agricultural machinery and tools.

Between 1963 and 1965 Chinese agriculture recovered, with grain production climbing back to its 1957 level in 1965. Although the collective character of agriculture was maintained, a limited degree of individual production was allowed in 'private plots' (small patches of land set aside for the peasants' personal use). But these gains were short-lived. Beginning in 1966, the Cultural Revolution restored the radical collectivist policies of the late 1950s, overturning most of the corrective economic measures adopted since 1962.

During the ten years of the Cultural Revolution, production of grain was emphasised under the policy of 'taking grain as the key link', but other areas of agriculture were neglected. Private plots of land were condemned as the 'tails of capitalism' which had to be 'cut off'. Raising of animals by individual peasants was severely restricted. For example, in some areas it was decreed that the number of chickens raised by a peasant was not to exceed the number of people in the household, so that any chickens over that number were regarded as symbols of capitalism and confiscated. The 'free markets' or country fairs were banned. Material incentives of all kinds were seen as antithetical to socialism. The allegedly successful example of collective agriculture, the Dazhai production brigade in Shanxi province, where brigade members had transformed nearly 5000 small plots of almost barren land into 1800 high-yield fields, was vigorously promoted as a national model of agriculture under the slogan 'learn from Dazhai', first put forward by Mao in 1964.

It should be added in fairness that the policies pursued during the Cultural Revolution produced no deleterious effects on the agricultural economy, such as had resulted from the Great Leap Forward. One major reason for this was the weather. Overall agricultural production, measured in fixed 1952 value figures, had fallen sharply between 1958 and 1962, but rose in most years from 1966 to 1976, in some years sharply. The emphasis on grain 'as the key link' was broadly successful with moderate or substantial increases over the previous year in nine of the eleven years from 1966 to 1976, the whole country producing 214 million tonnes in the former year and 286 million in the latter.

First-stage reforms

Since 1976, Chinese agricultural policies have de-emphasised collective farming and actively promoted individual farming. In addition to innovative schemes in production, there have been new and creative ideas for the storage and marketing of agricultural products. The two main aspects of rural economic reform have been the introduction of the household contract responsibility system and changes in marketing practices. The general strategy has been to employ material incentives to increase and diversify agricultural production. It was hoped that increased rural incomes would generate demand for industrial goods, thereby stimulating industrial production. The strategy has generally produced the desired results, while at the same time creating unwanted side-effects.

Under the household contract responsibility system, introduced in 1979, individual households enter into contracts with the state for the production of agricultural products, especially grain and some cash crops, on land leased from the state. The actual content and conditions of the contracts vary depending on the region and the commodity produced, but the general idea is the same everywhere: the peasant household is required to produce and sell a fixed quantity of grain or cash crop to the state. This system was not a product of any conscious plan adopted by the Party leadership or government — at least, not until later. Rather, the leadership observed the success of some regions in increasing grain production by making contracts for agricultural production with small groups of peasant households, and gave tacit approval to such undertakings on the condition that they should suit local conditions. It was not until 1980 that the Party and government gave full support to the signing of contracts between individual peasant households and the state. Early contracts remunerated peasants with work points which could be converted into grain and other commodities, a method not too different from methods used in the 1950s and 1960s. The work points system was abolished in the early 1980s, and since then new contracts have included a purchase price for the contracted portion of the total output. The household contract responsibility system, as it is now known, spread to various parts of the country after 1982, and by 1985 virtually every Chinese village had adopted it. Of course, differences still exist among regions in terms of the actual nature of contracts.

The responsibility system has to some extent overcome the former difficulties in creating incentive and initiative. It links remuneration to output and is based mainly on family management of the land. Giving major decision-making powers to individual peasant households has undoubtedly aroused peasant enthusiasm. Collective land ownership is maintained, but families are assigned rights to use the land, according to either the number of members in the household or the ratio of total household members to the labour force in the household, for periods extending up to 50 years in some cases. Land rights can be handed down to children, but they cannot be sold for profit. In some circumstances, the transfer of land from one family to another is permitted.

The household is responsible for the selection of crops and the organisation of production, relying on its own means of production and funds. It negotiates and signs contracts with the regional agricultural production co-operatives to undertake specific jobs. According to the terms of these contracts, the peasant household agrees to pay to the state an annual agricultural tax and also to contribute to a reserve fund held by the co-operative and used to fund public welfare activities in the area. As a result of the implementation of this system, the family has become the main player in Chinese agriculture. The co-operative plays a secondary but still important role, providing crucial help to the households by assuming responsibility for water conservation and irrigation work, pest prevention and control, and other related services.

The introduction of the household contract responsibility system was accompanied by changes in agricultural marketing and state procurement practices. As a first step, in 1979 the government raised basic agricultural procurement prices by 17.1 per cent (20 per cent for grain) at a cost to the state of 7.99 billion yuan.[3] Since the early 1950s, the Chinese government had used the 'unified purchase' (*tonggou*) system as the keystone of its grain control policy, procuring grain and other agricultural commodities from the rural areas at fixed prices and then selling them to urban residents at prices lower than the procurement prices. Although that meant the state had to foot a huge subsidy bill each year, it guaranteed stable agricultural supplies and food prices for both urban and rural residents. The increases in procurement prices announced in 1979 therefore further increased the state's subsidy bill. Increases in agricultural production following the introduction of the responsibility system contributed further to this burden by increasing the size of procurement. An essential feature of the unified purchase system had been the quota system, whereby each commune had to fulfil its annual quota of grain sales to the state, often leaving insufficient food for commune members to eat. The responsibility system shifted the quotas from the commune to the household, which had to specify the quantity of grain it would sell to the state at the fixed procurement price in the contract. The household, however, was offered an incentive in the form of higher prices for above-quota deliveries. After a household had fulfilled its contractual obligations, and kept enough food for its own consumption, the surplus (if any)

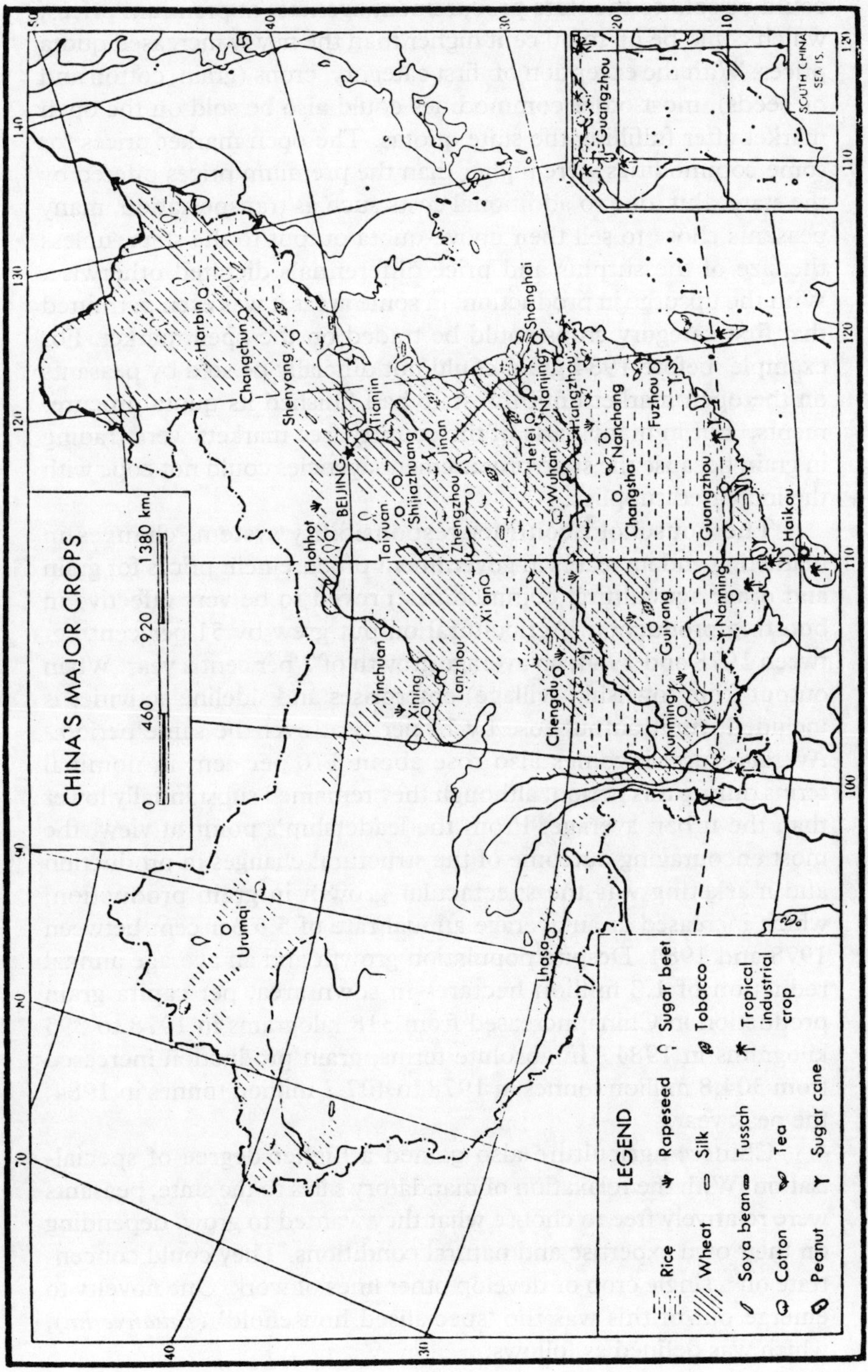
CHINA'S MAJOR CROPS
0 460 920 1380 km
LEGEND
Rice
Wheat
Soya bean
Cotton
Peanut
Rapeseed
Silk
Tussah
Tea
Sugar cane
Sugar beet
Tobacco
Tropical industrial crop
Harbin
Changchun
Shenyang
BEIJING
Tianjin
Jinan
Shijiazhuang
Taiyuan
Hohhot
Yinchuan
Lanzhou
Xining
Xi'an
Zhengzhou
Hefei
Nanjing
Shanghai
Hangzhou
Wuhan
Nanchang
Fuzhou
Changsha
Guangzhou
Haikou
Nanning
Guiyang
Kunming
Chengdu
Lhasa
Urumqi
SOUTH CHINA SEA IS.

could be sold to the state procurement agencies at premium prices, which could be up to 50 cent higher than the newly increased quota prices. With the exception of 'first category' crops (grain, cotton and oil seeds), most other commodities could also be sold on the open market after fulfilling the state quotas. The open market prices for some commodities were higher than the premium prices offered by the state. But, due to additional costs such as transportation, many peasants chose to sell their above-quota output to the state, unless the size of the surplus and price differentials dictated otherwise. With the upsurge in production, in some areas it was even permitted that first category crops could be traded on the open market. For example, before 1984 grain could not officially be sold by peasants on the open market until the state had finished its quota procurements,[4] but in many parts of the country free markets were trading in grain because the state procurement agencies could not cope with the increased supplies.

The household contract responsibility system, changes in marketing and increases in government procurement prices for grain and other agricultural commodities proved to be very effective in boosting production. Agricultural output grew by 51 per cent between 1978 and 1984, an average growth of 7 per cent a year. When output from township (village) enterprises and sideline activities is included, rural output rose by 71 per cent over the same period.[5] Average rural incomes also rose about 170 per cent in nominal terms during this period, although they remained substantially lower than the urban average. From the leadership's point of view, the most encouraging outcome of the structural changes in production and marketing was the spectacular growth in grain production, which increased at an average annual rate of 5.6 per cent between 1978 and 1984. Despite population growth and an average annual reduction of 1.3 million hectares in sown area, per capita grain production in China increased from 318 kilograms in 1978 to 395 kilograms in 1984.[6] In absolute terms, grain production increased from 304.8 million tonnes in 1978 to 407.3 million tonnes in 1984, the peak year.

Chinese agriculture also gained a higher degree of specialisation. With the relaxation of mandatory sales to the state, peasants were relatively free to choose what they wanted to grow, depending on their own expertise and natural conditions. They could concentrate on a single crop or develop other lines of work. One novelty to emerge out of this was the 'specialised household' (*zhuanye hu*), which was defined as follows:

> a household that devotes its ablest workers and at least 60 per cent of its work time to a single crop, product, or service (such as vegetables, poultry, or transport); sells at least 80 per cent of its products (60 per cent for grain producers); and has an income from sales of its products or services at least double the average of other local families.[7]

In 1984, there were 4.3 million specialised households,[8] and by the mid-1980s non-grain producing specialised households accounted for 13 per cent of all farm households.[9] This trend not only helped increase peasant incomes, but also improved the supply of fresh vegetables, fruits, eggs, meat and other commodities in both rural and urban areas.

While structural changes in agricultural policy until 1984 were responsible for increasing production and rural incomes, they also brought a series of new problems and further aggravated some old ones. With the dramatic rise in grain production, and consequently sales to the state, the financial losses to the state from subsidies also skyrocketed. Under the unified purchase system, the state was obliged to buy as much grain as the peasants had to sell. Further, increases in procurement prices were not matched by increases in sales prices for urban residents. Between 1979 and 1984, the state spent more than 30 billion yuan on grain subsidies.

The increased grain production also resulted in severe shortages of storage space. The state-run grain storage system was ill-equipped to cope with the rapid increase in grain production. In 1983, the national storage ratio was only 0.7 units of storage capacity for one unit of state-purchased grain.[10] While some regions were better able to cope with such a situation, others were utterly unprepared. Consequently, in some areas the state had to resort to storing the grain with the same households that sold it. Under this system, which was first used in the 1950s, the state pays about half or more of the price of grain in advance, even though the purchased grain does not leave the seller's house until there is room for it in the state's grain silos. The state also pays a fee to the peasants who agree to store the grain, thus adding to the cost of purchase. The shortage of storage space and the continuously increasing subsidy bill led to a lack of interest on the part of state procurement agencies in the purchase of grain from the peasants. Whereas in the past peasants used to hide grain from the state, now they were finding it hard to sell it to the state.

The lack of adequate storage space was at least partly due to a decline in investment in agriculture. The state's investment in agricultural capital construction dropped from 5.3 billion yuan in 1978 to 3.7 billion yuan in 1984.[11] The state's investment in maintenance and construction of water conservation facilities also dropped, from 3.5 billion yuan in 1979 to less than 2 billion yuan in 1984. As a result, the total irrigated area nationwide was reduced by 2.1 per cent between 1978 and 1985.[12]

Second-stage reforms

The period 1984–85, which followed the Third Plenum of the Twelfth Central Committee (see Chapter 3), is generally regarded as a period of accelerated change in agriculture and the formal beginning of the reform of the urban economic structure. Buoyed by the success of the early structural readjustments in boosting agricultural production, the central Chinese leadership decided to extend the reforms in production organisation that had been the focus of the first stage. There was widespread discussion about the question of ownership of land. Some Chinese economists, arguing that decentralisation of agricultural decision-making under the responsibility system had been the main reason for the improvement in production, advocated that ownership of land should be transferred to the peasants in order to bring their initiative into full play. But there was no major change in the contract responsibility system during the second stage. There was some attention to defects of the new system. By the mid-1980s the number of rules and regulations covering the implementation of the responsibility system had increased. Although the promulgation of new rules was intended to formalise the system by defining the precise powers and responsibilities of its participants, the inability of illiterate peasants to clearly understand their rights often meant that the new rules were misused by the local and regional officials to impose excessive taxes. Bureaucrats were accused of stifling peasant initiative by the peasants and the national media.

The main thrust of the second-stage reform was on improving marketing for agricultural commodities. Initiatives in this area were outlined in the principal rural policy document for 1985, commonly referred to as 'Document No 1', which foreshadowed major changes in the management of agriculture. The role of the market was to be extended to allow agricultural production to develop according to market demands. Rural transport services were to be improved so that the peasants could ferry their produce directly to the urban areas and government procurement centres. The major changes outlined in the document were:

- replacement of the old unified purchase system by a new 'contract purchase' (*hetong dinggou*) system for the major crop commodities;
- decontrol of prices for less important crops and many livestock products;
- increases in fixed prices for many foods sold to the urban residents through state shops, which coincided with price rises in urban free markets.

The contract purchase system was to further increase the decision-making powers of the household. Even after the readjustments of the early 1980s, the state monopoly over the marketing of major crops (the so-called first-category crops) had been maintained. The new system was seen as a move towards the elimination of state monopoly purchasing, introducing supposedly voluntary state contracts with individual peasant households involving cotton, major grains and oil seeds. The former fixed-quota and above-quota procurement price system was reversed. Since 1985, peasants have received the higher above-quota price for 70 per cent of their sales, and the lower basic price for the remaining 30 per cent. The state is no longer obliged to purchase all surplus grain at guaranteed prices. Unlike the system of the first-stage reform period, the new system provides no financial incentives to the grower to expand deliveries at higher prices. While the quantity of state purchases of grain had been reduced by the limits placed upon them (to avoid over-supply), they still made up about 80 per cent of total grain sales in 1985. But, in spite of the new 70:30 ratio for state purchases of grain, the contract price for grain was about 30 per cent lower than the open-market price. However, the peasants who had already signed contracts had to sell the contracted quantity of grain to the state. The prices of most other crops such as vegetables and fruits, and of meat, were decontrolled. Although the state still purchased large quantities for sale in state-run shops in urban areas, such purchases were no longer made on the basis of fixed-price and mandatory delivery.

One significant and, for the leadership, worrying effect of the introduction of the new policies was that they reduced grain returns relative to returns on commodities for which prices had been decontrolled. In other words, it was financially more rewarding for the peasants to grow crops other than grain. In the face of falling 'contract' prices for grain, it became increasingly difficult for the peasants to rely simply on growing grain, and diversification became a necessity for the vast majority of peasants. The output of meat (pork, beef and mutton) increased by 25 per cent between 1984 and 1986, while the output of aquatic and poultry products and fruits rose by over 30 per cent.[13] On the other hand, grain output fell 7 per cent in 1985 after peaking at 407 million tonnes the previous year. It was not until 1989 that there was to be a new record grain output of 407.5 million tonnes. The slow rate of growth in grain production was a source of much anxiety for many of China's senior leaders, who have always emphasised the need for not only national but also regional self-sufficiency in grain production. An inability to produce enough grain to feed China's people worries many Chinese leaders, who recall the severe famine at the end of the Great Leap Forward. Even though the situation today is quite different from what it was in the late 1950s or early 1960s — China is an active player in world trade, and it can afford to import grain from overseas to meet any shortfalls, provided its exports are doing well — its leaders are acutely aware of the daunting task of feeding some 22 per cent of the world's population with only 7 per cent of the world's cultivated land. And long-term reliance on imported grain could put a severe strain on the country's financial resources, diverting vital foreign exchange funds away from other important areas such as technology imports.

Price reform is always the most difficult part of economic reforms in centrally planned economies, and the Chinese experience has been no exception. Price changes since 1979 have given the peasants better value for their labour, but still neither agricultural nor industrial prices in China reflect their true market values. Higher prices for agricultural commodities have increased supplies by arousing peasants' enthusiasm, but the country's price system remains biased against agriculture. The fixed prices for many food items in state shops increased with the freeing of prices for vegetables, fruits, meat, etc. in 1985. These changes were aimed at rationalising the price system, increasing producer responsiveness to market signals, and reducing the strain on state outlays. But the government has feared an urban backlash because of the loss of real income, and has been quick to award subsidies to urban workers to compensate them for food price increases. Rural residents, however, have received no such subsidies for the increased costs of industrial consumer goods, transport and agricultural inputs.

Chinese leaders, economists and other government decision-makers remain divided in their evaluation of agricultural reforms. The major productivity effects of the household contract responsibility system seem to have been attained by 1984–85, while some

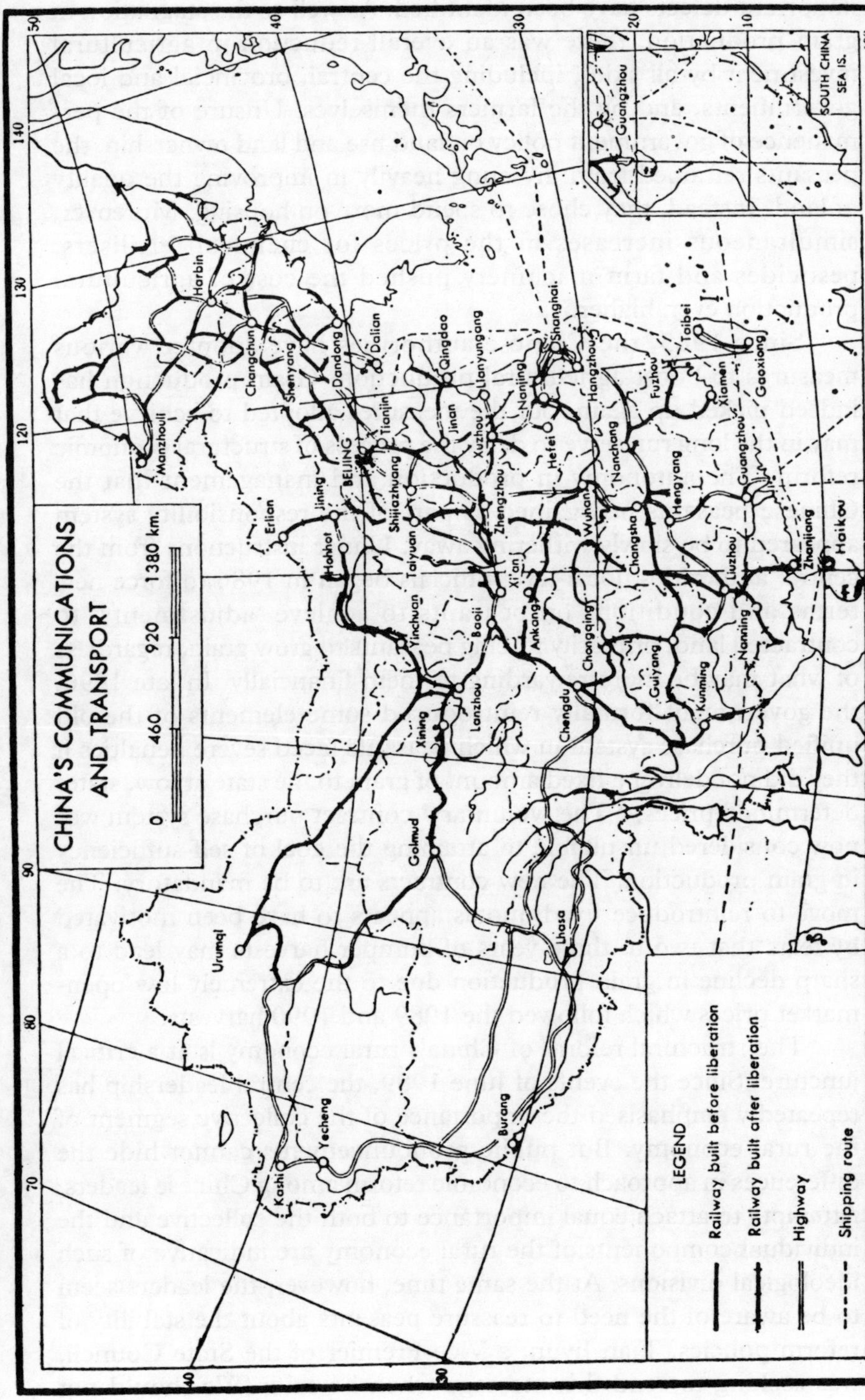
CHINA'S COMMUNICATIONS AND TRANSPORT
0 460 920 1380 km.
LEGEND
Railway built before liberation
Railway built after liberation
Highway
Shipping route
SOUTH CHINA SEA IS.
Manzhouli
Harbin
Changchun
Shenyang
Dandong
Dalian
Erlian
Jining
BEIJING
Tianjin
Qingdao
Lianyungang
Jinan
Xuzhou
Shijiazhuang
Hohhot
Taiyuan
Zhengzhou
Nanjing
Shanghai
Hangzhou
Hefei
Yinchuan
Baoji
Xi'an
Wuhan
Nanchang
Fuzhou
Taibei
Xiamen
Gaoxiong
Ankang
Changsha
Hengyang
Guangzhou
Zhanjiang
Haikou
Liuzhou
Nanning
Guiyang
Chongqing
Chengdu
Kunming
Lanzhou
Xining
Golmud
Urumqi
Lhasa
Burang
Yecheng
Kashi

important defects have been identified. As well as the stagnation in grain production, there was an overall reduction in agricultural investment by all sides, including the central, provincial and local governments, and by the farmers themselves. Unsure of the permanence of government policy on land use and land ownership, the peasants refrained from investing heavily in improving the quality of land. Instead, they chose to spend more on housing. Moreover, simultaneous increases in the prices for chemical fertilisers, pesticides and farm machinery pushed the cost of agricultural production even higher.

Since 1985, the Chinese authorities have adopted various measures to boost agricultural production. Grain production has indeed picked up again, but the measures adopted to achieve that may in the long run serve to delay the process of structural economic reform. The autonomy in production and management that the Chinese peasants had gained as part of the responsibility system appeared to be slowly withering away. Under instructions from the central authorities, local-level officials began in 1986 to force new terms and conditions on peasants to achieve 'adjustments' to contracted land, primarily forcing peasants to grow grain, regardless of what may be more rewarding to them financially. In late 1990, the government formally reintroduced some elements of the old unified purchase system in which peasants faced severe penalties if they did not deliver a fixed amount of grain to the state at low, state-determined prices.[14] The 'voluntary' contract purchase system was now considered unsuitable to attaining the goal of self-sufficiency in grain production. The new contracts are to be mandatory. The move to reintroduce fixed quotas appears to have been motivated by fears that two to three years of bumper harvests may lead to a sharp decline in grain production due to the extremely low open-market prices which followed the 1989 and 1990 harvests.

The structural reform of China's rural economy is at a critical juncture. Since the events of June 1989, the central leadership has repeatedly emphasised the importance of the collective segment of the rural economy. But public pronouncements cannot hide the differences in approach to economic reform among Chinese leaders. Attempts to attach equal importance to both the collective and the individual components of the rural economy are indicative of such ideological divisions. At the same time, however, the leaders seem to be aware of the need to reassure peasants about the stability of reform policies. Tian Jiyun, a Vice-Premier of the State Council, was seeking to send this message when he said: 'We should not boost the collective economy through taking back land already contracted to peasants.'[15] Whatever the outcome of policy debates and power struggles within the CCP, a return to the rural commune policies appears highly unlikely.

Notes

1 Carl Riskin, *China's Political Economy: The Quest for Development Since 1949*, Oxford University Press, New York, 1987, p. 320.

2 Xue Muqiao, *China's Socialist Economy*, Foreign Languages Press, Beijing, 1986, p. 33.

3 Jean C. Oi, 'Peasant Grain Marketing and State Procurement: China's Grain Contracting System', *China Quarterly*, no. 106, June 1986, p. 274.

4 ibid., p. 279.

5 Zhu Xigang and John Chapman, 'Rural Reforms in China: Current Challenges and Policy Aims', *Quarterly Review of the Rural Economy*, vol. 10, no. 4, December 1988, p. 405.

6 Guo Shutian, 'What's in Store for China's Grain Harvest?', *Beijing Review*, vol. 33, no. 8, pp. 19–25; February 1990, p. 14.

7 James Ethridge, *Changing China*, Foreign Languages Press, Beijing, 1988, p. 155.

8 ibid.

9 Zhu and Chapman, 'Rural Reforms', p. 405.

10 Oi, 'Peasant Grain Marketing', p. 275.

11 Andrew Watson, 'Investment Issues in the Chinese Countryside', *Australian Journal of Chinese Affairs*, no. 22, July 1989, p. 96.

12 ibid., p. 98.

13 Zhu and Chapman, 'Rural Reforms', p. 408.

14 Robert Delfs, 'State Incentives', *Far Eastern Economic Review*, vol. 150, no. 47, 22 November 1990, pp. 62–63.

15 See the Xinhua News Agency report of 16 September 1991 cited in the *Summary of World Broadcasts*, FE/1180/B2/1, 18 September 1991.

7 Industrial Economic Reforms

WHILE the changes in Chinese agriculture were relatively simple and began soon after the return to power of Deng Xiaoping, changes in industry were more complex and protracted. This was not only because ideologically industrial reforms required the resolution of many knotty problems, but also because of the resistance to reform arising from self-interest on the part of CCP officials, workers and state organisations. The greatest source of resistance to urban industrial reform was the state industrial sector — which was, incidentally, also the main target of reform. With more than 8000 large and medium-sized and 85 000 small enterprises, this sector produced nearly 70 per cent of industrial output and contributed the greatest share of taxes to the state's coffers. Despite obstacles, however, China's urban industrial sector has undergone dramatic changes since 1978, including decentralisation of decision-making, enhancement of the role of the market, rationalisation of the price system and the introduction of material incentives.

Decentralisation of decision-making

Decentralisation in centrally planned economies is often defined as a movement of decision-making powers from the higher to the lower levels of bureaucracy. A rapid increase in the number of enterprises, combined with a decline in the centre's ability to exercise effective control over them, had led to the transfer to regional control of a large number of enterprises in the late 1950s and in 1970. This created a multi-level and dualistic decision-making structure with both central and local bodies interfering in the operation of enterprises. Such regionalisation of operational planning was, however, purely administrative in nature. The superficiality of these past decentralisations was bluntly faced in an important 1984 CCP document:

> It is true that we tried to delegate power to lower levels on a number of occasions. But this was limited solely to readjusting the administrative power of the central and local authorities and of different departments and regions. The critical issue of giving enterprises decision-making power was not dealt with.[1]

One key element of post-1978 efforts to go beyond the former limits of administrative regionalisation is the Factory Director Responsibility System (FDRS), the showpiece of China's urban economic reform. Its objective is to place more powers into the hands of enterprise managers by loosening the grip of the specialised ministries and their subordinate bureaus and departments. In the centrally planned system China borrowed from the Soviet Union in the early 1950s, individual enterprises enjoyed little or no control over procurement of raw materials and intermediate goods and over marketing of products. Responsibility for these tasks rested with government bureaucrats. As a result, state-owned enterprises showed little concern for quality, market demand or profits. All their efforts were directed towards meeting the state output quotas, since whatever they produced was purchased by their ministry and offered to consumers or other state enterprises. An enterprise manager was also effectively subordinated to the CCP Secretary. Professional and technical personnel, including the manager, were responsible to the CCP branch in the enterprise, and all enterprise-level decisions had to be approved by the CCP committee.

The FDRS is meant to change all this through the devolution of decision-making authority to the enterprise managements (more precisely, to the plant directors), and separating the functions of Party secretaries and managers. The system, which was implemented on an experimental basis in six cities in the autumn of 1984 and later extended to other areas, is based on making the factory director (manager) responsible for most microeconomic decisions. The government has passed several laws and regulations in its effort to institutionalise the FDRS. The most important is the Law on Industrial Enterprises Owned by the Whole People, known informally as the 'Enterprise Law', which was adopted by the First Session of the Seventh National People's Congress in April 1988. It provides the legal framework for the enlargement of the powers of the enterprise by redefining the relations among the Party, the government and the enterprise. The functions and powers assigned to factory directors under the Law include making decisions on all projects of the enterprise, appointing or dismissing middle-management personnel, and planning the readjustment and the distribution of wages. Directors are appointed for three- to five-year terms, at the beginning of which they are required to set out both the long- and short-term targets of their enterprises, and reappointment depends partially on achievement of goals undertaken during their term of office.

The Law stipulates that a manager must act together with the management committee of the enterprise, especially on major plans. The management committee is composed of the secretary of the CCP committee, the head of the trade union, and the secretary of the Communist Youth League in the enterprise. The inclusion of the Party secretary does not help in separating the management of the enterprise from CCP control. Although there is some evidence of attitudinal change amongst Party officials, the vast majority of them find it hard to accept the changes that the reform policies demand.

Other reform initiatives designed to decentralise decision-making powers include the contract responsibility system and leasing. The former is based on agreements between the state and individual factory directors or groups of managerial personnel of the enterprises, and all contracts require specific economic commitments. These may be based on increasing profits, cutting deficits or on input–output indices. Such contracts are supposed to motivate enterprise managers to strive for greater efficiency, since there are material rewards inherent in the system for those who can produce a surplus after meeting their contractual obligations to the state.

While contract responsibility systems of all types have become commonplace in medium-sized enterprises since 1987, leasing is becoming prevalent in small state enterprises. Realising that trying to run tens of thousands of small industrial, commercial and service enterprises has always been an extremely difficult and onerous job for the provincial and local authorities, the reformist leaders in Beijing have actively supported the leasing of small state enterprises to groups of individuals or families. The lessees are required to pay a fixed amount or a proportion of their earnings to the state in return for the use of the state's assets. They are also often required to add to the value of these assets either by upgrading the building or equipment, or installing totally new machinery. In spite of the commitment to reform the economy, private ownership of the means of production is one area in which the CCP is reluctant to take any bold steps. Because of its ideological commitment to state ownership, and also because of the more practical considerations of clinging to power in the face of worldwide collapse of communist governments, the CCP finds leasing more acceptable than wholesale privatisation of state-owned enterprises. This is also one of the reasons why leasing of state enterprises to private citizens has not been extended to large enterprises. Control of the economy is seen as a bulwark against challenges to the CCP's authority.

Enhancement of the role of the market

Decentralisation of decision-making has been accompanied by reduction in the scope of planning and expansion of the market. This has created a dual system where the plan and the market play parallel co-ordinating roles in the allocation of resources and in the distribution of products. Each state-owned and state-managed enterprise engaged in the production of goods or materials covered by state plans receives stipulated compulsory output targets. It also receives material inputs at plan prices, which are generally lower than the prevailing market prices. The goods produced to meet the targets must be sold at fixed plan prices. In addition, the enterprise is required to maximise its output above the targets. To this end, it is free to purchase excess input requirements and to sell the above-plan output on the open market. The actual mix of plan and market components depends on the industry and product concerned.

Although the dual system in agriculture was firmly established by 1982, the market component in the industrial sector did not gain legal status until May 1984 when the State Council issued provisional regulations, known as the 'ten articles', authorising industrial enterprises to sell on the open market products in excess of state quotas, trial-produced or over-stocked items, and those refused by state purchasing agencies. Initially the prices of producer goods sold outside the state quota system could be manipulated within a range of 20 per cent of the state-set prices. This limit was abolished in February 1985,[2] but price ceilings on major producer goods were reintroduced in January 1988.[3]

Centralised planning as a means of economic regulation has certainly lost some of its importance in the Deng era. But the state still exercises a high degree of administrative control over the economy. The difference is in the nature and scope of planning. Whereas in the past the state tried to regulate almost every aspect of the urban economy through mandatory plans, the scope of such planning has been steadily reduced since 1984. Recognising the rigidities of the old system, the CCP Central Committee's 1984 document on the reform of the economic structure stated: 'If the state institutions were to directly administer and manage all kinds of enterprises owned by the whole people, it would be very hard to avoid serious subjectivism and bureaucratism.'[4]

Subsequently, two types of plan have emerged: a mandatory plan and a guidance plan. In the past, all plans were mandatory, with little room for the market. Now mandatory plans cover only those essential goods and materials which the government considers crucial — a total of 23 kinds of producer goods and nearly 80 kinds of light industrial and consumer goods. The guidance plan covers a wide range of goods and services not considered crucial. It sets targets which are not mandatory for the producers, but which still serve as indicators of market demand as estimated by the planning authorities.

The vexed issue of plan versus market always evokes strong sentiments among bureaucrats, economists and politicians in all centrally planned economies. Traditionally, CCP leaders have been unwilling to allow any more than an insignificant role to the market. Chen Yun has been an advocate of a greater share for the mandatory plan. He once compared the market to a caged bird, where the cage represents state planning, his message being that the market must have a place in a socialist planned economy, but it is the plan which must regulate the economy. Many young Chinese economists regard Chen as a conservative, and would like to see the market play a far greater role than that accorded to it up to the early 1990s. Indeed, most of them advocate comprehensive decontrol of prices and limited privatisation of state-owned enterprises, while a small minority completely reject state ownership and support the restoration of individual property rights. Deng Xiaoping and his cohorts decided to tread the middle path, but their gradualist approach has failed to satisfy either group. In the period after the political crisis of June 1989, Chen Yun's ideas received extensive coverage in China's official media, which conferred 'scriptural status on his economic doctrines'.[5] The ascendancy of 'Chen Yun Thought' in the post-June 1989 era was largely due to the rise to

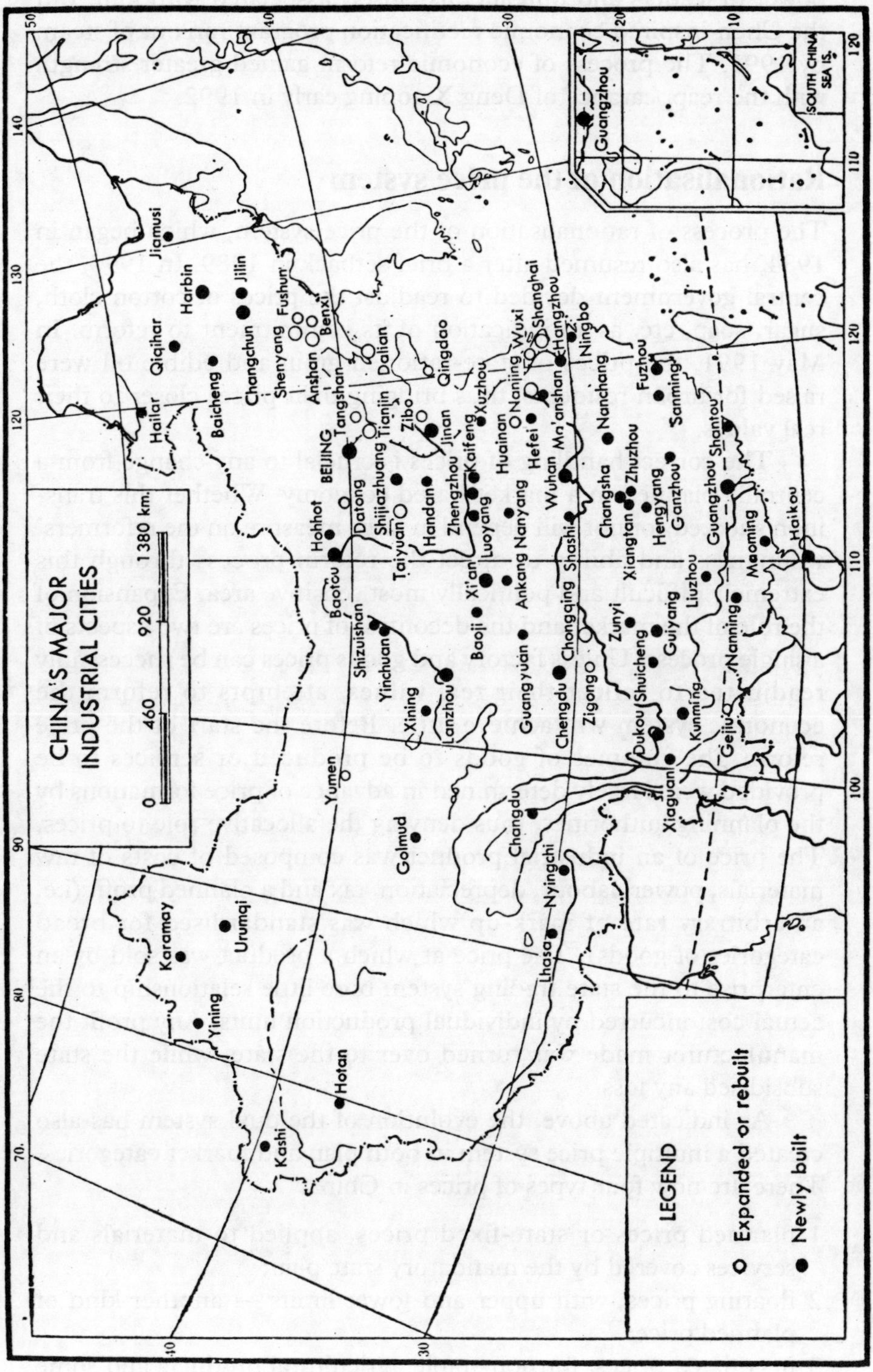
CHINA'S MAJOR INDUSTRIAL CITIES
0 460 920 1380 km.
LEGEND
Expanded or rebuilt
Newly built
SOUTH CHINA SEA IS.
BEIJING
Jiamusi
Harbin
Jilin
Qiqihar
Changchun
Fushun
Benxi
Shenyang
Anshan
Dalian
Baicheng
Hailar
Tangshan
Tianjin
Qingdao
Zibo
Jinan
Xuzhou
Nanjing
Wuxi
Shanghai
Hangzhou
Ningbo
Ma'anshan
Hefei
Huainan
Kaifeng
Zhengzhou
Luoyang
Handan
Shijiazhuang
Datong
Taiyuan
Hohhot
Baotou
Xi'an
Baoji
Ankang
Nanyang
Wuhan
Shashi
Nanchang
Fuzhou
Sanming
Changsha
Zhuzhou
Xiangtan
Hengyang
Ganzhou
Shantou
Guangzhou
Haikou
Maoming
Liuzhou
Guiyang
Zunyi
Chongqing
Chengdu
Zigong
Guangyuan
Shizuishan
Yinchuan
Lanzhou
Xining
Yumen
Golmud
Changdu
Nyingchi
Lhasa
Dukou
Shuicheng
Kunming
Gejiu
Nanning
Xiaguan
Karamay
Urumqi
Yining
Hotan
Kashi

power of leaders and bureaucrats closely associated with him. But the Chen-inspired economic rectification program ran out of steam by 1991. The process of economic reform gained greater strength with the reappearance of Deng Xiaoping early in 1992.

Rationalisation of the price system

The process of rationalisation of the price system, which began in 1984, has also resumed after a brief setback in 1989. In 1990, the central government decided to readjust the prices of cotton cloth, sugar, soap, etc. as an indication of its commitment to reform. In May 1991, the prices of state-rationed grain and edible oil were raised for urban residents, thus bringing their prices closer to their real values.

The correct handling of prices is crucial to any change from a centrally planned to a market-based economy. Whether this transition succeeds or not will depend in large measure on the reformers' willingness and ability to direct the reform process through this extremely difficult and politically most sensitive area. Expansion of the role of the market and the decontrol of prices are two aspects of a single process. Unless factory and goods prices can be successfully readjusted to reflect their real values, attempts to reform the economic system will achieve little. Before the start of the price reform, the volumes of goods to be produced or services to be provided were largely determined in advance of price formations by the planning authorities, thus denying the allocative role to prices. The price of an industrial product was composed of costs of raw materials, power, labour, depreciation, tax and a planned profit (i.e. an arbitrary rate of mark-up which was standardised for broad categories of goods). The price at which a product was sold by an enterprise to the state trading system bore little relationship to the actual cost incurred by individual production units. Any profit the manufacturer made was turned over to the state, while the state subsidised any loss.

As indicated above, the evolution of the dual system has also created a multiple price system in both plan and market categories. There are now four types of prices in China:

1 planned prices or state-fixed prices, applied to materials and services covered by the mandatory state plan;
2 floating prices, with upper and lower limits — another kind of planned price;
3 negotiated prices, for non-staple agricultural products and some

consumer goods, set through negotiations between local and provincial governments and the producers;

4 free-market prices, applicable to manufactured goods not covered by state plans and to goods sold on the free markets, determined by the producers and retailers according to demand and supply.

Two closely related outcomes have flowed from price reform: first, prices have come to reflect market demand and supply relations more directly than before; and second, price levels have substantially increased. But the price system is still far from being rational. Because of the politically sensitive nature of price reform, the government has been prudent in first targeting those areas where economic reforms have produced higher living standards, such as the coastal provinces of Guangdong and Fujian. The impact of price reform and the resultant inflation have, however, been felt by everyone in China. Although the incomes of both urban and rural residents have gone up since the reform began, Chinese people from all walks of life complain that income rises have not kept pace with inflation. But it is fair to say that in most of the reform years there has been real wage growth for most people.

The real impact of price reform became evident in 1988 when inflation jumped to 18.5 per cent as against 7.3 per cent in 1987. The urban Chinese were particularly angry about the inflation because they had been living with stable prices and guaranteed incomes for decades. In fact, urban residents continued to pay for rationed grains, cooking oils and rent at 1950s prices well into the 1980s. Unlike farmers, who were accustomed to income fluctuations associated with crop harvests, urban residents had received financial protection since the early 1950s by way of food subsidies, and medical and social welfare facilities. With prices changing every day, they no longer feel financially secure. While factory workers could rely on bonuses at a time when the economy was growing at 10–11 per cent annually, the steep rises in prices made life difficult for pensioners, academics and other fixed-income earners whose workplaces were either unprofitable or who were not in the business of making profits. The widespread discontent which led to the tragedy of June 1989 (see Chapter 5) was in part fuelled by soaring prices, as by then inflation was running at close to 25 per cent.

Reintroduction of material incentives

The use of material incentives as a means of worker motivation was never very popular with the Chinese leadership during Mao's time.

But for Deng Xiaoping, material incentives always had a certain appeal and a legitimate place in China's socialist centrally planned economy. During the periods when Deng held important government and CCP positions (even under Mao), he pushed for the use of a combination of material and moral incentives to boost agricultural and industrial productivity. This was one of the most important ideological issues on which he differed from the radical leftists and which led to his being branded a 'right deviationist'.

As a reflection of such ideological differences within the CCP, the motivational structure of the Chinese economic system until 1978 was characterised by swings between material and moral incentives. The Great Leap Forward and the Cultural Revolution were periods of heavy reliance on non-material, moral incentives such as the bestowal of 'model worker' or 'model enterprise' titles. Such incentives are still used today, but the criteria for their selection are now based more on economic performance than on soundness of political thinking. Moreover, titles and honours now have little meaning for the vast majority of workers, who are as much a part of the consumer society as those in any capitalist country. The emphasis on material incentives is reinforced by attacks on the long-standing practice of egalitarian distribution of income, which has been criticised as 'everybody eating from the same big pot'.

Although the principal forms of material incentives for urban workers still include wages and welfare benefits such as subsidised public housing, the actual schedules of incentives have been changing since 1978. Among urban Chinese, apart from the operators of private businesses, the main beneficiaries of these changes are the employees of manufacturing and commercial enterprises, including ordinary workers and managers, while cadres in government bureaucracy have also benefited. To take the wage system in industrial enterprises as an example, there have been significant general increases in wages for workers, but the government still seeks to exercise control (often without much success) over the range of wage scales and wage funds. The average annual wage in state enterprises almost doubled between 1977 and 1985. Most workers are still paid according to the old eight-grade wage system, while a few industries follow a seven-grade system. Actual wage scales and income differentials between grades vary among different branches of industry, trades and enterprises, and among regions. In 1985 the standard wage, a major element in the old wage system, was modified by introducing a basic wage, which forms only a part of the original standard wage at any given grade. This component of the wage is not linked to the worker's performance, but is meant to guarantee a minimum monthly income. Above the basic wage, the worker also receives a 'post wage', reflecting the responsibility and demands of the job. The other component of the total wage is the 'floating wage', based on enterprise profits, individual contribution and other criteria which vary depending on the industry and the region. In addition to the above wage components, most workers also receive bonuses which are more often than not indiscriminately distributed and rarely reflect differences in individual efforts towards increasing productivity — a reminder that the old egalitarian practice of 'everybody eating from the same big pot' is still prevalent. Nevertheless, according to Vice-Premier Tian Jiyun, the reform of the wage system is designed to link labour payment to performance.[6]

Such reintroduction of material incentives indicates a change of attitude toward values hitherto spurned by the CCP. It also reflects the pragmatic interpretations of Marxism used by Deng and his followers to justify almost every method that has been used to promote economic growth under the slogan of 'building socialism with Chinese characteristics'. Inherent in this change of attitude is the recognition of China's poverty and the need to improve Chinese living conditions in a region of high economic growth and unprecedented prosperity, and dominated by capitalist societies. In a clear denunciation of past economic policies, Deng once said: 'Poverty is not socialism . . . if it is to be superior to capitalism, it must enable us to eliminate poverty.'[7] To achieve this objective, principles and policies which were anathema to Mao, such as emphasis on material incentives, have been actively promoted by the Chinese leadership.

Conclusion

The economic reforms have fundamentally transformed China's industrial sector, in what can best be described as a transition from a centrally planned to a market-based economic system. That transition is not yet complete; nor can it be without a similar transformation of political institutions. And it has generated pressures and tensions which make change a very difficult and painful process.

Reform measures implemented so far have produced mixed results at best. Economic statistics show that the economy has grown rapidly since the beginning of the four modernisations program. Gross national product grew at an average annual rate of

9.7 per cent between 1979 and 1990, while the growth in national income was 8.4 per cent.[8] Foreign trade also boomed during this period, so much so that there was a trade surplus of over US$13 billion in 1990. While these figures are indeed impressive, there are also drawbacks in economic performance. Much of the growth in industrial production was due to the injection of huge amounts of foreign capital, mainly by overseas Chinese from Hong Kong, Macao and other places, but also by investors from many developed countries. According to the State Statistical Bureau, US$73 billion had been used in foreign investments and loans between 1979 and 1991.[9] The economic performance of foreign-funded enterprises was far better than that of state-owned enterprises. In 1990, for example, the output value of foreign-funded enterprises increased by 56 per cent, and private Chinese businesses, with registered capital of only 2–3 per cent of that of state and collectively owned enterprises, also grew at 21.6 per cent. State-owned enterprises, on the other hand, increased their output by a paltry 2.9 per cent.[10]

China's state industrial sector faces many other problems, apart from slow growth. Nearly 40 per cent of all state-owned enterprises are losing money, adding to the already very high subsidy bill. Furthermore, state enterprises are finding it hard to sell their products to consumers because of poor quality and declining real incomes. According to Chinese economists, in 1989–90 about 60 per cent of industrial production by state enterprises ended up in warehouses.[11] Unsold stock in state warehouses was valued at US$53.1 billion, or 12 per cent of gross domestic product, in September 1991.[12]

The inability of the state industrial sector to improve its efficiency and to compete with the foreign and private sectors has been a source of much concern to the CCP leadership, which sees the state sector as the backbone of the Chinese economy. The political importance of the state industrial sector was underscored by Premier Li Peng's comment in September 1991: 'to revitalise large and medium-sized state enterprises is an economic as well as political question that should be understood in light of consolidating and developing the socialist public ownership system'.[13] The process of reform appears to have reached a political deadlock. For it to proceed further towards the market, some hard political decisions will be required. In order to become more efficient and profitable, state-owned industrial enterprises will have to carry out further reforms. The initial attempts to change ownership patterns in the economy have met with resistance from within the CCP. While at least two Chinese cities, Shanghai and Shenzhen, have established stockmarkets and others are planning to follow, the central authorities are still evaluating the political costs of such moves. Li Peng has already criticised some aspects of the shareholding system on the grounds that the 'selling of stock will . . . cause some social and economic problems'. He warned that 'some people may get rich overnight' if the shareholding system in China were to follow the examples of capitalist countries.[14] Following the fall of governments in Eastern Europe led by Marxist–Leninist parties and the dismantling of the Soviet Union, China's leaders find themselves on the horns of a serious dilemma. If they continue with market economic reform, they risk becoming increasingly irrelevant. If they backtrack and reassert centralised control, they could force the economy into stagnation and face social and political crises. However, as of the end of 1992, the leadership has opted decisively for market economic reform, making such a backtrack most unlikely in the near future.

Notes

1 CCP Central Committee, *Decision of the Central Committee of the Communist Party of China on Reform of the Economic Structure*, Foreign Languages Press, Beijing, 1984, p. 7.

2 Wu Jinglian and Zhao Renwei, 'The Dual Pricing System in China's Industry', *Journal of Comparative Economics*, vol. 11, no. 3, September 1987, p. 312.

3 *Far Eastern Economic Review*, 7 April 1988, vol. 140, no. 14, pp. 16–17.

4 CCP Central Committee, *Decision on Reform of the Economic Structure*, p. 10.

5 Robert Delfs in *Far Eastern Economic Review*, vol. 150, no. 45, 8 November 1990, p. 19.

6 Tian Jiyun in *Beijing Review*, vol. 29, nos 6 and 7, 10 February 1986, p. x.

7 Deng Xiaoping, *Fundamental Issues in Present-Day China*, Foreign Languages Press, Beijing, 1987, p. 178.

8 Xinhua News Agency report of 21 September 1991, in *Summary of World Broadcasts*, FE/W0199 2 October 1991, p. A/1.

9 *Beijing Review*, vol. 34, no. 46, 18–24 November 1991, pp. 6–7.

10 Xinhua News Agency in *Summary of World Broadcasts*, FE/1005, 25 February 1991, p. C1/2.

11 Julia Leung in *Asian Wall Street Journal*, 1 November 1990, p. 1.

12 *The Australian*, 4 December 1991, p. 8.

13 Xinhua News Agency in *Summary of World Broadcasts*, FE/1176, 13 September 1991, pp. B2/5–6.

14 Xinhua News Agency in *Summary of World Broadcasts*, FE/1082, 27 May 1991, p. B2/4.

8 Special Economic Zones and Open Investment Areas

THE Deng era in Chinese politics marked a significant change in China's attitude to the outside world, and this had been especially important economically. China now wanted to be an active player in the world economy. Foreign trade was no longer seen as a means of balancing shortages and surpluses, and China's share in world trade grew from 0.65 per cent in 1977 to 0.93 per cent in 1980. Since 1978, China has promoted many forms of direct and indirect foreign investment, including co-operative exploration, exploitation and development of natural resources, equity joint ventures, co-operative joint ventures, wholly foreign-owned firms and compensation trade. By 1990, some 12 000 Sino-foreign equity and co-operative joint ventures had been set up. The former involve joint investment by both sides and profit or risk sharing according to investment percentages. In the latter, which are preferred by Chinese authorities, land and buildings are typically provided by the Chinese side, and the equipment by the foreign side, with each side sharing profits or losses according to the ratios set out in the contract.

Abandoning Mao Zedong's views on self-reliance and economic self-sufficiency, China also emerged as one of Asia's biggest borrowers in the mid-1980s, having become a member of the World Bank, the International Monetary Fund, the Asian Development Bank and many other multilateral organisations. According to official Chinese sources, by the end of 1986, China's total foreign debt stood at US$20.6 billion, of which US$7.6 billion comprised low-interest long-term loans.[1] This figure almost doubled, to nearly US$40 billion, in the following three years.[2]

An integral part of China's new open-door policy was the establishment in 1980 of four Special Economic Zones (SEZs) in the southern coastal provinces, where the old ports of entry for foreigners had been located. Three of the four SEZs (Shenzhen, Zhuhai and Shantou) are in Guangdong and the fourth (Xiamen) is in Fujian. In April 1988, all of Hainan Island was declared a Special Economic Zone, thus becoming the fifth and largest such zone.

The origins of the policy of delineating certain areas in coastal provinces as 'special zones' can be traced back to 1978,[3] when the idea was first considered by Chinese officials after observation of the Export Processing Zones (EPZs) in other parts of Asia — especially Taiwan, which had set up Asia's first EPZ in Gaoxiong (Kaohsiung) in 1966. The Chinese media were later to claim that the 'initiation of the SEZs was proposed by Comrade Deng Xiaoping' at the Central Work Conference in April 1979.[4] In July 1979, the CCP Central Committee and the State Council decided to establish 'Special Export Zones' in Shenzhen, Zhuhai and Shantou on a trial basis.[5] The areas were not officially designated as 'Special Economic Zones' until May 1980, and in August 1980 the Standing Committee of the National People's Congress officially approved their establishment and formally promulgated the Regulations on Special Economic Zones in Guangdong Province.

The functions of the SEZs

Before the EPZ concept gained such popularity in Asia, the protectionist economic environment which prevailed did not favour foreign investment in manufacturing. The successful establishment of EPZs in Taiwan and South Korea caused other Asian governments to revise their inward-looking policies, which had in the past hindered their attempts to attract export-oriented foreign investment. The main anticipated advantage of EPZs was the increase in employment and foreign exchange earnings without seriously threatening already existing domestically oriented manufacturing sectors. Other potential benefits were the transfer of technology, and skills in marketing and management. The activities and influence of foreign firms would, it was hoped, be restricted to the zones. Moreover, no major changes in government economic policies outside the zones would be required to successfully utilise foreign investment within them. Asian governments offered foreign investors in the EPZs an economic environment free of the industrial regulations and trade barriers that existed in the rest of the economy. Chinese SEZs have borrowed much from, but expanded upon, these features of EPZs elsewhere in Asia.

Deng Xiaoping described SEZs as 'windows for technology, management, knowledge and foreign policy to better serve China's modernisation programme'.[6] They are expected to help improve the quality and quantity of manufacturing and service industries, acting as a channel for the transfer of accumulated knowledge and experience to the inland industries. Thus SEZs are intended to serve as:

1 sources of foreign exchange earnings;
2 devices for technology transfer;
3 devices for managerial skills transfer;
4 a means of allaying the fears of the people of Hong Kong; and
5 laboratories for economic reform.

In spite of their isolationist policies in the past, Chinese authorities had not been totally indifferent to the importance of exports for the national economy. In the early 1960s, Premier Zhou Enlai proposed so-called 'production bases' for development of the manufacture of light industrial goods for export, using mainly domestic resources. But the SEZs differ greatly from such precedents. Unlike the production bases, the physical boundaries of the SEZs are clearly defined. The most important departure is that foreign investment and technology are expected to play key roles in SEZ development and operation. SEZs were conceived as segregated enclaves designed to attract foreign investment and technology in order to boost China's foreign exchange earnings through exports. While a strategy of export-led growth was not considered suitable for China as a whole, SEZs were to be launching-pads for entering international markets. They were to be integral parts of the revamped foreign trade policy, offering cheap labour, tax concessions and ready-made and subsidised infrastructural facilities to foreign investors. The SEZs are thus similar to the Asian EPZs, and many of their regulations are identical to those in most of the EPZs, which had been studied by Chinese officials, economists and legal experts. For example, according to SEZ regulations the products of their enterprises are mainly for exports; investors are promised freedom in the management of their enterprises; all raw materials and capital goods can be imported duty-free by SEZ enterprises; foreign enterprises receive a 'tax holiday' or pay taxes at rates lower than in other parts of the country, and so on.

Chinese SEZs, however, are more comprehensive than the EPZs in the range of activities they aspire to cover. In particular, the economic activities in the SEZs include not only manufacturing, but also tourism, agriculture, commerce and real estate development. The scope of business in the SEZ is set out in Article 4 of 'Regulations of the People's Republic of China on Special Zones in Guangdong Province':[7]

> All items of industry, agriculture, livestock breeding, fish breeding and poultry farming, tourism, housing and construction, research and manufacturing involving high technologies and techniques that have positive significance in international economic cooperation and technical exchanges, as well as other trades of common interest to investors and the Chinese side, can be established with foreign investment or in joint venture with Chinese investment.

It was thus indicated that the SEZs were to combine the standard features of EPZs with some new functions, such as export-oriented agriculture and tourism. Although Guangdong had traditionally been the major source of supply of farm produce to Hong Kong, Shenzhen was expected to enhance this role by attracting Hong Kong investment to such areas as poultry farming, fishing and dairying. It was also to attract foreign tourists, especially Hong Kong holidaymakers wishing to spend their weekends and holidays in relatively quiet places. The ill-fated Club Méditerranée joint-venture with the Shenzhen SEZ Development Company was one of several resorts built for this purpose.

The establishment of SEZs also had an important political motive, as they have implications for China's policy of reunification. Shenzhen and Zhuhai border Hong Kong and Macao respectively, both of which have long been held by foreign powers. Xiamen faces Taiwan, the alienated province the mainland government has been trying to bring back into its fold since the revolution. Both Hong Kong and Taiwan have achieved remarkable economic successes in the past three decades with their market economic systems. Macao, in general, has also done well. By locating the SEZs in such carefully selected areas, the Chinese authorities want to inspire confidence in the lost territories by creating economic buffer-zones adopting quasi-capitalist practices. These would provide opportunities for profit by entrepreneurs in Hong Kong, Macao and Taiwan, thus expanding their economic hinterlands. As Zou Erkang, Secretary-General of the Shenzhen SEZ, admitted: 'Some Hong Kong residents were worried that capitalists' property would be confiscated, and that their living standards would go down after 1997.

The establishment of the special economic zone has been a stabilising factor in easing those worries.'[8] Hong Kong pacification was clearly one of the original functions of Shenzhen. Now that the return of Hong Kong and Macao is certain, the focus is on preventing the flight of capital.

Another important function of Shenzhen and other SEZs was to experiment with systemic reforms in segregated areas. The zones were to function as laboratories where the government could try out changes to the economic organisation of the country as a whole. While growing dissatisfaction with the performance of the Soviet-style command system had combined with changes in the configuration of political forces to make reform of the economic system necessary, it was feared that attempts to introduce uncontrolled market forces throughout China could lead to a serious dislocation of the economy and to political upheaval. The SEZs were, therefore, to serve as sealed-off enclaves for experimentation with market economy practices. Adverse outcomes would not disrupt the whole economy and polity, while successful experiments could be replicated in other parts of the country.

Apart from the common considerations shared by most countries in setting up EPZs, fears over the economic and political risks involved in inviting foreign capitalists to operate on Chinese soil were an important motive for establishing SEZs. Obviously there were industrially advanced Chinese cities such as Shanghai, Tianjin and Dalian that already had infrastructure to cope with foreign investors' demands, but these cities were not made SEZs. Instead, the SEZs were established in remote and relatively underdeveloped sites which needed huge initial investments in infrastructural facilities before they could attract foreign investors. While Shantou and Xiamen did have some existing infrastructure, Shenzhen and Zhuhai were utterly underdeveloped, particularly in the area of industrial infrastructure.

The decision to set up SEZs in these areas may have been motivated by several factors, one of which was proximity to Hong Kong, Macao or Taiwan. Since the vast majority of Chinese living overseas hail from Guangdong and Fujian provinces, they were recognised as the ideal sites to lure overseas Chinese investors. Moreover, their very remoteness from China's main population centres and the country's economic and political power bases may have been regarded as a positive factor in containing both the anticipated and unexpected disruptive influences of market-oriented policies to be implemented in the SEZs.

Open investment areas

Impressed by the pace of development in Shenzhen and other SEZs, the central government in Beijing decided to open up other areas for foreign investment. In January 1984 Deng visited Shenzhen and announced that 'Shenzhen's development and experience prove that our policy of establishing Special Economic Zones is correct'. Soon afterwards, cities such as Shanghai and Tianjin were included in a list of fourteen coastal cities which were to be allowed to implement some of the SEZ policies, and to open one or more 'economic and technology development zones' (ETDZs). Although they would not enjoy exactly the same kind of privileges as the SEZs, the open cities would be granted greater local control over international economic policy. They would be able to lower tax rates, simplify administrative procedures and ease duty requirements in the ETDZs. While the primary objective would be to earn hard currency through export-oriented production in the zones, the open cities were also permitted to offer inducements to attract foreign investment and technology for the renovation of existing enterprises outside the ETDZs. The SEZs remained distinct from the open cities and their ETDZs, in the sense that their administrative structures enabled them to enjoy a greater degree of independence from the central and provincial authorities, whereas ETDZs were fully within the jurisdiction of established municipal authorities.[9]

The decision to implement SEZ-like policies in major coastal cities resulted in the creation of a series of foreign investment enclaves from Dalian in the north to Beihai in the south. Within six months of their formation, they had attracted more foreign capital than had been invested there during the preceding five years.[10] Encouraged by the response of foreign investors, the Chinese authorities decided in 1985 to set up three 'coastal economic zones' — the Yangzi Delta Economic Zone (around Shanghai), the Pearl River Delta Economic Zone (11 000 square kilometres around Guangzhou) and the South Fujian Economic Zone (a triangular area with Xiamen SEZ at its apex). In 1987, the entire Liaodong and Shandong peninsulas were opened up as part of a broad 'coastal strategy'. The local and provincial governments in relatively affluent areas of south and east China are also establishing 'Overseas Chinese Cities' to attract investments from people of Chinese origin who live abroad.

Shenzhen SEZ: The record

The popularity of the SEZ concept, as evident from the creation of so many 'zones' of all kinds, may give the impression that the SEZs have been extremely successful in achieving their goals. But down to the end of the 1980s, SEZ successes were only limited, even in Shenzhen, the most successful of all SEZs.

Some Chinese officials cite the high speed and volume of urban construction in Shenzhen as its greatest achievement. Its urban area grew from a mere 3 square kilometres in 1979 to 50 square kilometres in 1987. The capital construction investment increased at an average rate of 60 per cent each year between 1979 and 1987. By the end of 1986, RMB7 billion had been spent on capital construction in Shenzhen.[11] The funds for investment in capital construction projects came from varied sources, including direct foreign investment, domestic and foreign bank loans, and investment by central and provincial government agencies and enterprises. The main sources of capital construction investment were, however, domestic.

Although Chinese data vary widely, it is estimated that by 1989 Shenzhen had utilised about US$2.5 billion in foreign investment, a large portion of which went into real estate development. In 1985, for example, real estate and hotel projects absorbed more than 46 per cent of the total direct foreign investment (excluding loans and subcontracting arrangements) in the SEZ, whereas the industrial sector absorbed 38 per cent, and commerce and agriculture the remainder.[12] By 1985, foreign capital had made up only about 25 per cent of the total investment in Shenzhen. In terms of attracting foreign investment, Shekou Industrial Zone, a division of Shenzhen SEZ, seems to have been more successful than the SEZ as a whole. Apart from being more industry-oriented than the entire SEZ, Shekou has also become a support-base for oil companies engaged in exploration in the South China Sea.

The effects of foreign participation are most evident in managerial skills and methods of quality control, which are quite easily transferred to the locally hired managers and technicians. Additionally, China's service sector had become notorious for its inefficiency and unpleasant customer relations. It was, therefore, hoped that the establishment of hotels and shopping centres in the SEZs, with Hong Kong and foreign capital and management, would help improve service standards in China. On the other hand, the SEZs' other original function of bringing advanced foreign industrial and farm technology to China does not seem to have materialised to the extent expected by the planners. The history of the development of EPZs elsewhere in Asia reveals that the actual transfer of technology through such zones is very limited. Most foreign investors tend to be manufacturers of labour-intensive, low-technology products. Moreover, foreign firms which do have unique technological advantages guard them carefully.[13] They are understandably anxious to ensure that their technological secrets are not passed on to other local or foreign competitors.

In the early years of Shenzhen SEZ, only about 7 per cent of the imported technology was of an international standard. According to some Chinese economists, some of the technology imported consisted of disused 1940s and 1950s equipment from Hong Kong.[14] The SEZ's failure to attract advanced technology is related to the preponderance of Hong Kong and Macau investment. Until 1988, around 80 per cent of all foreign investment in Shenzhen originated in Hong Kong or Macau, neither of which is particularly well known for the production of technologically advanced production equipment. As late as 1989, Shenzhen's most profitable industrial activity was assembly and subcontracting work for Hong Kong manufacturers. In 1989, export processing constituted almost 60 per cent of Shenzhen's gross industrial output.

Although Shenzhen has attracted some advanced technology, such as for the Daya Bay Nuclear Power Station, this is not directly related to the SEZ. The power station is a project of national importance, which is partly funded by the central government and partly by a Hong Kong company. No doubt the generation of electricity from the Daya Bay plant will ease Shenzhen's power shortage, and thus contribute to enhancing its attractiveness in the eyes of foreign investors. It will also help existing enterprises to improve their competitiveness by increasing productivity through eliminating power cuts. It is believed that the completion of the Daya Bay plant will change Shenzhen from an importer of electricity from Hong Kong to a net exporter of electricity to that territory.

The ultimate test of Shenzhen's success in attracting modern technology has to be in manufacturing. In this sphere, however, Shenzhen is sadly lagging behind the old industrial centres in China, which have taken most of the foreign investment projects involving world-class industrial technology. The spillover of some technologies and management expertise could be arranged by rotating workers and managers in the zones, moving them outside, and replacing them with new personnel. But this is unlikely to happen because of resistance from those affected by such transfers.[15] Moreover, the numbers involved, especially in the case of workers, would 'strain the bureaucracy'. The transfer of technology to the rest of the economy is made even more difficult by the physical separation of the zones. Chinese authorities have tried to promote the transfer of whatever new technology has been brought into the SEZs by encouraging state-owned firms from other areas to establish joint ventures with foreign firms in the SEZ. But so far there is very little evidence to show that this is helping the transfer of foreign technology to China. In fact, the reverse is the case, as many Hong Kong investors want to use the technological prowess of the large and successful Chinese enterprises to improve the quality of their own products. Hong Kong certainly has an edge over China in certain fields, especially consumer electronics. But a combination of Hong Kong capital with the accumulated expertise of China's civil and military technologists is an idea that appeals to many Hong Kong capitalists.

With respect to foreign exchange earnings through exports, the SEZ as a whole has always run a trade deficit, which reached US$662 million in 1983. Despite a central government-initiated clampdown on imports in 1985–86, there was still a deficit of US$400 million.[16] The series of trade deficits was caused in part by the large-scale importation of machinery and raw materials by the SEZ, but mainly by the imports of consumer goods for sale within Shenzhen and in the interior. The SEZ has failed to live up to the expectation that it should be an export-oriented zone. Although Shenzhen's per capita income was almost three times the national average, its prosperity was based largely on its unintended function as an entrepôt between the mainland and foreign countries. In 1987, only about half of Shenzhen's industrial products were exported, the rest being sold on the domestic Chinese market.

Systemic reforms in Shenzhen

As a reform laboratory, Shenzhen was to provide the economic planners of China with new ideas on economic management. It was hoped that the insulation of Shenzhen would create an economic sub-system, where many economic (and perhaps political) ideas still regarded by many within China as 'revisionist' could be tried for future application more generally. The institutional characteristic of central planning were to be dismantled in the SEZ, to be replaced by institutional arrangements necessary for a market economy. To achieve these objectives, Shenzhen was physically cut off by means of a 85 kilometre long fence, known as the 'second line', finished in 1985. One reason for erecting the fence was to prevent tariff-free imported goods from finding their way into the interior markets, although such practices have persisted. It was also designed to prevent large-scale migration of people into Shenzhen.

The SEZ was also supposed to be removed from the pervasive influences of central planning. But no amount of policing was able to insulate Shenzhen from the commands of central bureaucrats. The fact that those commands are not always heeded is a different matter, and is symptomatic of the constant conflicts in which local bureaucracies try to resist pressures from the centre. But the central bureaucracies are not completely hostile to Shenzhen. On the contrary, many ministries have set up their own factories and built hotels and office blocks in the SEZ. Still, their pursuit of narrow interests and persistent adherence to the old ways are the cause of much friction with the SEZ administration.

Despite this, however, Shenzhen has broken some new ground in the reform of the economic system and in creating a market-oriented sub-system. It was the first city in China to use the tender system for a joint venture construction project in July 1981.[17] Under this system, the owner of the building to be constructed and the successful bidder enter into a contract containing clauses concerning construction work, materials, duration of the project, construction costs and the quality of construction. This marks a significant departure from the old system, whereby labour, finance and materials were all allocated according to the plan and the construction companies had no way of obtaining materials from other channels, resulting in long delays in the completion of projects, wastage and high costs. The tender system has now become the norm in Shenzhen and is increasingly being used in the construction industry in other parts of China.

In order to make the SEZ economy more responsive to market signals and for commodity prices to reflect their values more accurately, Shenzhen became the first city in the country to introduce price reforms. These reforms have also spread to other parts of China, but the slowness of price reform and frequent setbacks elsewhere have meant that wide price differentials have emerged between Shenzhen and other parts of the economy. Much of the prosperity of the SEZ has been based on these price gaps, which have provided SEZ firms, particularly state firms, with opportunities to make profits by selling tariff-free or low-tariff imported goods from Shenzhen to other areas.

Conclusion

With implementation of flexible foreign investment policies in most parts of China, the SEZs have lost some of their early attraction. In 1989, Shanghai was allowed to develop Pudong District as a foreign investment zone. Shanghai officials claim that Pudong will be more attractive to foreign investors than any of the existing SEZs. It already boasts China's first Free Trade Zone. At the same time, among the four places of Deng Xiaoping's southern visit early in 1992, two were to SEZs, these being Shenzhen and Zhuhai. What this suggests is that SEZs and the economic policy they imply remain very much on the agenda of the CCP leadership. They are likely to remain one of the most important planks of the open-door policy and are among the factors making it increasingly difficult to abandon.

Notes

1 *Beijing Review*, vol. 31, no. 31, 1–7 August 1988, p. 23.

2 *Far Eastern Economic Review*, vol. 144, no. 21, 25 May 1989, p. 64.

3 Thomas Chan et al., 'China's Special Economic Zones: Ideology, Policy and Practice', in Y.C. Jao, and C.K. Leung (eds), *China's Special Economic Zones: Policies, Problems and Prospects*, Oxford University Press, Hong Kong, 1986, p. 88.

4 *Liaowang*, 11 June 1984, in *FBIS Daily Report*, 18 June 1984, K1–7.

5 ibid. The decision was formally announced by Vice-Premier Gu Mu in September 1979: Sun Ru, 'The Conception and Prospects of the Special Economic Zones in Guangdong', *Chinese Economic Studies*, vol. 14, no. 1, Fall 1980, p. 68.

6 *FBIS Daily Report*, 18 June 1984, K1–7.

7 *Special Economic Zones of the People's Republic of China*, Hongkong and Shanghai Banking Corporation, Hong Kong, 1982, pp. 14–15.

8 *Beijing Review*, vol. 27, no. 48, 26 November 1984, p. 19.

9 George Crane, *The Political Economy of China's Special Economic Zones*, M.E. Sharpe, Armonk, 1990, p. 95.

10 James Ethridge, *Changing China: The New Revolution's First Decade, 1979–1988*, New World Press, Beijing, 1988, p. 122.

11 *Far Eastern Economic Review*, vol. 138, no. 40, 1 October 1987, pp. 102–3.

12 *Shenzhen jingji tequ nianjian* (*Shenzhen SEZ Yearbook*), Nianjian bianji weiyuanhui, Shenzhen, 1986, pp. 442–43.

13 Peter Warr, *Export Processing Zones in the Philippines*, ASEAN–Australia Joint Research Project, Canberra, 1985, p. 33.

14 Gu Shutang et al., *Shenzhen jingji tequ diaocha he jingji kaifaqu yanjiu* (*A Survey of Shenzhen SEZ and Studies on Open Economic Zones*), Nankai University Press, Tianjin, 1984, p. 8.

15 Kevin Bucknall, *China and the Open Door Policy*, Allen & Unwin, Sydney, 1989, p. 160.

16 *Far Eastern Economic Review*, vol. 138, no. 40, 1 October 1987, p. 105.

17 Chan et al., 'China's Special Economic Zones', p. 100.

9 Socialism with Chinese Characteristics

IN contrast to the collapse of regimes in Eastern Europe and the Soviet Union, China under Deng has remained one of the few state-socialist political systems. The main defining characteristics of such a system are clearly evident — an expressed commitment to the goals of 'socialism', adherence to Marxist–Leninist ideology, and explicit political dominance of the Communist Party. Nevertheless, the period since 1978 has seen significant changes in Chinese politics. Broadly, those changes have derived from two general orientations in reform. Firstly, political reform has been pursued as an end in itself. By the late 1970s there was widespread dissatisfaction with many aspects of the political system, both popularly and in the CCP. The Cultural Revolution had left a legacy of political instability and conflict. One objective of reforms has been to reduce political uncertainty by making political processes more regular and ordered and reducing the intrusion of political conflicts into many areas of social activity. Secondly, political reform has been seen as necessary for facilitating economic reform. The Party leadership has recognised that much of the economic reform program requires corresponding changes in political structures.

While both of these orientations have been widely accepted within the Chinese leadership under Deng, they have posed some difficult questions providing much room for disagreement over the scope and extent of political reform. How might the legacies of the Cultural Revolution be addressed? How far can political change go without endangering core aspects of the political system, including the commitment to Marxism–Leninism and socialism and the dominance of the CCP? The connection between the type of political structure and the success of economic development is an issue which has been contentious among analysts of many countries, not only China. Are liberal-democratic political forms more compatible with economic modernisation, as might be suggested by advanced industrial economies of Western Europe and North America? Or are forms of authoritarianism suitable for rapid industrial development, as might be suggested by East Asian examples such as South Korea and Singapore? In terms of reform of state socialist systems, many have pointed out that in the Soviet Union under Gorbachev, the political dimension of reform was emphasised, in contrast to emphasis on the economic dimension in China. Does the demise of the Soviet Union merely confirm the dangers (from the perspective of the Chinese leadership) inherent in allowing political reform to proceed too far and too rapidly? The process of economic reform itself constantly presents new challenges and tensions, with the introduction of new forms of economic activity and corresponding changes in social structures and ideological influences. How might these be accommodated within political structures and, again, how will this threaten core aspects of the political system? The need to confront all these sorts of questions has led to conflicting tendencies and vacillations. While the Chinese leadership since the late 1970s has constantly reaffirmed political reform, the actual implementation of reforms has been limited and hesitant (and sometimes reversed), reflecting differing views on the sorts of changes that are desirable or necessary and anxiety over some of the consequences.

This chapter considers the background for changes in terms of principal characteristics of the pre-reform political system, and then discusses general adaptations in the ideological framework and the articulation of 'socialism with Chinese characteristics'. The next chapter is concerned with some of the major aspects of political reforms, focusing on implications for the role of the CCP.

The pre-reform political system

As in all state-socialist systems, the key element of political processes in China was the centrality of the so-called 'vanguard Party'— the CCP. The role of 'Party leadership' was explicitly affirmed in terms of the fundamental character of the PRC. That affirmation was firstly based upon the origins of the state. As the leader of the revolutionary movement which triumphed in 1949, the CCP has presented itself as the creator of the new state. The establishment of the PRC was supposed to be a decisive break from the former political and social system. Chinese sources always refer to 1949 as 'Liberation' — evoking both nationalist themes (the freeing of China from subjection to foreign powers) and themes of social transformation (the removal of class exploitation and domination). But 'liberation' was not an end in itself — it was the basis for a long-term process of building a new form of society identified as 'socialist'. Hence the continued dominant role of the CCP was further justified in terms of its claimed necessary role in realising the objectives of 'socialism' in China.

This general justification for 'Party leadership' was reflected in the importance attached to ideology in Chinese politics. All political systems must include at least some of the understandings of political processes normally included under the term 'ideology' — such as explanations of political life, prescriptions of what is correct or appropriate political behaviour and specification of political goals. The assertion of long-term objectives of 'socialism' meant that political ideology was very prominent in China, in terms of looking forward to a better society and also establishing standards through which present actions could be measured. Marxist–Leninist ideology was supposed to guide all political activity, since it was claimed to provide general laws about all societies and to be an analytical tool allowing further and more specific understanding of social development in China.

Accordingly, ideology was referred to more often and more directly than in most other systems. It was more explicit — that is, political principles or objectives were not left as implicit or understood but were explicitly linked to political action, as justification or explanation. Following from that, ideology was directly connected to questions of power and political position. Because of the link between ideology and action, the ability to articulate the ideology became crucial in setting the parameters and the content of political activity. In particular, the basic rationale of Communist Party leadership was ideological. The main basis for the Party's claim to dominance has been in terms of its superior grasp of Marxism–Leninism, which allows it to understand and guide social development. This has led to the CCP's articulation of an ideological orthodoxy — that is, an official statement of the major aspects of doctrine intended to guide and limit political activity. And what this has usually meant is that the dominant leaders in the Party have established the ideological framework as an intrinsic part of their shaping of the political agenda.

The articulation of long-term objectives and their linking to current political practice also provided the rationale for the organisational role of the CCP. 'Party leadership' did not involve simply the articulation of generalised ideological propositions, but also the direct and specific supervision or guidance of all significant areas of social activity. This meant that the Party penetrated all major forms of social organisation. In other systems a ruling political party might be defined according to its ability to formulate policy and the placing of its members in the main structures of government. This certainly applied in China, as all major political institutions were directly subordinated to the CCP. Thus the legislative institutions (known as 'people's congresses') invariably endorsed without demur what was presented by the Party, and government ministries implemented policies formulated by the Party. But CCP leadership was much more pervasive, involving the establishment of Party organisations in industrial enterprises, rural production brigades, bureaucratic offices, the armed forces, schools and universities, trade unions and other mass organisations, and so on. In all such organisations there were Party branches and corresponding Party officials who exercised authority in all major aspects of decision-making.

Hence 'Party leadership' was not remote but directly tangible to almost all people. This was reinforced by the significance of the 'unit' (*danwei* — the place of work or study) in an individual's life. To take the important example of employees in state industrial enterprises:

> . . . the enterprise exercises authority not only over one highly specialized role, but over the whole person: the state factory is a branch of government and, through the factory's party branch, exerts a measure of the state's political rule over the worker as a citizen.[1]

The unit was not simply the place of work, but also the provider of welfare services such as pensions and health facilities, the means of obtaining housing, childcare and other services, the organiser of recreational activities, the channel for authorising travel or job transfers, and so on. Much the same applied in rural areas, as the focus of an individual's life was necessarily the collective agricultural organisations. Hence the form of social organisation, and especially the predominance of state and collective forms of economic activity, provided the framework for the pervasiveness of the Party's political penetration.

Such arrangements were typically used for fostering high levels of popular political activity of a peculiar kind. Characteristic of the Chinese system before the late 1970s were extensive mass mobilisation and a campaign style of politics. Party branches were responsible for ensuring that people within their units were regularly involved in political activity, which could include everything from routine ideological study to analysis of the significance of new general policies in the specific conditions of the unit or participation in national campaigns against political deviations of various kinds. Such participation was consistent with one of the CCP's hallowed principles, the 'mass line'. Derived from experiences during the pre-Liberation period, the mass line was supposed to require that Party organisations should be close to the people among whom they operated, remaining sensitive to popular wishes or aspirations and thereby acting as a channel for popular inputs into policy processes. There were, of course, often reasons to doubt that these prescriptions were followed — although it should not be assumed that this was always so, and that the mass line was nothing more than the manipulative imposition of political activity. Nevertheless, fostering and direction of mass political activity was one of the CCP's principal tasks and further reinforced the extent and scope of its political domination.

The emphasis on socialist objectives had another important implication in terms of the limitation of political participation. Not everyone was included in 'the masses' who were encouraged to be politically active. Generally, 'the masses' included those regarded as supporting the current processes of social transformation towards the objectives of socialism. By the same token, other groups were excluded from 'the masses' and were likely to become targets of political attack. This could apply to those identified with what had been categorised as a political deviation, inimical to socialism. But there was also a more systematic mechanism of categorising social groups according to a notion of political reliability. In 1949 some groups were identified as defeated enemies of the revolutionary victory, including rural landlords, those associated with foreign economic interests and those linked to officials of the old regime. Individuals from such groups were officially given 'bad' class labels, as opposed to the 'good' labels given to workers, poor peasants and revolutionary activists. With later stages of social transformation, other categories came to be regarded as 'bad' — for example, capitalists not associated with foreign economic interests. These labels were assigned to all individuals, and could be used as a means of discrimination, such as in the favouring of those with 'good' labels in access to higher education. Those with 'bad' labels were constantly objects of suspicion, and were likely to become targets of attack in any political movement. And the labels were inheritable, so that the children of former landlords still bore that label decades after the expropriation of their parents' lands.

Despite this, the CCP claimed that the system was 'democratic'. A standard argument was that democracy could not apply universally in any society having fundamental social divisions based upon economic classes. Thus, according to CCP sources, the claims of Western countries to be democratic were fraudulent because they simply disguised an effective dictatorship of the bourgeoisie over the proletariat in order to maintain capitalism. Similarly, it was argued, a socialist system would necessarily exercise dictatorship over the limited numbers of enemies of socialism. But its democracy was more authentic because it included the overwhelming bulk of the population. And the 'leading' role of the CCP was not seen as restricting 'democracy'; rather, it was a necessary condition for allowing effective mass political participation, directed towards realising the socialist objectives which were in the interests of all of the masses.

In sum, the post-1949 political system saw a heavy emphasis on the explicit use of ideology consistent with the realisation of socialist objectives, and was highly politicised in the sense of entrenching the CCP's dominance in all significant forms of social organisation and mobilising mass participation in political activity. These characteristics were reinforced and extended during the Cultural Revolution from 1966. A key theme of the Cultural Revolution was the constant danger of anti-socialist tendencies. As noted in Chapters 6 and 7, such tendencies could be identified in forms of economic activity, but they might arise in practically any area of life, including what in other systems would be regarded as 'private' matters — everything from what types of music or other art forms one enjoyed to religious beliefs to personal relationships. Hence official ideological standards were applied very rigorously and the scope of what could be regarded as politically salient expanded. The emphasis on anti-socialist dangers also fostered the search for enemies, and more groups came under suspicion — such as intellectuals, who were accused of promoting individualism in opposition to collectivism and of separating themselves from the masses of workers and peasants.

The actual forms of political activity during the Cultural Revolution also had enduring consequences. In 1966–67, some sections of the Party leadership, claiming that opponents of socialism had infiltrated the Party itself, sanctioned mass attacks upon Party organisations and officials. This destroyed the integrative role that the CCP had formerly played, and the unrestrained mass movement degenerated into factional conflicts and often violence. Party officials at all levels were punished and dismissed from office (including senior leaders such as Deng Xiaoping) and many were killed. From the end of the 1960s there were efforts to remedy many of these effects of the Cultural Revolution. Party organisations were rebuilt, mass political activity was restrained, and many of the victims of the movement were restored to official positions. But the traumatic effects of the Cultural Revolution persisted. The CCP's legitimacy was undermined by the demonstration of its internal divisions and by popular resentment of political disorder and repression. Frequent mobilisation of mass movements into the 1970s prevented the restoration of orderly processes in political institutions, even if the excesses of 1966–67 were avoided. Within the Party itself the antagonisms generated by bitter conflict persisted. There were efforts to restore the norms of political conduct which had been flouted in the Cultural Revolution, but they were largely disregarded and resentment over injustices in treatment of Party members and officials continued to simmer. Hence, while the Cultural Revolution had extended the characteristic emphasis on ideology and high levels of politicisation, which were directly associated with CCP dominance, it had also introduced severe strains within the Party itself and in its legitimacy among the Chinese people.

The ideological framework

The general trend since 1978 has been a substantial redefinition of 'politics' in China, in an effort both to remedy the legacies of the Cultural Revolution and to remove political practices seen as inhibiting economic development. Reform has thus involved the restriction of the sphere of political activity, consistent with the view that politics had become too inclusive and intrusive, impinging upon too many areas of people's lives. There have been efforts (to be discussed further in the next chapter) to reinforce political institutions and to distinguish their separate spheres of competence, in order to foster greater regularity and stability in political processes. Given the explicit ideological basis of the political system, all such reforms required substantial modifications of the ideological framework. Most directly, new policies often required changes in the content of particular official ideological formulations so as to remove evident inconsistencies. But the CCP leadership has also tackled the more fundamental underlying issue of how ideological direction should be understood. At the same time, processes of reform have generated new challenges to CCP authorities with the spread of ideological influences outside of the official framework.

Since the early 1940s, the orthodox ideology of the CCP has been identified as 'Marxism–Leninism–Mao Zedong Thought'. Mao's place was established through the process of 'Sinification of Marxism' during the Yanan period,[2] and the ability to define core aspects of the ideology was one important aspect of Mao's power until his death. This did not mean that the ideology remained static, since there were both continuities and novel departures in Mao's thinking from the 1940s to the 1970s. The 'Mao Zedong Thought' inherited by Mao's successors included the principal themes of the Cultural Revolution, such as the persistent danger of revolutionary retrogression and the need to guard against tendencies inimical to socialism. Such themes clearly militated against many aspects of reform proposals, especially in economic reforms. But the leadership under Deng was unwilling simply to repudiate the former official ideology, for fear that this would be too divisive and directly undermine the Party's position. Instead, it has deliberately manipulated 'Mao Zedong Thought' so that it becomes useful for present purposes.

The key tactic has been to sever the guiding ideology from necessary connection with Mao himself. According to the new orthodox view, Mao Zedong Thought refers to the accumulation of wisdom and understanding gained through the whole process of the Chinese revolution. Mao Zedong may have been the main individual who articulated or expressed the results of this collective endeavour. But there were other contributors to 'Mao Zedong Thought', such as Liu Shaoqi, Zhou Enlai and Deng Xiaoping himself, who also helped to express the accumulated wisdom of the revolutionary movement.

Such collectivisation of the guiding political ideology has done more than simply downgrade Mao. It has allowed two further important steps in the framing of a new orthodoxy. One is the selective use of Mao. The converse of severing the necessary link between Mao and Mao Zedong Thought is that not everything Mao said or wrote would necessarily be a part of Mao Zedong Thought. It becomes possible to claim that some of Mao's views were inconsistent with the general body of doctrine called 'Mao Zedong Thought'. This opportunity was quickly exploited, for example, in the official Party history published in 1981.[3] That document affirmed Mao Zedong Thought, but excluded from it many of Mao's words and actions during and after the Cultural Revolution. It could now be asserted that these were mistakes, inconsistent with the collective ideology of Mao Zedong Thought.

The other main consequence of this approach was the flexibility allowed by the possibility of continuing addition to the guiding ideology. Although Mao himself was gone, Mao Zedong Thought as a product of collective experience could continue to adapt and grow, as the revolutionary movement developed and assimilated new elements. This was especially useful for the process of self-justification. It became possible to provide ideological explanations for new departures, as responses to new conditions and experiences. It was not necessary to be tied by the ideological precepts which formerly applied. Someone like Deng Xiaoping can be an authentic contributor to guiding ideology, allowing the most flexible justification of new policies and programs.

This treatment of ideology was crucial in the reorientation of Chinese politics after 1978. In fact, the so-called 'turning point' was largely construed in these terms. The Central Party meetings at the end of 1978 were the scene of battles between two different approaches, which focused on key epistemological and theoretical issues.[4] The two groups which emerged were given the names of the 'whatever' and 'practice' factions. The first name derived from the injunction associated with the then Party Chairman, Hua Guofeng, in 1977 — to support whatever policies Mao had devised, and to observe whatever directives Mao had laid down. Those in the Central Party leadership who supported this type of proposition were the 'whatever faction' (although this was a name imposed upon them by their opponents, and not their own choice). The main proposition of the opposing group was that 'practice is the sole criterion for testing truth'. The argument here was that emphasis on practice was the only correct and comprehensive way to assimilate Mao Zedong Thought. Mistakes would inevitably follow attempts merely to sustain what Mao had said or done and to apply that to new situations. Rather, the Party would have to devise and test new policies according to current realities. Hence this group came to be known as the 'practice' faction. This conflict may seem rather esoteric, but it was very closely linked to questions of policy and power. The victory of the 'practice' approach allowed policy innovations which departed markedly from precedents associated with Mao. And the losers in the debates at these meetings inevitably suffered loss of political power. They were demoted, or rendered politically inactive, to be removed progressively from senior positions over the next few years.

The main trends resulting from the reformulations of 'Mao Zedong Thought' since 1978 have been a progressive erosion of much of the former content of official ideological formulations and a reduction in their political salience, although there have also been contradictory tendencies for the reassertion of ideological constraints. The dominant interpretation of 'practice' has reduced the significance of the articulated ideology by undermining its connection with practical activities, which are supposedly to be governed by other 'non-ideological' standards. Those objecting to the former emphasis on ideological principles have claimed that they inhibited flexibility and innovation which would have had desirable results. And they see such desirability as objectively self-evident. This has applied principally to economic matters, where higher levels of production assume the status of unchallengeable benefits. As discussed in Chapters 6 and 7, that has become the basis for removing former ideological 'obstacles', such as commitment to collectivism in agriculture and opposition to sole reliance on material incentives.

But reliance on 'practice' is not as straightforward, nor as objectively self-evident, as its adherents in the Chinese leadership maintain. There are always grounds for differing views on the criteria for assessing the success of 'practice'. In all areas of social policy, choices among competing values are inevitable. For example, in medical care it might be easily agreed that successful 'practice' is the prevention and treatment of illness, but there may be competing arguments over whether a successful medical system is one providing sophisticated technologies to a necessarily small clientele or one providing less advanced health care more widely. Even with economic growth, the Chinese leadership cannot entirely dismiss other standards, whether these be environmental effects or differential benefits of reform for different social groups. In other words, 'practice' does not provide objective standards, but is itself subject to interpretation according to values and understandings which are inherently 'ideological'. Thus there remain grounds for opposition to aspects of reform policies which the invocation of 'practice' cannot completely disguise. Such opposition has been expressed in various ways, although the line which has generally prevailed in the Chinese leadership has asserted the need to separate 'practical' activities from 'ideological' intrusions, especially in the pursuit of economic growth.

At the same time, though, CCP leaders have also adopted an inconsistent stance in their sensitivity to erosion of ideological controls. As discussed in Chapters 3–5, examples have included Deng's stipulation in 1979 of 'four fundamental principles' intended to limit the allowable scope of political activity and expression of political ideas, the complaints about 'spiritual pollution', the campaigns against 'bourgeois liberalisation' and warnings concerning the dangers of 'peaceful evolution'. There have been bitter battles in the CCP revolving around claims about ideological backsliding, most notably the dismissals of Hu Yaobang in 1987 and Zhao Ziyang in 1989, which were linked to their failure to combat 'bourgeois liberalisation'.

Since the late 1970s the CCP has faced increasing competition from alternative ideological influences. This is epecially linked to the process of 'opening up to the outside world', which has involved not only the importation of foreign technology and capital, but also ideas and cultural influences. Expansion of tourism, importation of literature, television programs and music, greater access to forms of telecommunication — all of these have rapidly increased the sources of information and opinion available to large sections of the Chinese people. While some in the CCP leadership have been worried by the popularity of rock music or the copying of foreign patterns of behaviour, they have been even more upset by the influence of foreign political ideas. Perhaps the best symbol of that was the 'Goddess of Democracy' erected in Tiananmen Square in 1989 (see Chapter 5).

Attempts to reassert the official ideology may do little more than generate cynicism, even if there is enforced nominal compliance. They are inconsistent with the Party's own repudiation of the relevance of ideology to many aspects of modernisation. Even worse, the Party appears to foster hypocrisy, by encouraging people to embrace ideological standards which are incompatible with the types of behaviour simultaneously promoted as necessary parts of economic reform. Further, because of processes of reform and the greater diversity of competing ideological influences, the themes of official ideology often simply appear naive and anachronistic. A good example of this was in the wake of the events of 1989, which saw the revival of a campaign to emulate Lei Feng, a model of political rectitude from the 1960s. The campaign was received with derision by many Chinese youth. The CCP thus faces a dilemma largely of its own creation. The hankering after higher levels of ideological commitment confronts the difficulty that the CCP's own program has created an environment which provides little basis for generating and sustaining such commitment.

Socialism

The most important single aspect of official ideological formulations must be the treatment of 'socialism', since this defines what is supposed to be the fundamental character of the social and political system. Its continued importance is demonstrated by the constant official references to 'socialism with Chinese characteristics'. Since the late 1970s there has been a fundamental reinterpretation of 'socialism', repudiating the conception which was inherited from the Cultural Revolution. The two main trends have been an economistic interpretation of socialism, and the definition of socialism in terms of current political arrangements. These trends are partially complementary and partially contradictory. Reflecting the general tensions between economic and political dimensions of reform, they illustrate the CCP's efforts to adapt political understandings to the perceived imperatives of economic development, but also the Party's fear of some of the consequences of such adaptation.

The economistic interpretation can be traced directly to December 1978, and the CCP Central Committee's announcement of a shift in the Party's focus to modernisation, understood primarily as economic growth. Progressively during the 1980s, the Party's platform was cast in terms of economic goals and criteria. By 1987 the Party was ready to present its new orthodoxy of socialism, in what was called the 'theory of the initial stage of socialism', which was given its authoritative expression at the Party's Thirteenth National Congress in 1987.[5] This is supposed to provide a theoretical explanation of the character and tasks of 'socialism with Chinese characteristics'.

There are two main aspects of the theory. The first is that China has already established a socialist society, which must be preserved. Hence China is said to have a socialist economic system, which is based on public ownership of the means of production; that, in turn, is said to mean that exploitation and exploiting classes have been eliminated. In terms of ideology, the 'guiding role of Marxism' is affirmed. And China also has a socialist political system — a crucial point we shall return to in a moment. The other aspect of the theory is that China's socialism is necessarily in the early or 'initial' stage only. This means that the socialist system is limited by China's poverty and backwardness. Scientific and technological levels remain low, much of the population is culturally deprived, and 'decadent feudal and capitalist ideologies' are still widespread. The main emphasis, however, is on economic backwardness, which is seen as constraining the further development of socialism in China. In the initial stage, therefore, it is necessary to bring about industrialisation and economic development to achieve the modernisation of production other countries achieved under capitalism. It is emphasised that this stage cannot be avoided and that it is inevitably protracted. Thus the Great Leap Forward and the Cultural Revolution are condemned as 'leftist mistakes', based on 'utopian' views of rapid development beyond China's objective capacities. By contrast, the official timetable for socialism in China now sees the initial stage lasting at least until the middle of the twenty-first century, ending with the 'basic realisation of socialist modernisation'.

The 'initial stage' notion clearly reinforces the priority accorded to economic growth in all Party programs. It can provide the general justification for whatever measures raise productivity, while other social or political criteria are more or less explicitly subordinated to economic development. In the words of the official ideologues, it is necessary to reform all parts of the production relations and the superstructure not suited to the growth of the productive forces. Anything conducive to the development of production can be considered intrinsically valuable in terms of the Party's current line. Factors such as widening inequalities, private use of labour or receipt of unearned incomes may be encouraged so long as they produce economic results. What emerges, therefore, is an effective denial of any authentic socialist values and objectives independent of economic development. Following from that, the meaning of 'socialism' itself can be drastically changed. Not only can any practices be encouraged if they boost productivity, but they can even be regarded as inherently 'socialist'. Within the conceptual constraints of the current orthodoxy, for example, widening inequalities can be presented as entirely compatible with socialism. If socialism is seen primarily in terms of increase in economic output, anything which is seen as economically useful can be justified as contributing to socialism.

While this notion of the initial stage of socialism can hardly be regarded as a significant contribution to Marxist theory, that misses the main point of its formulation, which is that the 'theory' is useful in officially justifying both present and future policies, especially in programs of economic reform. This sort of ideological juggling raises the question of whether 'socialism with Chinese characteristics' retains any substantial content. We must, however, also take into account the other main aspect of the 'initial stage' — the assertion that socialism has already been established in China. The socialist system is seen in an economic structure based largely on public ownership of the means of production, in the affirmation of Marxist–Leninist ideology, and in various political structures. The main basis of such assertions is simply definitional — that such characteristics are 'socialist' because they apply in China which is socialist by definition. But they can also be used to to impose some restraint on policy innovations.

Hence, while economic reforms have undermined much of what used to be regarded as necessary parts of a 'socialist economic system', some general propositions concerning the necessary characteristics of such a system remain. These include the need for planning rather than a complete reliance on markets, and the maintenance of high levels of state ownership in industry. Such constraints may not always be compelling, to the extent of preventing changes which are presented as boosting production. And the constraints may be rather formalistic, as in the technical continuation of collective ownership in agriculture, even though farming is effectively conducted as though the land were privately owned. Nevertheless, the constraints do remain — at least loosely. Perhaps their main significance is that they can be used by those in the CCP leadership who want to resist proposed economic changes. Similarly, as noted above, the repudiation of former formulations of official ideology has provided the basis for flexibility and adaptation, but there has also been concern over the erosion of ideological standards. The notion of a socialist system again provides a platform for those who wish to resist what they see as the attenuation of Marxist–Leninist ideology. In other words, the extent to which the affirmation of a 'socialist system' affects CCP policies and programs depends upon the outcomes of conflicts within the leadership.

Over recent years it has been the notion of a 'socialist political system' which has become the most sensitive, bringing us to the second main trend in the treatment of 'socialism' — that is, the definition of socialism in terms of current political arrangements. Most importantly, the dominance of the Communist Party is often presented as the principal characteristic of a socialist system. This was illustrated well by the suppression of dissidence in 1989. When Deng and the other political figures who ordered the suppression claimed to be protecting socialism, it was clear that they percieved the main threat to be the challenge to Communist Party authority, especially in the growth of autonomous political organisations outside of the Party-dominated political structures.[6] Their determination to crush such political activities derived from a conviction of the need to preserve the dominance of the Party, which they equated with the maintenance of 'socialism' in China. In other words, 'socialism' becomes embodied in existing political structures, and especially in the Party's position. Chinese leaders' views on this were confirmed by the collapse of 'socialist systems' in Eastern Europe later in 1989.

The two main trends of an economistic interpretation of 'socialism' and an affirmation of a 'socialist system' are, at one level, consistent, in that it is the CCP itself which has presented socialism in terms of economic targets. But there are also implicit contradictions between them. The economistic interpretation tends to undermine the principal grounds on which the Party's role had been justified, that is, the need for a directive force in a process of socialist transition. The key point about that justification was that objectives such as economic growth were pursued within a framework of social change led by the Party. To the extent that those objectives now stand independently, they have become separated from the Party's supposed 'vanguard' status.[7] Alternative grounds for claims to leadership are suggested, especially possession of expertise or abilities in the stimulation of economic growth. The Party has thus thrown into doubt the relevance of its own sphere of competence. At the same time, no challenge to the Party's political dominance will be tolerated. Thus the implicit contradictions within the interpretation of socialism are focused on implications for the Party's position.

In the period since the crisis of May–June 1989 there have been some official attempts to give more substance to the concept 'socialism'. The suggestion that no one can state clearly what the socialist road is (something of which Zhao Ziyang was accused) has been repudiated. There has been a stronger recourse to historical claims, about the necessity of socialist revolution to save China from its former parlous state. It is asserted that only socialism could avoid Chinese dependence on world capitalism, and prevent the drawbacks of internal growth, such as class polarisation. And there have been attempts to spell out objectives of social transformation. These sorts of statements are acceptable to all within the CCP leadership, but there have been tensions over how far they might be taken before they threaten reform programs. Some CCP authorities have gone beyond generalised and rhetorical affirmations, mounting an implicit challenge to the dominant economistic interpretation of socialism. In the context of the demise of regimes in the Soviet Union and Eastern Europe, they have warned about the dangers of 'peaceful evolution', questioning whether Chinese reforms have 'practised socialism or capitalism'. In response, Deng Xiaoping and others have strongly reasserted the centrality of economic construction, repudiating what they see as a resurgence of 'leftism'.

Hence, within the general affirmations of the benefits of 'socialism' shared by all CCP authorities, there have still been conflicting views on the precise characteristics of 'socialism with Chinese characteristics'. In October 1992, however, the Fourteenth CCP National Congress strongly reaffirmed the position associated with Deng. The revised Party Constitution included an explanation of the 'initial stage' in the Party's 'General Program'. And while the 'four cardinal principles' remain as part of the Party's 'basic line', the Constitution asserts unequivocally: 'In leading the socialist cause, the CCP must persist in regarding economic construction as its central task and all other work must be subordinated to and serve the central task.'[8]

Notes

1 Andrew Walder, *Communist Neo-Traditionalism: Work and Authority in Chinese Industry*, University of California Press, Berkeley and Los Angeles, 1986, p. 16.

2 See Nick Knight, 'Mao Zedong and the "Sinification of Marxism"', in Colin Mackerras and Nick Knight (eds), *Marxism in Asia*, Croom Helm, Kent, 1985, especially pp. 83–90.

3 *Resolution on CPC History (1949-81)*, Foreign Languages Press, Beijing, 1981.

4 B. Womack, 'Politics and Epistemology in China since Mao', *China Quarterly*, no. 80, December 1979, pp. 768–92.

5 The following discussion of the 'initial stage' is based upon Zhao Ziyang's Report to the 13th Congress, *Beijing Review*, vol. 30, no. 45, 9–15 November 1987.

6 See Luo Qiping et al., 'The 1989 Pro-Democracy Movement: Student Organizations and Strategies', *China Information*, vol. v, no. 2, 1990, pp. 30–43.

7 Cf B. Womack, 'Party–State Democracy: A Theoretical Exploration', *Issues and Studies*, vol. 25, no. 3, March 1989, pp. 45–46, 53–54.

8 'Constitution of the Chinese Communist Party', *Summary of World Broadcasts Part III: The Far East*, 22 October 1992, FE/1518 C1/2.

10 Political Reform and the Chinese Communist Party

WHILE there have been wide-ranging changes in political structures and processes, the approach of the leadership under Deng to political reform has been limited, consistent with the interpretation of 'socialism with Chinese characteristics'. The most obvious direct limit is imposed by the affirmation of a 'socialist political system', which especially prohibits any challenge to the dominant role of the CCP. More generally, the overall orientation to political reform has derived from the economistic interpretation of socialism. The leadership under Deng has certainly been intent on dealing with legacies of the Cultural Revolution, but its objections to the former political system mainly revolve around problems of incompatibility with the perceived imperatives of modernisation. Accordingly, the approach to remedial measures has been largely instrumental, and the main arguments have seen political reform as necessary for facilitating and promoting economic reform. This linkage has provided grounds for conflict within the leadership over the extent of political reform — that is, whether political reform should be pursued for its own sake or treated instrumentally; and, if the latter, what sorts of reforms are required to serve economic reform.

Almost all pronouncements on political reform by authoritative sources emphasise stability, which is seen as a fundamental condition of successful economic development. At the same time, of course, stability necessarily implies rejection of any challenge to the existing political system. Apart from suppression of any activity which is regarded as destabilising, the main strategy for encouraging stability has been the 'institutionalisation' of Chinese politics. This can be seen as a direct reaction to the Cultural Revolution, which was characterised by haphazard, arbitrary and unpredictable forms of political activity. The objective of institutionalisation in Chinese political reform can be understood as the effort to channel political activity within formal institutional structures, which routinely adopt generally accepted procedures within their defined and limited spheres of competence. This involves not only establishing political institutions, but also maintaining the regularity and predictability of their operations. A key aspect of this is the linkages between different institutional structures, something which especially concerns the role of the CCP. Overarching themes, given the experience of the Cultural Revolution, are the forms of political participation and the scope of political intrusions into other areas of social activity.

Party building

An important dimension of the process of institutionalisation has been reform of the CCP itself, in concert with its relationship with other structures. In broad terms, reforms have sought to strengthen the Party organisation, to remedy deficiencies in its operational procedures, and to change the composition of both membership generally and of leading bodies especially.[1]

For decades, the CCP has had a clearly articulated set of organisational principles, including both formal rules and prescribed operational procedures. The core principle is that of 'democratic centralism', which stipulates subordination of lower to higher levels and of individuals to the organisation, on the basis of 'democratic' procedures of discussion and election of Party officers. A major principle is 'collective leadership', which encourages the participation of individual members in decision-making by Party organs, while all abide by the decisions reached. Although it is doubtful how far such principles applied in earlier periods, it is nonetheless clear that they were severely eroded by the Cultural Revolution.

Party authorities have constantly condemned the lack of discipline, and a clear demand of reforms has been that all members and officials must obey the Party's rules and subordinate themselves to the organisation. It is also recognised, however, that indiscipline is a symptom of the more general problem of the loss of commitment of many Party members and officials to maintaining the integrity of the Party organisation, and working within the prescribed Party framework. Members no longer bothered to take part in the affairs of, and thus submit themselves to the supervision of, Party branches. The collective solidarity of Party organs had been undermined by the factionalism generated during the Cultural Revolution, as attachment to a faction (extending beyond the Party organisation) prevailed over loyalty to the Party as a whole. Most generally, members relied on their personal connections or relationships *(guanxi)*, undercutting the Party organisation by bypassing it or treating it merely as a shell in which these more personalised links were mobilised. Collective leadership was also obstructed by the 'patriarchal' behaviour of Party officials, who stifled participation by other members and used the organs they led as a means for imposing their own wills.

CCP leaders have seen all such deficiencies of 'work style' as reflections of underlying ideological problems among the Party membership. As they claim, members infringe the proper standards of political behaviour because they lack dedication to the Party's objectives. The question of ideological standards relates firstly to acceptance of the reformist direction pursued since 1978. Whatever the supposed rights of expressing competing views within the Party, it is clear that acceptance of the 'line' formulated by the Central authorities is mandatory. The other main aspect of lack of dedication refers to self-seeking motives. Those applying to join the Party may be concerned primarily with enhancing their prospects for career advancement rather than expressing a commitment to political objectives. Further, *guanxi* can be mobilised for personal privilege and material benefits. And the exchange of favours which provides the basis for *guanxi* networks easily extends into more straightforward corruption, as Party officials use the powers of their positions for embezzlement or extortion of bribes. Such practices generate popular resentment, which undermines the Party's authority.

From the perspective of the leadership, therefore, there are several layers of organisational, behavioural and ideological problems besetting the CCP. One remedial measure has been to reinforce the organisational structure of the Party. In 1980 the Central Secretariat, an organ responsible for managing the Party's daily affairs and handling crucial areas such as personnel placements, which had been abolished during the Cultural Revolution, was restored. This has been accompanied by efforts to ensure the effective operation of 'organisation departments' throughout the Party structure. The Central Party organs have also sought to provide a model for more regularised procedures. A simple example is that National Party Congresses are now held at regular five-yearly intervals. The proceedings of the Congresses have become far less secretive. And there have been more 'democratic' procedures, both in selecting delegates to congresses and in election of leading party organs. Although such moves are still very limited, they have had some impact, including Central Committee election results which differed from those the leading political figures had planned.

Since 1978, a system of 'discipline inspection commissions' has been charged with checking on Party members and organisations. Consistent with the range of problems within the Party, these commissions have not only been concerned with investigating and punishing disciplinary infringements and corruption, but have also addressed more general questions of 'work style'. Along the same lines, from 1983–87 there was a broad-ranging 'rectification' movement. The process of 'rectification' was first devised in the early 1940s, and has since been used periodically, with differing objectives and differing punitive and educative emphases.[2] The aims of the 1983–87 movement included the fostering of ideological commitment in the sense of acceptance of the current 'line' of the leadership, the strengthening of discipline, the re-establishment of prescribed organisational procedures, and punishment or expulsion of members found unsuitable in terms of ideological standards or organisational behaviour.[3]

Another overlapping strand of Party reform has focused on personnel issues, concerning the qualities of Party members and especially of those in responsible positions. In the early period of Deng's dominance, a principal focus was on the generational differences among Party cadres produced by the Cultural Revolution. The 'new cadres' — that is, those who had been recruited or promoted during the Cultural Revolution — were often regarded as unreliable or unsuitable, because of their connection with the types of policy orientations which were now repudiated and their culpability in nefarious political practices within the Party organisation. Many such cadres were removed from their positions, often to be replaced by 'old cadres' (i.e. those who had been victims of the Cultural Revolution but were later rehabilitated, with a rash of such rehabilitations since the late 1970s), who were considered to be more favourable to post-1978 policy orientations and better trained in appropriate standards of political conduct. From the early 1980s, however, this orientation was superseded by a new emphasis on personnel changes intended to be more consistent with the Party's 'modernisation' approach. The stipulated standards for cadres were now summarised as the 'four transformations' — that is, that cadres should be younger, better educated, more vocationally qualified, and 'revolutionised'.

The emphasis thus shifted from political and ideological credentials and length of experience in the Party to managerial and technical expertise. That may be qualified by the fourth standard, but only partially. While 'revolutionisation' involves continued insistence that Party members and cadres should have the necessary commitment to socialism, that is likely to mean little more than simply fitting in with the views propounded by the Central Party authorities. Given the offical interpretation of 'socialism', a cadre's 'revolutionisation' might itself be interpreted in terms of managerial or technical abilities contributing to economic development, plus acceptance of the inviolability of CCP dominance and avoidance of any taint of 'bourgeois liberalisation' (both of which were more strongly emphasised after the events of June 1989).

One difficulty in the transformation of the cadre ranks was the need to remove the incumbents of responsible positions, including the 'old cadres' favoured in the earlier efforts to redress Cultural Revolution grievances. The usual former practice in the CCP had been that cadres would remain in their positions until death, so long as they were not purged for political reasons. To counter that, the Party leadership has introduced mechanisms for encouraging or enforcing retirement. It has directly attacked the notion of 'lifelong tenure of office'. And it has provided various inducements for retirement, including material benefits and the provision that retired cadres should retain 'advisory' positions.

The various strands of Party reform have achieved some degree of success. There have been measurable changes in the composition of Party leading bodies, most notably at the central level, but also at lower levels. Consistent with the intended 'transformation', average ages have declined, the proportions of those with higher education levels have risen markedly, and those with vocational expertise, especially in engineering and science, have become increasingly more prominent. Standards of youth, higher education levels and abilities useful in economic development have also been applied in Party recruitment, leading to increasing numbers of members who are identified as 'intellectuals' or have specialist or technical qualifications, at the expense of declining proportions of peasants and, to a lesser extent, manual workers.[4] Nevertheless, there remain tensions within the Party over the extent to which ideological and political criteria should be subordinated to those relating to economic success. Thus objections to the favouring of successful entrepreneurs and newly rich farmers in Party recruitment have questioned whether such people are suitable members of the supposed 'vanguard of the proletariat'. Such objections implicitly challenge the economistic interpretation of 'socialism'.

In other aspects of reform the results have been at best mixed. While there have been frequent reports of members expelled or punished in other ways for corruption and violations of discipline, these have been predominantly at the lower levels and have undoubtedly merely scratched the surface of such practices. Even more difficult has been the promotion of prescribed operational procedures. The models of ideological commitment and proper organisational conduct may be regarded simply as pious pronouncements which should be given rhetorical support but are too divorced from actual practices to be realised. In particular, the personalistic character of the Party's operations is very resistant to change, as *guanxi* networks close ranks to obstruct any outside attempts to forbid political relationships that their members find personally beneficial, to the extent of providing protection for those guilty of indiscipline and corruption. As a result of these sorts of inhibitions, even official sources admitted that the 1983–87 rectification was far from successful. A major reason, as one analyst has noted, was that of 'non-compliance' by Party organs and members.[5] The CCP is now a gigantic organisation of over 50 million members, so any efforts at reform confront the problem of sheer size in addition to the depth to which practices regarded as wrong have become entrenched.

A consequence of inability to deal with identified problems has been the CCP's continuing low standing in popular evaluation. For example, a 1987 survey revealed that a majority of all occupational groups rated the CCP as 'not good', ranging from slightly over 50 per cent among workers up to nearly 70 per cent among intellectuals.[6] Other surveys have revealed low assessments of the qualities of Party members, and a very general belief that those wishing to join the Party have selfish motives. A key theme in popular protest during 1989 was anger at official privilege and corruption. The leadership under Deng can use this sort of evidence to push for more efforts in Party reform, but that response can also be treated cynically. The spread of corruption is closely linked to the leadership's own economic reform program, which has sanctioned a 'get rich' attitude and provided far more opportunities for engaging in extortion, bribery and so on. Party leaders may condemn *guanxi* networks, but one focus of resentment is the so-called 'prince's party' — that is, the children of high-level cadres who have conspicuously enjoyed privileges and career opportunities, and who have often been implicated in corruption facilitated by their family connections.[7] While the lack of success in Party reform so far is reflected in Party leaders' continual demands for 'strengthening Party building', there are good grounds for scepticism not only over the likelihood of success but also over the credibility of the demands themselves.

Party and government

The objective of institutionalisation in the government system has involved the resuscitation or reorientation of old political structures and creation of new ones, many aspects of which have been discussed in Chapters 3 and 4. Among the most important was the abolition of the former system of revolutionary committees as the basis of administration at all hierarchical levels below the Centre, and their replacement in 1979–80 with the system of people's governments which were supposedly accountable to the legislative organs, the people's congresses. From 1979 new regulations were applied for elections to people's congresses, with the extension of direct elections to congresses at county level. In 1982 a new Constitution of the PRC was promulgated. It restored the office of President, or Head of State, which had been eliminated with the dismissal of Liu Shaoqi in 1968. Another institution which lapsed during the Cultural Revolution, but has since been restored, is the Chinese People's Political Consultative Conference, a consultative body consisting mainly of people considered to have relevant expertise in areas of social policy. The national-level Consultative Conference has met annually, and corresponding bodies have been revived at lower levels. Similarly, the so-called 'democratic parties' (which became part of the CCP-led 'United Front' in the pre-Liberation period) have resumed their activities and recruited new members.

In terms of 'institutionalisation', an important point beyond the formal establishment or change of structures is the commitment to their regularised operations. To take an important example, the National People's Congress (NPC), the 'highest organ of state power', had met only sporadically in the wake of the Cultural Revolution. During the 1980s it was established that the NPC met annually, and its Standing Committee holds several sessions every year. The proceedings of both bodies are well publicised, with announcements of agenda and decisions reached. The NPC has also set up a system of functional sub-committees, in areas such as finance and economics, education, foreign affairs and so on, which are intended to have input into relevant legislation and to maintain oversight of the corresponding activities of government organs. Hence there is at least the form of a developed institution operating according to regularised procedures.

Reforms of government institutions have also been directed towards improving efficiency, which is linked to effective programs of modernisation. There have been constant calls for the streamlining of executive organs of government and for a reduction in the number of ministries and other organs and in their levels of staffing. Deng Xiaoping has been prominent in the condemnation of 'bureaucracy', under which he has included a formidable list of faults — 'divorcing oneself from reality and the masses; spending a lot of time and effort to put up an impressive front; indulging in empty talk; sticking to a rigid way of thinking; being hidebound by convention . . . circulating documents endlessly without solving problems; shifting responsibility to others' and so on.[8] As with reforms in the Party, emphasis has been placed on personnel issues. Again, a principal focus has been on corruption among government officials. Life tenure of office has been condemned as contributing to the ossification of bureaucratic structures and preventing the appointment of more competent officials. Competence is understood primarily according to standards of expertise, education and youth. An intention to strengthen institutionalisation was demonstrated by the moves towards a 'public service' system in some areas of government staffing, involving more systematic procedures operating according to stipulated rules in matters such as recruitment, training, performance appraisal and wages.[9]

Other criticisms of 'bureaucratism' have focused on overlapping and duplication of functions, the practice of one person holding positions in different structures, and overconcentration of powers in too few hands. These sorts of problems are part of a crucial dimension of institutionalisation, which is the clearer differentiation among structures and the reinforcement of ability to perform within defines spheres of competence. Once again a primary consideration has been efficiency, especially in terms of successful economic development. For example, the major 1984 Central Committee decision on economic structural reform, in dealing with the relationship between industrial enterprises and government administration, stated:

> . . . since social demand is very complex and in a state of constant flux, since the conditions of enterprises differ in a thousand and one ways and since the economic links between enterprises are complicated, no state institution can know the whole situation fully and cope with everything in good time. If a state institution were to directly administer and manage various kinds of enterprises owned by the whole people, it would be very hard to avoid serious subjectivism and bureaucratism, with a consequent suppression of enterprise vitality.[10]

The operation of an enterprise as 'a relatively independent economic entity' was seen as improving flexibility in production and marketing, allowing 'modern methods of scientific management' and increasing incentives. Government administration, on the other hand, would be better able to concentrate on its proper roles in economic management, including 'formulat[ing] the strategy, plans, principles and policies for economic and social development', coordination among regions and economic entities, provision of infrastructure, and natural resource development.[11]

The most significant — and most sensitive — aspect of institutional differentiation concerns the role of Party organisations. The prescribed role of the Party is to exercise 'political and ideological leadership', which is distinguished from the operational responsibilities of other institutional structures. According to the Party Constitution adopted in 1982, the Party organisation within a unit:

> . . . discusses and decides on major questions of principle and at the same time ensures that the administrative leaders fully exercise their functions and powers, but refrains from substituting itself for, or trying to take over from, the administrative leaders.[12]

'Party leadership' is supposed to provide the framework within which other institutions operate, but not directly undertake those operations. Hence the Party should determine policy at all levels, from the national to the 'major questions of principle' in any particular unit. It should also exercise a 'guarantory and supervisory role' by monitoring the observance of policy and the extent to which other structures meet stipulated objectives. And it should be concerned with more general aspects of 'mass political work', which involves the spread of ideological influence and propagation of the Party's line and policies. But guidance and supervision is distinguished from the actual performance of tasks in other structures. This sort of distinction is seen as necessary to improve the effectiveness of the work of those other institutions and of the Party itself. That is, operational matters can be handled more effectively by giving responsibility to those able to adopt appropriate standards — economic, technical, professional and managerial — without Party intrusion. On the other hand, Party organisations themselves can give proper attention to their guidance and supervisory roles by avoiding entanglement in and responsibility for operational matters.

Such prescriptions for differentiating the functions of the Party and other structures are inherently difficult to apply. This is not to say that they have been entirely ineffective. The blurring of Party and government structures which followed the Cultural Revolution has been reduced. There is more possibility for those holding responsible positions in various structures to assert some degree of autonomy from Party organisations, by appealing to the standards recognised as more appropriate for handling operational matters. In particular, the thrust of economic reform has strengthened the hand of enterprise management. Nevertheless, the background of the Party organisation 'substituting itself for, or trying to take over from' other structures is very strong and, despite the current prescriptions, there are several factors encouraging its persistence. One is the lack of clarity in any distinction between 'policy' and 'operations'. In China, as elsewhere, it is difficult to specify matters which are purely operational without attendant policy implications and effects. The distinction becomes more problematic when Party organisations are enjoined to 'play a guarantory and supervisory role to see that the production targets or operational tasks assigned to their own units are properly fulfilled'.[13]

The restrictions on the Party's intrusions have also been resisted by Party officials. While it may be claimed that the differentiation of functions serves to strengthen the Party's role, that may not be persuasive to officials who wish to maintain their own power within a unit. And such people are likely to interpret the scope of 'policy' more widely than the official formulations would suggest. This is especially significant because the prescriptions concerning the relations between Party and other structures have to depend on behavioural changes, since the overall organisational framework for

Party intrusion remains basically intact. Although there have been some modifications,[14] the system whereby the Party parallels and penetrates other structures persists. And that is greatly reinforced by the Party's control of personnel matters. Again there have been changes relating to multiple office-holding — such as the provision that a Party secretary should not simultaneously hold the top administrative position (e.g. acting both as Provincial Governor and Party First Secretary). But it is still routine that almost all significant political figures at any level will also hold Party posts, or at least membership. The highest government official, Premier Li Peng, is a member of the CCP Politburo's Standing Committee. This sort of linkage applies at all levels, so that it should be expected that a large proportion of enterprise managers or government officials at any level will be Party members. More generally, the system requiring approval by the Party of those who hold important posts in any institution (the so-called *nomenklatura* lists) also remains largely intact, despite some modifications such as the 'public service' proposals mentioned above. Any notion of differentiation of functions cannot be understood simply in terms of relationships between structures, but must recognise that people have places in more than one structure, and will be subjected to cross-cutting loyalties, commitments and obligations.

In sum, attempts to separate Party and government necessarily face many obstacles deriving from the former (and in many ways continuing) patterns of Party penetration, and there are corresponding difficulties in assessing their success. The extent to which Party organs still go beyond the role prescribed in official formulations will often depend upon particular local factors, such as the respective ambitions and assertiveness of Party officials and those responsible for operational matters in a unit. While there has certainly been a trend away from the blurring of functions which prevailed after the Cultural Revolution, it is also clear that 'institutionalisation' in terms of defining and maintaining distinct spheres of competence has not been achieved.

Political participation

In reaction to the legacies of the Cultural Revolution, the Chinese leadership under Deng has promoted two broad complementary trends in the scope and content of political activity: restriction and regularisation. One objection to the Cultural Revolution was that 'politics' had become too inclusive and too intrusive because it revolved around 'class struggle', which was seen as pervading all aspects of social activity. The official formulation of socialism adopted from the late 1970s asserted that 'class struggle' persisted in only limited forms, and this allowed the view 'that there exist certain areas of autonomy in economic and social life into which political power cannot and should not intrude'.[15] Within this more restricted sphere, the leadership has attempted to establish more ordered forms of political activity, so as to create the environment of stability necessary for concentrating on the tasks of modernisation. Such efforts are also claimed to foster 'democratisation' of the political system.

Restriction and regularisation of political activity have involved repudiation of the campaign style of politics, which had reached its greatest heights during the Cultural Revolution. Mass campaigns were seen as having been manipulated by political figures for their own purposes, as being arbitrary and leading to injustices, and especially as creating disorder at the expense of the economy. Consistent with the effort to reduce the former inclusive view of what was relevant to 'politics', many of the types of matters which had been the focus of campaigns were now to be removed from the political agenda. And what remained was to be treated according to formal procedures, most notably through elections and representative institutions. This implied a shift in the understanding of the basis of popular political participation. People were to participate not as masses mobilised for political movements, but as citizens involved in the routine functioning of established institutions. One consequence was that some people who had been excluded from political participation, because they were objects of suspicion and targets of mass movements informed by 'class struggle', could now be included. In the early period of Deng's dominance, the pejorative 'class labels' attached to social groups were removed. This allowed political participation by groups such as intellectuals who, rather than being seen as likely class enemies and thus targets of political attack, could participate as citizens (indeed, especially valuable citizens because of their contributions according to the economistic interpretation of 'socialism').

In terms of institutionalisation, a notable innovation has been the more regular operations of representative structures — from village committees, neighbourhood committees in urban areas and workers' congresses in enterprises to the system of people's congresses. To take the last as an example, the PRC Constitution describes people's congresses as the 'organs of state power' and gives them responsibility for legislation and for choosing and supervising the executive organs of government. They are thus central to a process of institutionalisation. An obvious criticism of the system of people's congresses which applied before the late 1970s was that they acted merely as a 'rubber-stamp', as they were entirely subservient to the CCP. People's congresses now cannot be so easily dismissed as 'rubber stamps', but nor do they fully exercise the range of responsibilities stipulated in the Constitution.

At the highest level, the NPC has become a much more lively body. In contrast to the former automatic unanimous endorsement of whatever was presented to it, more recent sessions of the NPC have seen vigorous debate, criticisms of government actions, and dissenting votes on legislation presented (including nearly one-third of deputies voting against the Three Gorges Dam Project in 1992) and nominations for government office. There have been cases in which deputies' criticisms have led to amendments of and delays in legislation. At the 1992 NPC session there were many revisions in the government's work report, presented by Premier Li Peng, resulting from deputies' comments. These more assertive tendencies within the NPC have no doubt influenced legislation and the performance of government organs, but not to the extent that they have exercised any sort of independent legislative role or directly confronted the executive arm of government.[16] Nor is that likely to happen, as the CCP continues to maintain overall control over NPC proceedings. In addition to the large proportion of deputies who are Party members, the CCP decides the NPC agenda and determines who will hold all key positions within the NPC. The operations of both the legislative and executive branches of government, and the relations between them, are still conducted within the framework of 'Party leadership', and the more lively activity within the NPC is tolerated because so far it does not challenge that framework.

Similar constraints apply in the election system. Innovations since 1979 have included the extension of direct election to people's congresses at county level, and electoral contest (i.e. that there should be more than one candidate per constituency).[17] There have been cases in which candidates opposed by Party authorities have been successful in the direct elections to the lowest two levels of people's congresses. There have also been reports of local Party officials being punished for infringing the Electoral Law — for example, by attempting to coerce voters or to nullify electoral results of which they disapproved. But generally such incidents are likely to be exceptional; Party organisations usually do not need to interfere illegaly because they routinely have a large degree of control over elections. Matters such as the drawing of boundaries, the organisation of 'voters' groups' and the selection of candidates are handled by commissions organised by the relevant people's congresses, but are also subject to 'leadership' by Party organisations. The opportunity for the CCP to manipulate electoral processes is perhaps greatest in the nomination of candidates. The nomination process is very open, in that a candidate can be nominated by any group of ten voters. But the Electoral Law stipulates that the final election is to be contested by a limited number of candidates. The reduction of the large number of potential candidates produced by the open nomination process to the small number actually contesting the election is supposedly achieved through 'consultation', and the local Party organisation's guidance of the process of consultation allows it to vet those who might be elected.

In these major areas of political participation, therefore, any moves towards institutionalisation are qualified by the maintenance of firm political controls, predominantly by the CCP. Programs of reform may be intended to reduce political intrusion into many areas of social activity, but there is little notion that individual or group activity should be unconfined in areas which are still part of 'politics'. And since the CCP itself decides what should be construed as 'political', it determines what is directly subject to its intervention,[18] and may expand those areas (as in the period after June 1989).

Nevertheless, the CCP faces new constraints in exercising political controls. An increasingly significant factor is that economic reforms such as agricultural decollectivisation, promotion of various forms of individual enterprise and the greater opporunities for labour mobility have separated many people from the *danwei* stuctures, thereby tending to undermine the organisational basis of Party penetration among large sections of the population. Furthermore, the Party must consider the potential economic costs of tighter controls. Processes of economic reform depend on contributions of groups such as scientists and other intellectuals, enterprise managers and new entrepreneurs. The imposition of restrictions on such groups and a failure to take account of their interests could endanger prospects for economic growth.

This last factor has led many analysts to consider the possibilities of growth of 'civil society' in China. Although that term can have varying connotations, its key dimension is a notion of social activity and processes which are autonomous of imposition or regulation by the state (which, in this context, includes both government and party institutions and processes). Thus one commentator suggests several 'common elements' in an analysis of 'civil society' relevant to China:

> First, the use of 'civil society' reflects an attempt to define a type of relationship between state and society, regarding them as separable, distinct spheres roughly to be equated with the 'public' and 'private' spheres; second, it implies a certain power relationship between state and society such that there are limitations on the state's capacity to pervade and control society, and a certain power on the part of members of a society to insulate themselves from, and exert influence upon, the state; third, in this realm of autonomous social power and space, 'civil society' denotes an associational realm in which autonomous organisations are formed through voluntary association to represent the interests and aspirations of members of society.[19]

According to this conception, the post-1949 Chinese system was explicitly antagonistic to the operation of a civil society, since it imposed state penetration and direction of all significant forms of social activity. Attention to the possibilities of growth of civil society has been encouraged both by the consequences of reform policies in China itself, and by considering the experience of the decline of socialist regimes elsewhere — in which one of the main trends has been identified as the loosening of social forces from the state-imposed framework, which eventually encouraged the undermining of and direct challenge to that framework.

In this context, the events of 1989 were significant in that there emerged groups which called themselves 'autonomous' and which directly challenged the regime. According to one analyst, '1989 witnessed the formation of a genuine civil society in urban China', as there was 'an unprecedented expression of Chinese society's separation from the omnipresent state'.[20] Others, however, have suggested more qualified assessments of emergent civil society. Certainly all of the 'common elements' quoted above have become more evident since the late 1970s. Most generally, criticism of the former state intrusiveness into all areas of social activity has acknowledged the distinctiveness of a 'private' sphere. There has also been a proliferation of forms of social organisation — including religious, sporting and cultural organisations, professional associations and organisations based upon economic activity. Many such organisations are explicitly concerned with advancing the interests of members, including economic interests, as in organisations of those engaged in private enterprise or those in a particular type of industry. Even the old official 'mass organisations', such as the Women's Federation or the Trade Union Federation, have become much more vigorous in advancing their members' interests, in contrast to their former role of top-down mobilisation.

In terms of autonomy, however, social organisations largely remain enmeshed with the state. That obviously applies to the official mass organisations, but other types of economically or politically significant organisations can be regarded as 'semi-official'. Their office-holders are likely to hold posts in state institutions, and their finances may be derived at least partly from the state.[21] Members of economic organisations may combine to advance their own interests, but that is likely to be seen in terms of providing better access to state authorities. And government authorities themselves may encourage the formation of such organisations, in order to allow more effective regulation of an industry or type of economic activity with the decline of more direct administrative controls. The political reins may be looser, but not to the extent of sanctioning independent pursuit of interests outside of, let alone against, the state-imposed framework. As one analysis suggests, the Chinese system lacks 'a kind of social trellis of autonomous, self-organising associations and networks willing and able to dissociate from the policies and values of the state. Without this political diversity, all opposing forces tend to be penetrated by or reproduce the state.'[22]

In terms of 'civil society' since the late 1970s, therefore, several trends have been very significant, though still limited. Social organisations which are voluntary, or at least not entirely imposed from above, have become more prominent; the activities of organisations have been less restricted by the state; and they have had greater scope in seeking to influence the state, including acceptance of a role in pursuing their members' interests. State authorities have at times tightened controls, most notably after the 1989 crisis, in reaction to what they regarded as too threatening assertions of autonomy. But there are good reasons why political leaders are reluctant to restrict social organisations too much. In particular, allowing economic organisations or professional associations to operate according to their own concerns is seen as beneficial to modernisation programs. And restriction may itself generate antagonism. Thus one reason for allowing greater latitude to the official trade union structure in more effectively representing workers may be to forestall the demands for genuinely autonomous unions, the stirrings of which so alarmed Party leaders in 1989. In sum, civil society in China is still no more than embryonic. Despite continuing restrictions on social activity and organisation, there have been marked changes in the relationship between state and society over a decade or more, and extension of such changes may encourage the longer-term consolidation of a far more robust and mature civil society.

What then of 'democratisation' in China? If democracy is understood as autonomous political activity, trends in that direction are still subjected to firm controls and limits. There is certainly no notion of competition among political parties — the CCP explicitly rejects such Western 'bourgeois liberal' conceptions. But the CCP's claim that democracy is being advanced by institutional reforms through which the people become 'masters of the state' are, at best, only very partially confirmed by the operations of election systems and people's congresses. Many of the Party's pronouncements suggest that democracy is understood largely in terms of expanding consultation in policy processes — allowing expression of diverse views from groups concerned with areas of social policy. This sort of approach is demonstrated by the value placed on the role of the so-called 'democratic parties' and consultative conferences. Such consultation partially sanctions the expression of competing interests, but it is mainly based on a notion of 'scientific decision-making', suggesting that it is useful because it allows policy to be informed by harnessing knowledge and expertise. Most importantly, consultation is to occur within the framework of Party domination over political structures. The common theme in any treatment of democracy within official programs of political reform is that it must be consistent with maintenance of 'Party leadership'.

Notes

1 The following is discussed more fully in Graham Young, 'Party Reforms' in Joseph Y.S. Cheng (ed.), *China: Modernization in the 1980s*, The Chinese University Press, Hong Kong, 1989, Ch. 3.

2 See Frederick C. Teiwes, *Politics & Purges in China: Rectification and the Decline of Party Norms 1950–1965*, M.E. Sharpe, White Plains, New York, 1979.

3 Bruce J. Dickson, 'Conflict and Non-Compliance in Chinese Politics: Party Rectification, 1983–87', *Pacific Affairs*, vol. 63, no. 2, 1990, pp. 170–90.

4 Stanley Rosen, 'The Chinese Communist Party and Chinese Society: Popular Attitudes Toward Party Membership and the Party's Image', *Australian Journal of Chinese Affairs*, no. 24, July 1990, pp. 51–92.

[5] Dickson, 'Conflict and Non-compliance'. There was another process of 'rectification' in the wake of the crisis of 1989 which again met internal resistance and 'demonstrated the inability of higher levels of the Party to mobilize lower level Party members to cleanse Party ranks': Kenneth Lieberthal, 'China's Political System in the 1990s', *Journal of Northeast Asian Studies*, vol. 10, no. 1, 1991, p. 73.

[6] Rosen, 'The Chinese Communist Party and Chinese Society', p. 81.

[7] Jae Ho Chung, 'The Politics of Prerogatives in Socialism: The Case of *Taizidang* in China', *Studies in Comparative Communism*, vol. xxiv, no. 1, March 1991, pp. 58–76.

[8] *Selected Works of Deng Xiaoping (1975–1982)* , Foreign Languages Press, Beijing, 1984, p. 310.

[9] Important proposals along these lines were announced at the Party's 13th National Congress in 1987: see John P. Burns, 'Chinese Civil Service Reform: The 13th Party Congress Proposals', *China Quarterly*, no. 120, December 1989, pp. 739–70. In his report to the 14th Party Congress in 1992, Jiang Zemin urged that: 'The system of public service must be put in place as soon as possible.' *Beijing Review*, vol. 35, no. 43, 26 October–1 November 1992, p. 24.

[10] *Beijing Review*, vol. 27, no. 44, 29 October 1984, p. vi.

[11] ibid., pp. vi, x.

[12] *Beijing Review*, vol. 25, no. 38, 20 September 1982, p. 18.

[13] ibid.

[14] Tony Saich, 'The Reform Decade in China: The Limits to Revolution from Above' in Marta Dassu and Tony Saich (eds), *The Reform Decade in China: From Hope to Dismay*, Kegan Paul International, London and New York, 1992, pp. 33–38.

[15] Tang Tsou, 'Back from the Brink of Revolutionary–"Feudal" Totalitarianism' in Victor Nee and David Mozingo (eds), *State and Society in Contemporary China*, Cornell University Press, Ithaca and London, 1983, p. 62.

[16] There are more (although still limited) examples of greater independence among lower-level people's congresses — for example, vetoing nominations for local government appointments, exercising the right of recall of officials considered guilty of dereliction of duties, and rejecting budgetary and development plans submitted by local governments.

[17] A good discussion of election processes is J. Bruce Jacobs, 'Elections in China', *Australian Journal of Chinese Affairs*, no. 25, January 1991, pp. 171–99.

[18] Cf. the distinction between a 'zone of immunity' and a 'zone of indifference': Brantly Womack, 'Modernization and Democratic Reform in China', *Journal of Asian Studies*, vol. xliii, no. 3, May 1984, pp. 424–25.

[19] Gordon White, 'Prospects for Civil Society in China: A Case Study of Xiaoshan City', *Australian Journal of Chinese Affairs*, no. 29, January 1993, p. 69.

[20] Lawrence R. Sullivan, 'The Emergence of Civil Society in China, Spring 1989' in Tony Saich (ed.), *The Chinese People's Movement: Perspectives on Spring 1989*, M.E. Sharpe, Armonk, New York, 1990, pp. 126–27, 130.

[21] White, 'Prospects for Civil Society in China', p. 80.

[22] David Kelly and He Baogang, 'Emergence of Civil Society and the Intellectuals in China' in R.F. Miller (ed.), *The Developments of Civil Society in Communist Systems*, Allen & Unwin, Sydney, 1992, p. 24.

11 The Law

ONE of the principal components Deng Xiaoping and his supporters have specified for 'socialism with Chinese characteristics' and reform is the rule of law. So one of the early decisions the CCP reached after Deng Xiaoping returned to power was to re-establish a legal system. This represented a very sharp break with the preceding period of the Cultural Revolution, when 'the law of rule' by Mao Zedong and a few other top leaders masquerading in the name of mass participation had been the order of the day.

Background

China is not traditionally a legally minded society. While it is true that there have for many centuries been institutions involved in law, by tradition it is the ruler or the official — rather than the institution — who pulls weight and power. Moreover, the concept of the separation of powers which dictates that the legal system must be able to operate independently of the government is notable by its absence in China until the twentieth century, and its hold has never been more than shaky. In imperial China the judge was more than dependent on the official: he was the same man.

Because the law was extremely savage in imperial times, with a whole plethora of barbaric corporal punishments, people avoided any recourse to it like the plague. One result of this fear was that mediation and conciliation were regarded as the ways to solve problems. This was strongly in accord with the Confucian outlook, which dominated imperial China. So when disputes, even very bitter ones, arose, the tendency was to appeal to some third independent party. The emphasis on mediation, very strong throughout the ages, remains so to this day.

When the PRC was established, its leaders took immediate action to overthrow whatever legal system had earlier existed, on the grounds that it was a bulwark for the previous political regime. They set up their own legal structure, based on that of the Soviet Union.

In addition to the public security system, there are two main arms of the legal system: the courts, and the procuracy or procuratorate. The function of the procuracy is to establish an *a priori* case against a defendant, to check the evidence and to issue warrants for arrest.

Mao Zedong had stated his belief that the police and courts were instruments 'by which one class oppresses another', as a result of which the people's state, including the people's police and people's courts, must be designed for the protection of the people's interests.[1] In other words, class was to be a definite factor in the legal system. From the 1950s to the 1970s, a worker or peasant could expect better treatment from the law than a member of the bourgeoisie, let alone a former landlord.

During the Cultural Revolution, the power of the legal structures which continued to exist was seen in terms of class. 'Public security organs are a knife in the hands of the proletariat' stated one document of the time. They could be used either by the enemy classes or by those of the people, but the dichotomy was always there.[2]

Mao Zedong appears to have believed that the proper way to handle law was by mass participation under CCP leadership or direction. The classes belonging to the people would need protection and would manage the law. The enemy classes ought not to be protected anyway. The trouble with this method is that it can easily lead to tyranny if one group within society holds too much power. That is precisely why formal legal structures developed in Europe and it is just what *did* happen during the Cultural Revolution.

The separation of powers

Article 78 of the Constitution of 1954 states that 'in administering justice the people's courts are independent, subject only to law',[3] giving an unambiguous declaration that law should be independent of the CCP and the government. Laws were passed at about the same time, specifying how the courts and other legal bodies, such as the procuracy, were to operate. However, the anti-rightist movement of 1957 changed any trend in favour of legal independence. The CCP was not prepared to share power with the legal system. The 'model judge', Liu Zejun, wrote in 1959 that he believed 'judicial work must be absolutely obedient to the leadership of the Party', and acknowledged that in any cases which 'required arresting and sentencing, had a relatively strong policy nature, or involved village or cooperative cadres' he 'asked instructions from the Party committee both before and during the process of handling the cases' and reported to the Party committee afterwards.[4]

Any lingering independence was destroyed during the Cultural Revolution. In order to prevent the class enemy from seizing control of legal bodies such as the public security organs, it was declared that all public security work 'can only be under the direct leadership of the Party Committee' and not 'under the vertical leadership of the relevant government department'.[5]

The Third Plenum of the Eleventh Central Committee, which introduced the reform period, also had something definite to say on the subject of the separation of powers and the independence of the legal system:

> Procuratorial and judicial organizations must maintain their independence as is appropriate; they must faithfully abide by the laws, rules and regulations, serve the people's interests, keep to the facts; guarantee the equality of all people before the people's laws and deny anyone the privilege of being above the law.[6]

Article 126 of the 1982 Constitution repeats that 'the people's courts shall, in accordance with the law, exercise judicial power independently and are not subject to interference by administrative organs, public organisations or individuals'.[7] However, the clear implication of this notion, if taken quite literally, was that the CCP would share power extensively with organisations over which it had very little control. This was too extreme for Deng Xiaoping and Peng Zhen, whose view was that, when it came to the crunch in matters seen as relevant to state political power, the CCP and not the law system should prevail.

Two cases which tested the limits of independence came up very quickly. The first was the trial of Wei Jingsheng, one of the leaders of the democracy movement at the end of 1978 which had actually helped Deng Xiaoping in the period leading up to the Third

Plenum. Wei believed that a 'fifth modernisation' — democracy — was necessary for China. He edited a magazine called *Explorations (Tansuo)*, which the authorities came to regard as subversive. Wei was accused of handing over military secrets to a foreigner. It is extremely unlikely that this was the real reason why Deng Xiaoping and his leadership distrusted Wei so much, but the court duly upheld the charge and sentenced him to fifteen years' imprisonment. Wei appealed, but was unsuccessful.

The other case was the trial of the gang of four and six other living persons, the political significance of which is discussed in Chapter 3. Numerous concrete charges were made against them and, although they had defence lawyers, there was never any real possibility that they would be acquitted, or even that the punishment meted out to them would be anything but extremely heavy. This was a showcase trial, staged to show the world that China was serious about politico-economic and legal reform. But the reality was that, in cases which involved political matters on which Deng Xiaoping felt strongly, the legal system was still used to corroborate his view. It was not independent of the CCP at all.

A third example came much later in the 1980s, following the Beijing massacre of June 1989. Since Deng and other leaders portrayed that disaster as a 'counter-revolutionary rebellion' which threatened to overthrow the CCP itself, they had the excuse they had been seeking to treat intellectual dissent as subversive. Until the political crisis was resolved and stability restored, the legal system was hardly more than a servant of the CCP. One observer wrote that, in that crisis, law became 'completely subordinate to political needs of the party leadership'. She claimed that, because of intense pressure to express political loyalty, legal officials were 'more concerned with the swift rounding up of "counter-revolutionaries" than . . . genuinely distinguishing the ringleaders from the average participants and the onlookers of the May–June agitations'.[8]

These observations are perfectly fair for the crisis period. One of the unfortunate results of the Beijing massacre was its impact on the legal system. The extent of independence of law undoubtedly suffered a serious setback. In the short term after the crisis, more worker than student dissidents were punished and received heavier sentences. However, in fairness, it is necessary to point out that when trials of the most prominent dissidents were eventually held in 1991 and 1992, the sentences imposed were, with some significant exceptions, rather lighter than expected. Among the student leaders, Wang Dan and Liu Xiaobo had both been arrested at the time of the massacre. Early in 1991 Wang was sentenced to four years in prison, but Liu was released. Wang Dan was released in February 1993, ahead of time. In July 1992 one of Zhao's former chief advisers, economist Bao Tong, was put on trial for counter-revolutionary incitement and sentenced to seven years' imprisonment, three of which had already been served since the crisis of 1989. The two who were most severely treated were Chen Ziming and Wang Juntao, neither of whom had been particularly prominent in 1989 in the world press. In February 1991 the authorities found them guilty of taking a leading role in the 'counter-revolutionary rebellion' and 'showing no willingness to repent', and sentenced them each to thirteen years in prison. It was a human rights breach to keep the political dissidents in prison for so long without a trial in the first place. On the other hand, the trials of 1991 and 1992 suggest some degree of recovery in the law system following the 1989 crisis.

Although such cases as these gain the most headlines, they are not the most typical. The run-of-the-mill court cases in the 1980s, and even in the early 1990s, bore no relation to sensitive political matters, let alone the highest levels of leadership. The extent of dependence is far slighter when politics are not involved, or when they are involved only indirectly.

Law and criminal law in the period of reform

Although the legal system had begun to recover very soon after the fall of the gang of four in 1976, the Third Plenum gave a crucial impetus to China's development in the direction of the rule of law. The issue of the separation of powers was of enormous significance, but only one aspect of the very global approach adopted by the Central Committee:

> In order to safeguard people's democracy, it is imperative to strengthen the socialist legal system so that democracy is systematized and written into law in such a way as to ensure the stability, continuity and full authority of this democratic system and these laws; there must be laws for people to follow, these laws must be observed, their enforcement must be strict and law breakers must be dealt with. From now on, legislative work should have an important place on the agenda of the National People's Congress and its Standing Committee.[9]

A Commission for Legal Affairs was established. It was headed by Peng Zhen, who had been among the first to fall as a result of the Cultural Revolution and who was acutely aware of the tyranny its lack of formal law had been able to perpetrate. In mid-1979, he had the National People's Congress adopt seven laws, the first step in the process of building a formal system of codified law.

One of these seven was the PRC's first Criminal Law. In introducing it to the National People's Congress, Peng Zhen emphasised the principle that nobody should be above the law, and that such evil practices as extortion of confessions through torture, unlawful incarceration and frame-ups on false charges would henceforth be absolutely prohibited. He suggested that such practices had been quite widespread during the Cultural Revolution. The Criminal Law came into effect on 1 January 1980.

One of the effects of economic reform was a major rise in the crime rate. In 1979 there were revelations for the first time that juvenile delinquency was a serious problem in China. During the 1980s several major crackdowns on crime took place, the main one beginning in 1983 and lasting for several years. It featured public trials with culprits executed on the spot. Foreign observers' estimates of the total number of people executed in this crackdown varied substantially, but ran into thousands.

Among the many types of crime, one which loomed particularly large because of its impact on Chinese society as a whole — and because of its effect on China's image abroad — was official corruption, which has been mentioned in other chapters. In July 1983, the Secretary of the Central Commission for Discipline Inspection, Han Guang, revealed that smuggling, graft, bribery and fraud had reached their highest level since 1949. On 20 March 1989, in his report to the Second Session of the National People's Congress, Li Peng made a special point of appealing to the procuracy at all levels to take more action in trying to curb criminal corruption. He urged them to 'shift the focus of their work to investigating and punishing graft, bribery, extortion, extravagance, waste and abuse of power for personal gain'.[10]

Figures released by senior legal officials gave some idea of how the problem worsened as the 1980s progressed. From 1983 to 1986 some 40 000 CCP members had been expelled for such corrupt practices as nepotism, bribery, graft and embezzlement, but in 1987 alone the figure was 109 000. In 1987 the number of cases of embezzlement, bribery, smuggling, speculation and fraud uncovered was 77 386, representing a 54.4 per cent increase over the preceding year.[11] In 1988, a total of 74 923 people were sentenced for economic crimes like embezzlement, bribery, profiteering, smuggling and tax evasion. In the same year, the Supreme People's Court sentenced 111 embezzlers and bribe-takers to death or life imprisonment, and 5642 to prison terms, of whom 3754, or more than half, were CCP members, suggesting that the scale of the crimes committed by cadres was very serious indeed in many cases.[12] In May 1989, the Vice-Governor of Hunan, Yang Huiquan, was dismissed for abuse of power and corrupt practices and in September the same year Liang Xiang, the Governor of the newly created island province of Hainan in the far south, suffered the same fate. In other words, open and proven corruption went very near to the top echelon of leadership. One could be forgiven for asking how many more there were who could use their connections to get away with corruption, or for suspecting that even the most senior leaders had something to hide.

The issue of official corruption occupied a major place in the student demonstrations of April–June 1989. Despite serious government attempts at some levels to curb it, criminal corruption has remained a pressing and unresolved problem.

The Criminal Law lays down precisely what constitutes a crime and the types of punishment which should be meted out to criminals. These range from 'control', by which a minor criminal continues to work and receive a salary 'while undergoing the supervision of the public security organs and the masses',[13] through imprisonment, to the death penalty, which the Criminal Law lays down as being by shooting. It specifies that 'if immediate execution is not essential', a two-year suspension may be implemented and any criminal who 'truly repents and demonstrates meritorious service' may be spared.[14]

The Criminal Law also lays down in considerable detail the maximum (and often also minimum) sentences to be applied to particular crimes. One example in the category of 'crimes of counter-revolution' is a minimum of ten years and maximum of life imprisonment for colluding with foreign states in plotting to harm China's sovereignty or security. Included among crimes of infringing upon the rights of the person and the democratic rights of citizens are rape, for which the punishment is between three and ten years' imprisonment, and sexual relations with a girl under the age of 14, which is deemed to be rape. If the circumstances are serious enough to result in injury or death, the punishment ranges from ten years' imprisonment to death.[15]

The slogan applied in China is 'leniency for those who confess, but severity for those who remain obdurate'. The slogan, which we have already seen applied in the trials of dissidents of 1991 to 1992, has very clear Confucian overtones in its emphasis on moral suasion, and may well induce some people to reform. On the other hand, such a slogan also runs the risk that innocent people will confess to crimes they have not committed.

The criminal process is designed not to protect the rights of the individual, but to suppress crime. Consequently, the law tends to be very harsh against suspected criminals. Under the Criminal Procedure Law, the police may detain suspects for up to two months without trial, but exceptions can be made in serious cases.[16] Moreover, the People's Armed Police, established as a crack surveillance unit to defend public security, have turned out to be very savage in several instances, most notably during the Beijing massacre itself and in Tibet. Amnesty International, among several other international bodies, has issued very damning reports about human rights in China.

The Chinese authorities have reacted to accusations of human rights abuses in several ways. Firstly, they have argued that the primary human right is subsistence, with which China has not done too badly. This was the focal point in a very long statement entitled 'Human Rights in China' issued in November 1991.[17] Secondly, they have stated that human rights are an internal matter, not one for international surveillance, so that foreigners should 'mind their own business'. The third reaction, however, is to acknowledge very serious problems in the legal processes in China. For example, in 1987 the Supreme People's Procuracy, the highest organ of public prosecution in China, reported that cases of abuse of power had risen substantially in the first half of 1987, including cases of extorting confessions through torture, frame-ups and unlawful incarcerations, the very evils which Peng Zhen had condemned in introducing the Criminal Law to the National People's Congress.[18]

Another important point concerning the criminal process in China is that conviction rates are extremely high, over 99 per cent. One of the reasons for this is the existence of the Procuracy. Even before any suspect comes before the courts, the procuratorates are supposed to have checked the case out fully. For a suspect to be declared not guilty after these processes have been carried out would imply that the Procuracy was not doing its job properly. Although everybody who comes before the courts has a right to defence, in fact the main function of the 'people's barrister' is to lessen the punishment meted out to the criminal, rather than to prove his or her innocence.

Civil law in the period of reform

It is true that civil law did exist during the Cultural Revolution, mainly in the form of those divorce cases which the units of individual couples were unable to handle. The emphasis was always on conciliation. However, with the period of reform, both the number and the range of civil cases rose substantially. Whereas 53 per cent of cases were civil in 1977, the proportion had risen to 76.1 per cent by 1982.[19] The types of case now coming under the heading of civil law include not only divorce, but a whole range of matters in family law, economic disputes and disputes involving tourists. Of these, the first two also subdivide into numerous different categories. Family law includes property settlements, custody of children and support to elderly parents. Chinese society has become much more complicated, with the reforms and problems which were once kept within the family or production unit now sometimes going to law.

The expansion is possibly greatest in the area of economic cases. Like society, the economy has become very much more complicated than it was during the Cultural Revolution, and people are much more open about their problems. Economic contracts between businesses, organisations, the collective and individuals have mushroomed, especially in the countryside, because of the introduction of the contract system there (see Chapter 6). One implication is the substantial growth in the number and importance of economic disputes.

Before 1979 there were no business cases; nor (since it did not come into existence until that year) were there any based on the rural contract system. However, figures from the early 1980s give some idea of just how rapid the growth of this kind of legal case at that time was. Business cases numbered 89 494 between 1980 and 1983, including over 73 000 contract disputes.[20] Others included cases in which the rural contract system was involved, concerning tax payments, patents, trademarks and foreign economic activities. The number of legal documents handled by notaries suggests a continuing increase in the influence of law: from 2 797 000 in 1985, it climbed to 5 149 000 in 1989 and 9 907 000 in 1991, the great majority of them in each year being economic contracts.[21]

How do these developments affect the conventional wisdom that the Chinese much prefer mediation and fear and dislike the law? This attitude still remains strong, as shown by the vast number of mediators compared with the number of lawyers. In 1991 there were 9 914 000 mediators, or well over 200 times the number of lawyers.[22] At the same time, commentators have expressed surprise at the speed and extent with which the idea of going to law has spread among ordinary people. One observed that, as far as laws affecting the day-to-day lives of ordinary people — matters such as housing and family property — were concerned, 'the new confidence shown in legal process is truly remarkable'.[23] Clearly a change has occurred in the way people regard the law. In addition, cadres have been encouraged to undertake legal training and schools have begun to offer legal studies courses. According to one report, about 95 per cent of all primary and middle schools offered legal studies courses in late 1989.[24] In the area of contract law, considerable efforts were made through public education and other means to change the idea of a contract much more from implying merely a sense of moral obligation to being fully binding. The basic motivation for this trend was to gain more foreign investment by offering better protection to potential investors.[25] But it is definitely in line with overall developments in civil law, all the same. The speed of legal change in China may have been retarded by the crisis of 1989, but in the long term it is probably already irreversible.

The legal profession

One of the most important features of the formal or external approach which it has been the aim of Deng Xiaoping and his leadership to promote has been an enlarged legal profession with a raised social status. The alternative informal or internal system which prevailed during the Cultural Revolution had a very small and weak legal bureaucracy with a low social status. A large legal profession with a high social status raises inherent contradictions in a poor and underdeveloped socialist society, because there is very little point in a legal system which is not open to poor people. On the other hand, a legal profession which is going to be prepared to take on the job of implementing the law must be highly trained. And if such a profession is going to attract good and talented people, they may need to be paid high salaries. Therefore the state must bear the costs of opening the law to the masses. But in a poor country such as China, the kind of law system which will guarantee individual rights to ordinary people is most unlikely to occupy a very high priority in development. What matters most is a legal system which will guarantee rights to rich foreigners who may wish to invest in China and thus advance its modernisation.

In the 1950s, China began to develop a very small legal profession, with Soviet assistance. But the split with the Soviet Union and the Cultural Revolution had a devastating effect on the incipient profession. The result was that when legal reform began at the end of the 1970s, there was hardly anybody in China in any position to implement the new laws. Moreover, China lacked not only professional lawyers, but also the institutions which might begin the enormous task of training a legal cadre. As a result, the government had to rely to a considerable extent on foreign countries, especially those of the West and Japan, where formal law remains by far the most highly developed in the world. But there were problems here too. To send students overseas to be trained as lawyers was one way out, but because salaries and conditions were incomparably better there than they were likely to be in China for many years, a significant proportion of the students elected to remain overseas if they could. Of course, the problem was greatly exacerbated by the troubles of 1989, which added to the determination of large numbers of students not to return to China and also made the governments of Western countries quite willing to let them stay.

The other possibility was to invite foreign legal specialists to China to teach. There were disadvantages to this option too, because they required high salaries and good conditions and could reach only quite small numbers of students in China. Moreover, the Beijing massacre had disastrous effects in this respect as in so many others, because it greatly reduced the number of foreign legal specialists who were prepared to work in China.

The number of lawyers of all kinds in China in the early 1960s was about 3000, a minute figure for a country the size of China. Even that number fell when the Cultural Revolution began. When legal reform began in the late 1970s, the legal profession began to recover and the number of lawyers in 1980 had again reached the approximately 3000 of the early 1960s. The number rose consistently and dramatically during the 1980s, to reach 43 715 in 1989, of whom 23 606 were full-time professionals and 20 109 were part-time. It then fell off greatly in 1990, no doubt due to the 1989 crisis, and recovered to 41 639 in 1991, still being below the 1989 figure.[26] As a proportion of the total population, the number of lawyers in China is extremely low by world standards.

One of the reasons why China's legal cadre is so deficient is the paucity of law schools. As of 1990 there were only 47 universities and institutes with special focus on law and politics, and 57 colleges for jurists of different levels. In the same year the Ministry of Justice set up a centre in Beijing to train senior lawyers and notaries.[27]

Most lawyers are paid a small state salary in China. However, from the mid-1980s a few began to start up private practices. Some charged 50 yuan for a divorce suit, equivalent at that time to about US$25.[28] Although this is an extremely small fee by Western standards, it was still much more than they could earn by staying in the state system. If fees rise, then law becomes inaccessible to all but an elite few; if they remain low, the incentive for lawyers to get really good training and thus advance their profession and the legal system itself remains weak. Either way, the situation presents serious problems for the future of Chinese law.

Conclusion

China's performance in law in the period of reform has been extremely mixed. On the one hand, the objective of a system independent of the Party and the government has been met only to a very limited extent. It is still very rare for an individual citizen to find protection against the state through the law system. Human rights are not properly met through law.

On the other hand, progress over the decade 1978 to 1988 was remarkable. Even taking into account the seriously damaging impact of the Beijing massacre and its aftermath on the legal system, the law is still very much better developed, and a very much more important part of social and economic development, than it was during the 1950s and early 1960s, and even more than during Cultural Revolution. Moreover, the rising numbers of lawyers suggest that in the 1990s the profession is recovering reasonably quickly from the 1989 crisis. A limited number of cases emerged in the early 1990s in which an individual challenged the authority of the government and even the CCP. In November 1992, in a case observers saw as being unusual in protecting the rights of an individual, the prominent author Yang Mo actually won a libel suit against a magazine columnist she claimed had defamed her character and faked an interview.

It is important to remember that legal systems are not set up in a short time. It took the West centuries to develop a good law system, and even now it is not without its failings, even serious ones. To create a law system requires a particular attitude on the part of the people, one totally lacking in China during Mao's period of power. It requires a series of codified laws, which likewise take time to produce. Above all, it requires a body of trained legal cadre, a legal profession. That takes a long time to create, especially in circumstances where the structures for training lawyers and the popular attitudes which will assist legal development exist only in a very rudimentary form. In addition, the combination of China's gigantic population, its still-serious poverty, its lack of a democratic and legal tradition, and its enormous and backward peasantry militates strongly against the development of an effective legal system other than one which merely oppresses the people even more than would be the case without it. What is surprising under these circumstances is perhaps not so much how little has been achieved, but how much.

Notes

1 'On the People's Democratic Dictatorship', in *Selected Works of Mao Tse-tung, vol. iv,* Foreign Languages Press, Peking (Beijing), 1969, p. 418.

2 Quoted by Victor Li in 'The Role of Law in Communist China', *China Quarterly*, no. 44, October–December 1970, p. 105.

3 The 1954 Constitution is given in full in Harold C. Hinton (ed.), *The People's Republic of China 1949–1979, A Documentary Survey, Volume 1, 1949–1957, From Liberation to Crisis*, Scholarly Resources Inc., Wilmington, Delaware, 1980, p. 105.

4 See Jerome Alan Cohen, *The Criminal Process in the People's Republic of China 1949–1963, An Introduction*, Harvard University Press, Cambridge, Mass., 1968, p. 501.

5 Quoted by Li in 'The Role of Law in Communist China', p. 105.

6 'Communiqué of the Third Plenary Session of the 11th Central Committee of the Communist Party of China', *Peking Review*, vol. 21, no. 52, 29 December 1978, p. 14.

7 See *Beijing Review*, vol. 25, no. 52, 27 December 1982, p. 28.

8 Louise Do Rosario, in *Far Eastern Economic Review*, vol. 145, no. 27, 6 July 1989, p. 12.

9 'Communique of the Third Plenary Session of the 11th Central Committee of the Communist Party of China', p. 14.

10 See *Beijing Review*, vol. 32, no. 16, 17–23 April 1989, p. xviii.

11 See the figures in Colin Mackerras and Amanda Yorke, *The Cambridge Handbook of Contemporary China*, Cambridge University Press, Cambridge, 1990, pp. 63, 70.

12 *Beijing Review*, vol. 32, no. 15, 10–16 April 1989, p. 6.

13 'Control' was defined in *People's Daily* of 10 December 1982. The above translation is from *The Criminal Law and the Criminal Procedure Law of the People's Republic of China*, Foreign Languages Press, Beijing, 1984, p. 17.

14 'The Criminal Law of the People's Republic of China', in *The Criminal Law and the Criminal Procedure Law of the People's Republic of China* , pp. 21–22.

15 ibid., pp. 35, 49.

16 'The Criminal Procedure Law of the People's Republic of China', p. 142.

17 See the full statement, in English translation, in *Beijing Review*, vol. 34, no. 44, 4–10 November 1991, pp. 8–45.

[18] See Edward Epstein in *Far Eastern Economic Review*, vol. 139, no. 12, 24 March 1988, p. 81.

[19] *Beijing Review*, vol. 27, no. 7, 13 February 1984, p. 22.

[20] *Beijing Review*, vol. 27, no. 16, 16 April 1984, pp. 6–7.

[21] *Zhongguo tongji nianjian 1992* (*Statistical Yearbook of China 1992*), China Statistical Press, Beijing, 1992, pp. 803 and 804.

[22] ibid., p. 803. The precise figure for lawyers in 1991, including both professional and part-time categories, was 41 639.

[23] Epstein, Edward, in *Far Eastern Economic Review*, vol. 135, no. 12, 19 March 1987, p. 106.

[24] See Xiao Xianfu, in *Beijing Review*, vol. 32, no. 44, 30 October–5 November 1989, p. 17.

[25] Henny Sender in *Far Eastern Economic Review*, vol. 156, no. 6, 11 February 1993, pp. 42–44.

[26] *Zhongguo tongji nianjian 1992*, p. 803.

[27] *China Daily*, 14 December 1990, p. 3.

[28] *Sunday Mail* (Brisbane), 21 April 1985, p. 34.

12 The Environment

DEVELOPMENT versus the environment is a hard choice for all nations as they strive to continually improve the living standards of their people. But this choice becomes even more difficult for the developing countries, whose primary concerns are to provide adequate food, shelter and clothing for their citizens. In a rapidly developing world, even these most basic of all needs cannot be met without at least some degree of industrialisation, which has become almost synonymous with modernisation. But industrialisation has come at a price, extracted in the form of damage to our physical environment, upon which our very existence is based. All countries, regardless of their geographical location and stage of development, are affected by environmental problems. While some problems may affect only a limited area, the most threatening environmental problems are global in nature.

In China, with its vast size and population, the four modernisations and reform program, while promoting economic growth, have also contributed to environmental degradation by adding to already existing problems and creating new ones. Although some efforts have been made to repair the damage and to prevent further damage from occurring, environmental problems continue to grow. China's economic development, backed by rapid industrialisation, is seen by many as potentially the world's greatest source of environmental pollution. The spectre of every Chinese family owning and driving a car, with its damaging impact on the depletion of the ozone layer, is often raised. It may be the dream of a large proportion of Chinese to own a motor car and the improvement in individual incomes that has come with the reform policies will ensure that some among them will fulfil their dreams. The possibility of this happening is limited only by the rate of development and the space on China's already congested roads. But can the Chinese people and their government be blamed for aspiring to expedite their economic development and for trying to catch up with the developed countries in individual incomes and living standards? After all, many of the global environmental problems were created by the developed countries, which concentrated on industrial development to the neglect of the physical environment. China and the other developing countries are indeed latecomers to the ranks of guilty nations who have, for example, contributed to ozone depletion. Chinese leaders argue that the blame for such environmental destruction should be apportioned fairly and the developing nations should not be penalised for the past and present mistakes of developed countries. They reason that if developed nations want to stop using technology and chemicals that are harmful to the environment, then they must use their vast material and scientific resources to develop alternative technologies and provide the developing countries with access to them. Such differences of opinion on the sources of environmental problems and on approaches to solving them have hampered international negotiations on several occasions.

The magnitude of the problem

It is by now widely recognised throughout China that the country's physical environment is heavily polluted. Environmental issues have attracted the attention of decision-makers at the highest levels of government, while a network of government institutions has been created. But the scope of the problem is so great and its nature so complex that government intervention alone is not enough to improve the situation. Since 1949, government preoccupation with economic growth has meant that the environment has become the main casualty of industrial development, while the problems have worsened since 1978 simply because industrial growth has been much faster.

The First Five Year Plan (1953–57), which concentrated on the development of heavy industry, did not take into account the environmental impact of industrialisation. Although for economic reasons the government emphasised the importance of recycling industrial waste, there was as yet no realisation of the need for environmental protection. The Soviet machinery, which formed the basis of industrial development during this period, was not designed to eliminate or minimise the impact of industrial emissions on the human environment. Consequently, the areas worst hit by industrial pollution even today are those where much of the Soviet machinery was installed in the 1950s. The concept of 'environmental hygiene', also borrowed from what was then the Soviet Union, was limited to the provision of clean water to the cities. Although health workers in major industrial cities had conducted investigations to study the impact of industrial pollution on public health, and found serious health problems among urban workers, the measures adopted and the regulations enacted to deal with the problem fell far short of incorporating proper environmental safeguards in industrial planning.

The Great Leap Forward period (1958–60) witnessed further erosion of environmental safety standards. Small-scale industrial units that were established within the communes either disregarded or were simply not aware of the regulations governing the siting of industrial enterprises. Even if there were adequate environmental laws, their enforcement would have been impossible in the politically highly charged atmosphere of the Great Leap Forward. Following the end of the Great Leap Forward campaign, further environmental regulations were promulgated, setting maximum legal limits for some types of industrial emissions. But with the launching of the Cultural Revolution in 1966, whatever little progress had been made in the field of environmental protection was lost to the radical socio-economic policies of the period. It was not until the early 1970s, still during the Cultural Revolution, that the Chinese authorities began to pay serious attention to the environmental problem. The reasons for the change of attitude are not entirely clear, but it seems likely that the official thinking in China was influenced by the growing debate on the subject in the West. It was around this time that the term 'environmental hygiene' was abandoned in favour of the term 'environmental protection', which is more widely used in the West and suggests a link between ecology and development. Having resumed its legitimate seat in the United Nations a year earlier, China sent a delegation to Sweden in 1972 to attend the United Nations-sponsored Stockholm Conference on Human Environment, which led to the creation of the United Nations Environment Program. The government also convened the first National Environment Conference in 1973 to chalk out strategies for environmental protection.

As described in Chapters 6–8, since the implementation of the reform policies, the Chinese economy grew at an average annual rate of over 9 per cent between 1978 and 1990. The economic structure also underwent radical change; the economy is more pluralistic, with private and collective sectors matching the state sector in economic importance. But one cost of all this development and change was damage to the environment. If China today is economically richer, its environment has positively deteriorated. In fact, the industrial growth of the past twelve years has become the main source of environmental pollution. In agriculture, too, the shift from collective to private farming has resulted in the decline of environmental standards in the countryside.

Environmental problems include acid rain, deforestation, soil degradation and water pollution, to name just a few. The idyllic image of China with its lush green peaks rising in the clear blue skies already appears to be a thing of the past. Carbon dioxide emissions from hundreds of thousands of chimneys across the country make China the world's fourth biggest contributor to global warming, after the United States, the former Soviet Union and Brazil.[1] Coal is the most widely used fuel in China's industries and homes, though the country is also self-sufficient in oil production. With increases in industrial production, consumption of non-renewable energy resources rose by 63 per cent during the decade from 1981 to 1991. At 70 per cent, the rate of increase in the consumption of coal was even higher.[2] Toxic fumes produced by the fossil fuel-burning industries and homes shower most industrial cities and the surrounding countryside with acid rain, causing severe health problems, especially lung cancer. The problem is most serious in the cities, where between 17 and 31 persons in every 100 000 are likely to die of lung cancer, although the national average is only four to five.[3] Two of the areas worst affected by the industrial pollution include the cities of Benxi and Shenyang, the coal and steel centres in north-eastern Liaoning province; this area is also one of the worst in the world. The haze of coal dust over Benxi is sometimes so thick that the city is invisible to satellite monitors. Both Benxi and Shenyang were the industrial high-achievers of the 1950s and 1960s; their economic growth was aided by central government policies which favoured the development of heavy industry. But the industrial development, which attracted hundreds of thousands of people from other parts of the country to Benxi and Shenyang, has made the area almost uninhabitable. According to the United Nations Environment Program, Shenyang's level of total suspended particulates, or inhalable ash particles, is ranked second in the world.[4] The city's sulphur dioxide level is also far above the World Health Organisation's guidelines.

With a 70 per cent rise in coal consumption during the past ten years, it was only to be expected that the sulphur dioxide emissions caused by coal burning would rise proportionally. Although the industrial growth of the past decade is largely responsible for increased sulphur dioxide emissions, the environmental situation in Benxi was in fact even worse during the 1970s. In 1973, shortly after China attended the Stockholm conference, Benxi adopted 270 practical measures to reduce emissions. It is now a pilot city for the study and control of both air and water pollution, a scheme funded by a special US$15 million grant by the central government. The city's particle discharge has been cut in half by the installation of anti-pollution devices since 1978.[5] Meanwhile, there are other cities and regions where sulphur dioxide emissions have already reached alarming proportions. The area that covers the Guangdong–Guangxi basin, Sichuan basin and most of Guizhou province has become one of the worst acid rain zones, not only in China, but also in the world. The problems of Chongqing in Sichuan province are compounded by high humidity and little wind, which has earned it the dubious honour of the title the 'acid-rain capital' of China. Chongqing's level of sulphur dioxide in the air exceeds the levels in Benxi. An acid rain zone is also forming around Nanchang, Xiamen, Fuzhou and Qingdao. Shanghai's petrochemical works, steel plants and thousands of other coal-burning industries pollute the air not just in that city, but also across neighbouring Jiangsu and Zhejiang provinces. The famous tourist spots of Suzhou in Jiangsu and Hangzhou in Zhejiang are also badly affected by the acid rain.

Coal provides 76 per cent of China's energy. Heavy reliance on coal as an energy resource is undoubtedly the main cause of air pollution in China, but the problem is accentuated by the use of outdated technology which also leads to inefficient use of natural resources. For example, although in the late 1980s China's average annual energy consumption was about 850 million tonnes hard coal equivalent (HCE), which was less than double that of former West Germany, dust emissions in China were more than fifteen times higher than in West Germany.[6] China's sulphur dioxide emissions at 15 million tonnes annually were also at least four times higher than West Germany's. Apart from the use of old and inefficient technology, the low quality of coal used by many of China's industries is also a major contributory factor in environmental pollution, especially air pollution. According to Glaeser, four-fifths of all emissions are caused by the combustion of low quality coal, washed inadequately and used wastefully, in power plants, industrial boilers, steam locomotives, ships and household stoves.[7] Most Chinese coal is high in sulphur. The National Environmental Protection Agency, a central government bureaucracy set up in 1988 to supervise the implementation of environmental laws, has set a goal: to keep industrial sulphur dioxide emissions in the year 2000 to 1990 levels. Taking into account future economic growth and continued increases in coal consumption, this means that sulphur dioxide emissions will have to be cut by 5 million tonnes. This is a great challenge. Given the fact that most state-owned industrial enterprises rely on government subsidies for their survival, it will be interesting to see how they respond to the seemingly mutually contradictory goals of increasing their profitability and strengthening environmental protection.

Another serious environmental problem facing China is deforestation. About 79 million hectares of forest have been lost over the past 40 years, accelerating the processes of wind and water erosion.[8] Forests cover only about 12 per cent of the total land area. More importantly, nearly one-third of all arable land is affected by erosion and silting. The problem of soil erosion is manifestly serious in the Loess Plateau, an area of bald mountains spread across half a million square kilometres north of Xi'an along the Yellow River. Scientists have estimated that loess deposition in this area began more than 2 million years ago, 'with the shift to cooler, drier conditions at the end of the Pliocene'.[9] It is therefore clear that the problem of soil erosion in this region is not directly related to the development of modern society. The economic needs of modern humans and their approaches to fulfilling them do, however, add to the destructive natural processes that afflict the region. The Loess Plateau is currently one of the areas of the world most affected by soil erosion. The amount of soil lost through erosion each year varies between 1000 and 10 000 tonnes per square kilometre. The loss of topsoil in this manner causes the erosion of 30 million tonnes of nitrogen, phosphorus and potassium each year.[10] The loss of topsoil leads to a worsening of conditions for agriculture because the natural elements lost through erosion cannot be compensated for by increased applications of fertilisers.

What worries China's environmental scientists even more is the transformation of formerly fertile land into desert over the past 20 to 40 years. Between the 1950s and the 1970s, an average of about

700 000 hectares of land turned into desert each year, and topsoil from an additional 16 000 hectares lapsed into potential desert land. Nearly 6.6 million hectares of farmland and grassland were also buried in sand by wind erosion.[11] Natural forces do play an important part in the transformation of formerly fertile land into desert in these parts of the world, but human factors also exacerbate the problems. While the urban Chinese are increasingly turning to natural gas or cleaner burning briquettes for cooking, rural residents still rely on firewood for use in home stoves. Logging of forests for commercial and domestic use reduced the forested area of Yunnan by 13 per cent over a period of ten years. Forests in Sichuan have also been reduced by about 30 per cent since the 1950s.[12] The impact of deforestation has been felt both by humans and animals. Many bird and animal species have become extinct, and only a worldwide campaign has been able to save the giant panda from extinction. There are now about a thousand giant pandas in the wild, their number actually having slightly increased during the past ten years as a result of close co-operation between the Chinese Ministry of Forestry and the Worldwide Fund for Nature.

Water pollution is another area of concern for the Chinese. The country's waterways carry a whole range of pollutants, from organic wastes to chlorinated hydrocarbons, nitrates, sulphates, cyanides and heavy metals such as lead, chromium and mercury. Nearly a quarter of all fresh water is polluted, and 85 per cent of the river water flowing through the urban areas is so heavily polluted that fish cannot survive in it. Millions of tonnes of industrial and household waste are discharged into rivers and irrigation systems every day. In 1990 a total of 24.9 billion tonnes of industrial waste water were discharged, a slight drop of 1.4 per cent over the 1989 level.[13] Coal-fired power plants discharge approximately 15 million tonnes of ash into the rivers each year. Only a small fraction of the industrial waste water and domestic sewage is treated before it finds its way into rivers and canals. In Shanghai, for example, drinking water is taken from the Suzhou and Huangpu Rivers. Together they receive 4 million tonnes of industrial waste water and domestic sewage daily, of which only 4 per cent is treated.[14] The failure of the municipal authorities to treat water for use by local residents often results in serious health problems. The untreated waste water eventually finds its way into the sea, where it affects the marine life. In 1988, an accumulation of wastes contaminated shellfish beds off Shanghai, causing an outbreak of hepatitis which affected 300 000 people. Overtapping of underground water has depleted underground water reserves in more than 20 cities. The ground water table in Xi'an has dropped so much that the ground level is sinking five times as fast as it did in 1972.[15]

While most of the environmental problems outlined above have existed for some time, Deng Xiaoping-initiated economic reforms have extended the scope of the problems. At the same time, however, the government has adopted positive measures to contain the environmental damage caused by agricultural and industrial growth. But Deng's return to power in the late 1970s has been marked by high-speed economic development through structural adjustments to the centrally planned economic system, which has seen agriculture decollectivised and decision-making in industry decentralised. These significant economic changes have also affected the ways in which the environment is managed in the country. The implementation of the household contract responsibility system in agriculture (see Chapter 6) has resulted in what the economists have called 'miniaturisation' of agricultural production. By making the family the basic unit of production, including land management, the responsibility system is gradually eroding the institutional basis for many of the previously successful agricultural improvement programs. For example, in the 1970s China pioneered an advanced form of pest control called integrated pest management, which uses a combination of biological, chemical and physical techniques in conjunction with traditional farming practices. Although integrated pest management is still used, the distribution of small blocks of land to individual families has reduced its effectiveness, since it can only be applied effectively over large areas.[16] Similarly, the bio-gas program in which China has gained considerable experience is better suited to collective farming than individualised farming. Individual peasant households also do not pay enough attention to land improvement, since they only have the right to use the land for a limited period. In 1991 about 80 per cent of arable land was classified as medium- or low-yield, compared with just 66 per cent in 1989.[17]

More importantly, the reform of the industrial economic structure has produced two related outcomes that affect the environment. Firstly, it has significantly boosted production, and increased industrial production almost always means more pollution. Secondly, it has made managers at least partly responsible for the profits or losses of their enterprises, which makes them less willing to spend money on costly anti-pollution technology. There is little incentive for managers at the factory level to use environmentally friendly technology. Further, such technology is expensive and often not available in China. In an economic environment where some 40 per cent of enterprises in the state sector (which accounts for 50 per cent of industrial production) are losing money, securing compliance with environmental safety regulations is not an easy task.

The Three Gorges Scheme

The best example of a project with the potential to damage China's environment in the long term is the proposed Three Gorges dam on the country's biggest river, the Changjiang, or Yangzi. Although the idea of building the dam has been advocated for a long time, it was not until April 1992 that the Chinese parliament, the National People's Congress, formally approved the plans for the work to begin. In the mid-1940s, the United States Bureau of Reclamation co-operated with the Nationalist government of China in assessing potential hydroelectric sites on the Yangzi.[18] After the victory of the CCP in 1949, various Chinese planning organisations also gave serious thought to the idea and a plan was prepared and approved at higher levels in 1958.[19] It was, however, the massive cost of the project that had until recently prevented the Chinese government from including the project in its Five Year Plans and actually constructing the dam.

The Four Modernisations program that began in 1978 led to renewed calls within the CCP and government to build the dam. The energy sector was identified as one of the 'weak links' in the national economy, along with raw materials, communications and transport. A high priority was given to the development of these sectors. The Three Gorges hydroelectric project was seen by many government officials as an important way of meeting the country's growing energy needs. A feasibility study was initiated in 1986 with financial help from the Canadian government. The World Bank also provided funding for evaluating environmental aspects of the project. The high rate of economic growth during the 1980s, coupled with the accumulated expertise in raising funds overseas, has finally given the Chinese authorities the confidence — and arguably the means — to go ahead with the project.

The sheer size of the project and the costs involved are mind-boggling. The giant scheme, which incorporates the biggest hydropower station and the largest ship-lift in the world with a series of five consecutive ship locks, would cost about 57 billion yuan, according to current estimates.[20] But as is well known, such projects have a tendency to exceed the original cost estimates, sometimes more than doubling the original price tag. The final cost, in monetary terms alone, may turn out to be much higher than the government estimates. About half the cost will have to be raised before the power plant starts generating electricity, while the rest would come from selling that electricity to industry and private households.

While the money for the project will somehow be found — although undoubtedly many hurdles will have to be overcome — the cost to the environment could be immeasurable and the damage caused irreparable. Even in economic terms, hundreds of productive enterprises and mines will be submerged. According to one newspaper report:

> . . . the reservoir will flood 19 counties and municipalities in the two provinces of Sichuan and Hubei. It will swamp 13 cities, including Wanxian and the city of Fuling, population 100 000. A total of 140 towns and hundreds of villages will be inundated, . . . as well as 23 800 hectares of arable land, 657 factories and mines, 139 power stations and 956 kilometres of roads.[21]

Over a million people in Sichuan and Hubei provinces will have to be moved from their homes and villages to new townships being developed by the state. Nearly one-third of the total cost of the project is to be spent on the resettlement of these people. Even for a government with considerable experience in resettling people affected by the construction of reservoirs, the Three Gorges Scheme poses a serious challenge. Many peasants who are to be moved from their mountain villages to even less-hospitable terrain will have to learn to grow new crops or abandon farming altogether.

The Chinese leadership acknowledges at least some of the problems that may be caused by the construction of the dam. Vice-Premier Zou Jiahua was being very cautious when he told the National People's Congress delegates in March 1992 that the construction of the dam could 'sharpen contradiction between land and people'.[22] But the authorities maintain that the environmental impact of the project will be minimal and well within manageable limits. Western environmental experts and conservationists disagree. In 1986, a group of fourteen Western environmental organisations known as the 'Tropical Forests Action Group, a Coalition' (TFAGC) described the Three Gorges Scheme as an 'ill-conceived megaproject'.[23] Some foreign and Chinese environmentalists fear that, in addition to environmental problems associated with the resettlement of such a large number of people, many species of rare plants and animals (such as the white-flag dolphins) would also be lost.

According to a group of Chinese scientists commissioned by the government to study the environmental impact of the project, however, the Three Gorges Scheme will not 'materially affect the growing and breeding of rare animals and plants' around the dam.[24] These scientists, based at the Yangzi Institute of Sciences in Wuhan, argue that their research shows that when the Three Gorges project is finished, in about 20 years' time, most rare animals and plants will still have an 'appropriate' living environment. They contend that the project will have varying effects on land animals and mammals at different heights. If their findings are to be trusted, a group of 26 rare species will remain unaffected by the dam because they live at a relatively high altitude. But the researchers agree that the natural habitat of aquatic animals will shrink by 20 per cent. Somewhat inconsistently, however, they also maintain that the spawning environment and feeding conditions for these animals will primarily remain the same. The breeding of Chinese sturgeons, finless porpoises and a few other rare Yangzi species will not be affected. White-flag dolphins will have to move to more 'receptive' waters, although the dam will not affect those dolphins living in the lower reaches of the Yangzi River.

The scientists from the Yangzi Institute have also warned that forests and other vegetation will have to be protected from destruction. The proposed reservoir basin area is home to 47 varieties of precious plants, many of which are supposed to be protected by China's environmental laws. Of the 47 varieties, four are found at less than 175 metres above the sea level, and will therefore be lost.

Given the generally pro-government bias of such studies in China, it is difficult to take these findings at their face value. But the fact that even officially commissioned studies find considerable potential for environmental damage by the Three Gorges Scheme is an indication of unprecedented divisions among China's leaders and scientists on the issue of the environmental impact of the project. When the National People's Congress voted on 3 April 1992 on the resolution to build the controversial dam, of the 2633 deputies, 1767 voted in favour, 177 against, 664 abstained and 25 did not vote, reflecting the extent of disagreement in China's otherwise docile parliament. Nevertheless, for a country struggling to enter the next century as a major economic power, government decisions are influenced more by the expediency of economic growth than by environmental concerns. When completed, the project will generate 84 billion kilowatt hours of electricity a year, representing one-eighth of China's 1991 output. The government officials also say that the project will reduce reliance on coal-fired power stations, which pollute the environment by spewing harmful gases into the air, in addition to protecting Shanghai and other downstream areas from periodic flooding.

Environmental protection

Ever since China attended the Stockholm Conference, it has recognised the importance of controlling environmental pollution and the consequences of unbalanced ecology for economic development. It also acknowledges that the environment is a global issue which requires joint efforts by all countries to solve the major problems which exist. It has signed a dozen international environmental protection agreements and protocols, including the Vienna Convention for the Protection of the Ozone Layer, the treaty banning nuclear weapon tests in the atmosphere, in outer space and underwater, and the International Convention for the Regulation of Whaling.[25] Chinese representatives regularly attend international conferences on environmental issues, including Premier Li Peng at the United Nations Conference on the Environment and Development, or Earth Summit, of June 1992 in Rio de Janeiro.

In recent years, the government has established an institutional framework for environmental protection. The work of pollution control is co-ordinated by the Environmental Protection Commission under the State Council, which is chaired by the State Councillor, Song Jian. The commission serves as a forum between environment and economic ministers and officials. The subministerial National Environmental Protection Agency and environmental protection bureaus at provincial, city and county levels share the responsibility for guiding the country's pollution control work. Although the environmental protection bureaus receive technical guidance from the National Environmental Protection Agency, they take administrative direction from the provincial governments and are authorised to punish environmental polluters. As is the case in other areas of the centre–province relationship, co-ordination between the National Environmental Protection Agency and the environmental protection bureaus is not always easy. Because they are under the administration of provincial or municipal governments, the environmental protection bureaus can be persuaded by the local authorities to overlook breaches of environmental laws by enterprises under their control.

Apart from providing formal institutional structures for environmental protection, the government has also supported the establishment of many research centres for environmental studies in universities around the country. Together they produce about 2000 environmentalists each year, who can be expected to play a major role in raising the level of public awareness on environmental issues. In addition to environmental education, both at secondary and tertiary levels, the government has also promulgated a series of laws aimed at protecting the environment. Article 26 of the 1982 Constitution makes the protection and improvement of the environment a state obligation.[26] In 1979, the Fifth National People's Congress adopted the Environmental Protection Law of the PRC for trial implementation. Since then, many laws and regulations have been enacted by the central, provincial and local governments. They include the:

- Law on Marine Environmental Protection;
- Law on Prevention of Air Pollution;
- Water Law;
- Forest Law;
- Regulations on Prevention of Noise Pollution; and
- environmental protection laws of the various special economic zones.

Despite growing emphasis on raising public awareness through education, the main thrust of China's approach to environmental protection remains punishment rather than persuasion. In 1990, fines totalling RMB 1.6 billion were imposed on various organisations for violations of environmental laws.[27] Moreover, in line with its traditional approach to dealing with social problems, the CCP relies on mass mobilisations to solve environmental problems. This approach has been particularly successful in tackling some labour-intensive tasks, such as planting trees or collecting rubbish on a designated day each month. Since 1978, however, mass mobilisation methods have been used in conjunction with material rewards. The Chinese Ministry of Forestry plans to add 30 million hectares of forest by the end of this century. To achieve this objective, it was decided to extend the responsibility system to forestry. Peasants in many areas facing desertification are given deeds to farmland they reclaim, provided they plant and maintain trees as barricades against the drifts. All this is part of a mammoth project to create a 7000 kilometre-long protective green belt known as the Green Great Wall, which extends from Heilongjiang province in the east to Xinjiang in the west. Between 1978 and 1985, the first phase of the project, a total of 6.05 million hectares were planted with trees.[28]

Environmental protection measures such as the green belt project have been widely praised by the United Nations and other international organisations. But the implementation of such projects requires enormous amounts of money, and that is what China demands from the developed nations in exchange for compliance with international environmental agreements. The government has said that it is 'ready to assume responsibilities commensurate to our economic possibilities'. In practical terms, the government has shown that it is prepared to make some sacrifices by promoting an environmental and economic development strategy that links expenditure on environmental protection with a percentage of the gross national product — currently claimed to be about 2 per cent of the GNP,[29] although the *Far Eastern Economic Review* reported it to be only 0.7 per cent.[30] In addition, the government hopes to raise more funds by introducing new taxes for chemical discharges by industrial units. One of the taxes being considered is the sulphur dioxide discharge tax. Collecting taxes or fines from state enterprises is, however, not easy, as most of the factories found guilty of discharging excessive quantities of chemicals are state owned. Taxes or fines paid by them would ultimately come from the funds that they are supposed to transfer to the state, which would simply mean that funds were transferred from one account to another.

Chinese demands for financial and technical help from the developed nations are supported by many other developing countries, including India and Brazil. They argue that the developing countries should not be penalised by setting limits on their growth. In its acceptance of the Montreal Protocol on Substances That Deplete the Ozone Layer, China made it clear that it would not be able to comply with international environmental protocols unless financial and technical assistance was forthcoming. At the Earth Summit of June 1992 in Brazil, its stand was to demand that the advanced industrialised world should assist the developing countries with funds and technology to improve their environment, as well as demanding that no country should use environmental protection as a pretext for interfering in the internal affairs of other countries. In terms of financial assistance, China already receives aid from the United Nations' Global Environmental Facility and from several

Western governments on a bilateral basis. It is also eligible for aid from a special US$200 million fund established by the parties to the Montreal Protocol.

The lack of funds will continue to be a major factor in China's efforts to contain environmental pollution. At this stage of its economic development, few people would expect China to slow down its rate of growth. But there is greater awareness among Chinese politicians that they need to strike a better balance between economic growth and environmental protection. At the Third Environmental Protection Work Conference in Beijing, Song Jian went to the extent of saying that, if necessary, China should 'slow down the economic development'.[31] In spite of such signs of political maturity on the issue, the Chinese approach to environmental protection is marred by the country's political system. Obsessed with political stability and control, the CCP is unwilling to allow any independent public initiative to address the problem. In the past, those dissatisfied with government-sponsored efforts to control pollution have been reprimanded and even arrested for speaking out. The Hong Kong people's concerns about the potential dangers from the Daya Bay Nuclear Power Plant on their doorstep were similarly brushed aside. Reaching the right balance with environmental protection is going to be an extremely difficult task, no matter who is in power.

Notes

1 Sandra Burton, 'The East is Black', *Time Australia,* vol. 6, no. 17, 29 April 1991, p. 12.

2 Xinhua News Agency, 'State Councillor on Extremely Urgent Need to Control Growing Acid Rain Problem', *Summary of World Broadcasts,* FE/1172, 9 September 1991, p. B2/1.

3 Bernhard Glaeser, 'The Environmental Impact of Economic Development: Problems and Policies', in Terry Cannon and Alan Jenkins (eds), *The Geography of Contemporary China,* Routledge, London, 1990, p. 256.

4 Burton, 'The East is Black', p. 13.

5 ibid.

6 Glaeser, 'The Environmental Impact', p. 259.

7 ibid., p. 256.

8 Burton, 'The East is Black', p. 15.

9 Edward Derbyshire, 'Loess and the Loess Plateau of North China', in Cannon and Jenkins, *The Geography of Contemporary China,* pp. 100–101.

10 Han Guojian, 'Green the Land: A Nation Mobilized', *Beijing Review,* vol. 33, no. 26, 25 June–1 July 1990, p. 14.

[11] ibid.

[12] Glaeser, 'The Environmental Impact', p. 260.

[13] Robert Nadelson, 'The Ruined Earth', *Far Eastern Economic Review*, vol. 153, no. 38, 19 September 1991, p. 39.

[14] Glaeser, 'The Environmental Impact', p. 256.

[15] Burton, 'The East is Black', p. 14.

[16] Glaeser, 'The Environmental Impact', pp. 261–62.

[17] Nadelson, 'The Ruined Earth'.

[18] Philip M. Fearnside, 'China's Three Gorges Dam: "Fatal" Project or Step Toward Modernization?', *World Development*, vol. 16, no. 5, 1988, p. 616.

[19] M. Gaines, 'China Reevaluates Three Gorges', *International Dams Newsletter*, vol. 2, no. 1 (1987), p. 6. Cited in Fearnside, 'China's Three Gorges Dam'.

[20] Yvonne Preston, 'Goodbye Gorgeous Gorges', *Age*, 18 April 1992.

[21] ibid.

[22] *Age*, 23 March 1992.

[23] Fearnside, 'China's Three Gorges Dam', p. 615.

[24] *China Daily*, 31 August 1992.

[25] Li Ping, 'Environmental Protection in China', *Beijing Review*, vol. 33, no. 29, 16–22 July 1990, pp. 15–16.

[26] See *Beijing Review*, vol. 25, no. 52, 27 December 1982, p. 15.

[27] Nadelson, 'The Ruined Earth'.

[28] Han Guojian, 'Green the Land', p. 14.

[29] Li Ping, 'Environmental Protection', p. 17.

[30] Nadelson, 'The Ruined Earth'.

[31] Li Ping, 'Environmental Protection', p. 14.

13 Education

THE crucial importance of education in a modern society hardly needs emphasis. Success or failure in modernisation depends to a great extent on general literacy rates, on the attitudes of the population towards modern phenomena, and on the the size of the highly qualified cadre of people with the expertise to introduce and maintain modern technology.

China was not without achievements in the educational field when the period of reform began in 1978. Not only did traditional China place enormous weight on education as a social phenomenon, but the twentieth century — and the 1950s to the 1970s in particular — had seen a good deal of progress towards the popularisation of education at primary and secondary levels. However, the changes which have accompanied modernisation and reform have been very significant, especially in terms of policy, quality and curriculum.

Policy and reality

The Cultural Revolution of 1966–76 was characterised by an extreme emphasis on class and the propaganda function of education. In addition, students and intellectuals were expected to devote a considerable, even inordinate, amount of time and energy to physical labour. One of the more pithy of Chairman Mao Zedong's directives during the Cultural Revolution was 'Education must serve proletarian politics and be combined with productive labour'. At the end of January 1967, the Central Committee of the CCP had issued a 'Preliminary Opinion on Reforming the Education System', which had called for raising the proportion of workers and peasants among tertiary level students and for the abolition of all examination systems. The disdain for examinations was pushed further when, on 19 July 1973, the *Liaoning Daily* published and approved a letter from a student called Zhang Tiesheng justifying himself for having handed in a blank examination paper because he had been working hard on his people's commune. On 10 August 1973 the CCP's official *People's Daily* even reprinted the letter approvingly.[1]

Another of Mao's views on education which was constantly quoted during the Cultural Revolution was: 'Our educational policy must enable everyone who receives an education to develop morally, intellectually, and physically and to become a worker with both socialist consciousness and culture.'[2] Although there was much to be said for such a policy, the demand for a stereotyped 'correct' view of socialist consciousness and culture was taken to unprecedented lengths — indeed so extreme as to result in the serious disruption of educational institutions at all levels, especially universities, and even their closure for varying lengths of time.

No sooner had the gang of four fallen in October 1976 than there was a violent swing against ultra-radical opinions on education. In mid-March 1977, Zhang Tiesheng was criticised at a rally in Shenyang, the capital of Liaoning, and arrested as a fraud put up by the gang of four.[3] Schools at all levels began attacking the gang of four for undermining knowledge and professional competence at the expense of the 'proletarian politics' which Mao had stressed so strongly and for allowing the social status of teachers to be pushed down to a humiliating level.

Even before the Third Plenum of the Eleventh Central Committee in December 1978, Deng Xiaoping was moving actively to reform the education system. On 22 April 1978 he gave a speech on the opening day of a National Conference on Education in Beijing. He called for improvement in the quality of education 'so as to serve socialist construction better' and denounced the gang of four for turning China's youth into 'illiterate hooligans'. He demanded that examinations be reinstated as 'a necessary way of checking on the performance of students and teachers'. On the crucial issue of the relationship between ideology and expertise, Deng had the following to say:

> Beyond all doubt, schools should always attach first importance to a firm and correct political orientation. But this doesn't mean they should devote a great many classroom hours to ideological and political teaching. Students must indeed give top priority to a firm and correct political orientation, but that by no means implies that they should abandon the study of the sciences, social sciences and humanities. On the contrary, the higher the students' political consciousness, the more consciously and diligently they will apply themselves to the study of these subjects for the sake of the revolution. Hence the Gang of Four were not only being utterly ridiculous but were actually negating and betraying proletarian politics when they opposed efforts to improve the quality of education . . .[4]

The balance between politics and expertise continued to change in favour of the latter throughout the 1980s until the crisis of mid-1989. Postgraduate degrees, which the Cultural Revolution had scorned, were reintroduced at the beginning of 1981, while in mid-1983 doctoral degrees were conferred on the first batch of research students to be trained by China's own staff. The sending of university students to labour in the countryside, which the Cultural Revolution had justified under the rubric of combining education with productive labour, was discontinued.

Although ideology remained important for Deng Xiaoping and other leaders, who were intent on using the educational system to keep the people loyal to the CCP, another imperative turned out to be even more significant, namely that education 'should respond to the needs of the economy'.[5] The change from the 1970s was perfectly natural, since the direction of Deng Xiaoping's new revolution has been based on the modernisation of the economy.

The overall thrust of the CCP's and government's actions on education was to raise its status in society, and to that end a greatly increased budget was allocated to it. In May 1985 the CCP Central Committee announced a series of major educational reforms, claiming it had undertaken wide consultation over how to proceed. The main elements of the reform were:

1 the staged introduction of universal nine-year education;
2 the rapid increase of technical and vocational secondary schools;
3 more autonomy for higher education; and
4 the development of postgraduate education and research, and of exchanges with industrialised countries.[6]

In June 1985, the government replaced the Ministry of Education with a State Education Commission, arguing that such a higher-level body would be better able to lead and implement the reforms. On 21 April 1986, the National People's Congress followed the CCP's lead and adopted the Law of the PRC on Compulsory Education, which stipulated nine years' compulsory education in the cities and developed areas by 1990 and almost everywhere in the country by the end of the century. The nine years refer to six years of primary school and three of junior secondary education.

In the interests of modernisation, China's leaders have seen it as important that foreign experts teach in China and that a number of their own scholars and young people go abroad to study. Such exchanges were not new when adopted as part of the educational reforms of 1985, but have gathered momentum since then. They have brought many benefits in the form of knowledge and technological and other expertise, but also serious problems. Because the standards of living in the industrialised countries are incomparably higher than in China, and opportunities for further education and research are very much better, most students have opted to stay away if they can. Like the very similar problem applying to the legal system (see Chapter 11), this one in education was enormously exacerbated by the Beijing massacre of 1989, since the great majority of students studying overseas at the time supported the student movement in China and denounced the Chinese government for the massacre, and Western governments generally allowed the Chinese students to stay.

This was only one of the problems with grave long-term implications to emerge as educational reform proceeded. As far as the government was concerned, the most serious of all was an erosion of student belief in the ideology of the CCP, especially at the tertiary level. Deng Xiaoping may have been prepared to insist that students maintain 'a firm and correct political orientation', but a number of factors combined to disseminate doubt in the minds of students as to whether the CCP had really done such a good job in China as they had been led to believe.

There were many factors leading to this erosion of confidence in the CCP. Probably the main one was the drastic change in overall policy in the late 1970s. Students had been the main supporters of the radical Cultural Revolution in its early stages. When Mao decided to withdraw support from them, many were shunted off to the countryside. With Mao's death and the new regime, they were told that they had been hoodwinked and had wasted ten years of their lives. In addition, returnees from study abroad told their colleagues that conditions were very much more favourable in the West than they had been led to believe and incomparably better than in China. News and information flooding in from the outside world under the open-door policy made it obvious to the meanest intellect that China was not doing nearly as well as a whole range of other countries. The effects on China in terms of the student movements of 1986 and 1989 are discussed in greater detail in Chapters 4 and 5.

In the aftermath of the 1989 crisis and crackdown, the CCP leaders again tried to revive interest in Marxist–Leninist ideology and patriotism among the students. At a major meeting of the State Education Commission on 17 January 1990, the new CCP General Secretary, Jiang Zemin, put his focus on instilling patriotism, national integrity and a sense of pride in their own country among students and teachers through schooling. Other speakers emphasised the strengthening of CCP leadership in education, pushing the economy ahead through the education system and serving the people.[7] Tighter ideological prescriptions were placed on student admission to universities. Political study was stepped up everywhere and measures such as sending first-year students for a stint in the army were introduced at Beijing University, possibly China's most prestigious educational institution. Considering how obviously and extensively the student body had defected from the government during the demonstrations of May and June 1989, and the savage retribution which had been taken at the massacre on 4 June, it would not be surprising if the government felt it needed to take some initiative to win back the youth. However, it is also highly likely that the concerns about gearing education to China's needs were also 'a form of punishment' on the students and intellectual elite because of the student movement.[8]

The change in policy which followed the crisis of 1989 may have convinced some young people, including students, to rethink their 'bourgeois liberalisation'. But it seems that most young people are still much more interested in making money and pursuing family life than in Marxist–Leninist ideology. One student said that she believed young people were 'confused' and no longer believed in communism. In very sharp contrast to the period of the Cultural Revolution, however, they make no secret of views such as these. What this means is that the gap between the ideology they are expected to accept and the realities of daily life and making a career is still a wide one and could eventually produce further student activity hostile to the CCP.

The emphasis on making money which has created such an impact on China as a whole since the early 1980s has produced a deleterious effect on the social status of teachers at all levels and consequently on the public education system. Salaries of teachers and academics have hardly risen at all, whereas the prices of consumer goods have risen considerably since the early 1980s. An intelligent young person can make far more money by driving a taxi or by going into business than by becoming a teacher. As a result, a large proportion of the best qualified people simply avoid the teaching profession.

Good academics or teachers moonlight regularly in order to make more money. Competent English-language teachers can make much more through private tuition than their normal salaries bring. Although the standard of living of most academics and good teachers has risen enormously, many teachers in rural areas still live in desperately poor conditions.

The rise in government expenditure on education has not been nearly enough to satisfy the needs of modernisation. Teacher training has remained totally inadequate and the standard of teaching has even fallen in some places. In April 1988 a report in the press claimed that in Hebei province conditions were so poor 'that teaching in primary and middle schools simply could not be carried out', while in one township teachers were owed four months' back pay.[9] One of the grievances of the students and intellectuals during the movement of 1989 was that the government never paid any attention to their views. In the wake of the crisis, CCP organs have stated very clearly that any suggestion of intellectuals as an social elite must be rejected totally.[10]

Structure and curricula

The structural changes which the Chinese education system has undergone have been much less dramatic than the policy changes. One of the most obvious relates to the length of schooling. The aims of the Cultural Revolution had included shortening the period of education, with the number of years to be spent at primary and secondary schools in order to graduate being reduced from six to five. In the 1980s, the trend was to revert to the period before the Cultural Revolution. This means that the norm is again six years, although in the countryside five-year primary schools are still common.

Children begin schooling at a very young age. Many attend nurseries from their first year; kindergartens cover the ages of about 3 to 6; children begin primary school at about 6; and they enter secondary school at about 12. Junior secondary covers three years and senior secondary another three. While junior secondary school is now very widespread in China, the same cannot be said of senior secondary. There is a system of adult education which runs courses ranging from basic literacy and numeracy to university-level programs.

The curriculum at the primary level is heavy. It includes Chinese language, arithmetic and numeracy, history, geography, physical culture, music, art and a foreign language, usually English. Chinese language and arithmetic take up about two-thirds of the scheduled time. Another particularly important subject is 'moral education' *(deyu)*, which covers good manners, hygiene, truthfulness, good speech and discipline. There is a standard list of ten regulations for primary school pupils, the first of which is 'Have a warm love for the motherland and the people. Study well and make progress every day'.[11] The school year covers nine and a half months, with two vacations — a longer one in summer and a shorter one in winter.

The secondary school curriculum includes Chinese language, mathematics, physics, chemistry and other sciences, a foreign language, history, geography, politics, physiology, music, fine arts and physical education. In junior secondary school, nearly two-fifths of the time is devoted to Chinese and mathematics and 16 per cent to foreign languages, while in senior secondary school the natural sciences and mathematics take up about half the students' time, and Chinese and a foreign language about 30 per cent. In the 1980s population education was introduced into some senior secondary schools because of the fundamental importance of the one-child-per-couple policy (see Chapter 15). The school year is nine months, with two months' summer and winter vacation and a month or so for physical labour. In the countryside, secondary schools allow students to substitute farm work for organised manual labour.

In accordance with the policy decision of 1985, there was a big expansion of technical and vocational secondary schools during the 1980s. Fields covered by these schools are very diverse, ranging from commerce and legal work to the arts and forestry. In the countryside, agricultural secondary schools have been established so that students can acquire some knowledge of agricultural science and technology and thus improve their productivity as farmers.

The normal period of study at tertiary level is four years, although there are variations, depending on the field. The best universities are designated as 'key' (*zhongdian*), and they stress teaching, research and postgraduate study. Institutions at a lower level are less focused on research and devote almost all energies to teaching. Lower still are a range of two- and three-year colleges, many devoted to specialist training in particular fields. Another way to categorise universities in China is comprehensive, which include humanities, social and natural sciences and other faculties; specialist, teaching such subjects as foreign languages, engineering, commerce or law; and teacher training.

The reforms of 1985 have handed considerable authority back to the universities themselves, and have thus reduced state intervention. There are now some privately run institutes in China. However, there are still no fully private universities. Admission to university is mainly through national competitive examinations, although physical health and ideology are also taken into account. The specific university is determined by a series of government committees on the basis of state needs and student preference. Since the 1985 reforms, the universities themselves have enjoyed more influence over enrolments than was the case before.

Some statistical data and implications

Table 13.1 shows the numbers of students in selected years at all three levels of the Chinese education system.

These figures show actual declines in the numbers of students at both primary and secondary levels in the 1980s compared with the 1970s, and explanations are clearly demanded. As far as the primary level is concerned, two reasons have been suggested. The first is the birth control campaign which began in the early 1970s. This had brought the size of the cohorts in the urban areas down very substantially by the late 1970s, with cities like Shanghai, Beijing, Tianjin, Nanjing and Guangzhou reporting 'declining primary school enrolments for this reason' as early as the late 1970s.[12] The one-child policy may not have met with the success the government hoped for in the 1980s (see Chapter 15), but its results were no doubt good enough to continue the fall in the size of the primary school-age cohort.

The other factor is the decline of the locally run or *minban* schools in the period of reform. These expanded greatly in number during the Cultural Revolution and the state gave the communes money to run them. However, in the wake of the Cultural Revolution policies, and with greater emphasis on profit and money-making, many of them closed down. Teachers could find other

Table 13.1 Number of students (millions)[1]

Year	*Primary*	*Secondary*	*Tertiary*
1950	28.924	1.57	0.14
1965	116.21	14.32	0.67
1978	146.24	66.37	0.86
1980	146.27	56.78	1.14
1981	143.33	50.15	1.28
1982	139.72	47.03	1.15
1983	135.78	46.35	1.21
1984	135.57	48.61	1.40
1985	133.70	50.93	1.70
1986	131.83	53.22	1.88
1987	128.36	54.03	1.96
1988	125.36	52.46	2.07
1989	123.73	50.54	2.08
1990	122.41	51.05	2.06
1991	121.64	52.27	2.04

[1] The figures come from *Zhongguo tongji nianjian 1992* (*Chinese Statistical Yearbook 1992*), Chinese Statistical Press, Beijing, 1992, pp. 702–3.

more remunerative work in the growing service sector, and in some places nobody was prepared (or had the money) to keep the schools going. The fall in the number of the locally run schools is reflected also in Table 13.2, which shows the totals for the numbers of schools at primary and secondary levels.

As regards the secondary educational level, the figures both for students and schools clearly show that, although the rise in the numbers by comparison with the 1960s has turned out to be permanent, the 1970s did very much better than the 1980s. Perhaps one explanation for this is the birth control program, which may have affected the secondary level about six years later than the primary, because the relevant cohort is some six years older by the time it enters secondary school.

But a more important reason relates to the attitude of various Chinese governments towards secondary education. During the Cultural Revolution it was government policy to popularise junior secondary schooling as far as possible. This was accomplished largely by reducing the length of primary schooling by one year, but adding two-year junior secondary classes to the village primary schools. However, with the negation of the Cultural Revolution, the government quite consciously reduced the number of secondary schools, arguing that this policy spread financial resources too thinly and 'aggravated the shortage of qualified teachers', with the result

Table 13.2 Number of schools[1]

Year	Primary	Junior secondary	Senior secondary
1952	526 964	3 117	1 181
1965	681 939	13 990	4 112
1977	982 291	136 365	64 903
1978	949 323	113 130	49 215
1979	923 532	103 944	40 289
1980	917 316	87 077	31 300
1981	894 074	82 271	24 447
1982	880 516	80 775	20 874
1983	862 165	77 598	18 876
1984	853 740	75 867	17 847
1985	832 309	75 903	17 318
1986	820 846	75 856	17 111
1987	807 406	75 927	16 930
1988	793 261	74 968	16 524
1989	777 244	73 525	16 050
1990	766 072	71 953	15 678
1991	729 158	70 608	15 243

[1] *Zhongguo tongji nianjian 1992*, p. 699.

that the quality of both junior and senior secondary school education declined.[13] During the 1980s, the number of secondary schools continued to fall, although the junior secondary sector did so very much more slowly than in the late 1970s. The ethos of glory attached to getting rich contributed even further to the decline in the number of students attending secondary school, since many students and/or their parents saw greater value and certainly more money in taking a job than in pursuing further schooling.

The 1980s saw a very large growth in tertiary level education in China, with the number of students nearly doubling. This was in line with the policy of using education to further modernisation. However, on 21 July 1989 a spokesman of the State Education Commission announced that the student intake numbers for 1990 would be reduced, which no doubt accounts for the fall registered in that year (see Table 13.1). The reason for the government's decision was probably to punish the student body for the demonstrations which had just taken place and to ensure the ideological reliability of the intake.

Enrolment rates — that is, the proportion of children of the relevant age cohort who begin schooling — have risen dramatically under the PRC. From 49.2 per cent in 1952, they rose to 84.7 per cent in 1965. From 1979 to 1982 they remained fairly constant at about 93 per cent and then rose fairly evenly to reach 97.4 per cent in 1989.[14]

There is clearly a relationship between the numbers who attend schools and literacy. The 1964 census showed that the illiteracy and semi-literacy rate was 38.1 per cent. This figure had fallen substantially to 23.5 per cent by 1982. An illiterate or semi-literate was defined in these two censuses as a person of more than 12 years of age who knew no characters at all, or very few of them. The 1990 census adopted a different definition of illiteracy or semi-literacy, raising the minimum age from 12 to 15. According to this definition, the illiteracy and semi-literacy rate was 22.81 per cent in 1982, but only 15.88 per cent in 1990. The 1982 and 1990 censuses also gave some proportions of those who had graduated from the various levels of educational institution. The results show a rising educational level everywhere in society.[15]

Among other matters, this is important for the population issues covered in Chapter 15. There is a general, although by no means universal, tendency for people to want fewer children as their educational level rises. In particular, the more people who attend school and the longer they do so, the greater the opportunity is for the Chinese authorities not only to add population education to the curriculum, as noted in the previous section, but also to instil attitudes favouring family planning. As usual in such matters in China, it is the peasantry who need the most education. They are the ones with the lowest educational level, the lowest desire for education and the greatest resistance to reducing the size of their families. Among the peasantry, the education of girls contributes more directly to reducing the birth rate, improving family nutrition and lowering the morbidity rate.

The literacy and other figures suggest that a great deal of effort has gone into bringing basic education to the population, especially the youth. However, there are some very serious problems awaiting solution. One is that, as illiteracy is being wiped out among some people, others are growing up without having received any education: the 'new illiterates'. Despite the rises in enrolment rates, there are still quite a few children who do not stay at school long because of the employment opportunities which now exist in the countryside. There has been a substantial, even alarming, growth in child labour over recent years, with very young people migrating from poorer to richer areas as hired hands. In March 1990, the Chinese representative at a UNESCO Conference on Education held in Bangkok disclosed that the 'new illiterates' totalled 2.7 million in China, accounting for 3 to 4 per cent of all school-age children, which is more than half the number who throw off illiteracy every year.[16]

There are also serious social inequalities in the realm of illiteracy and semi-literacy. For instance, illiteracy is considerably worse among most of the minority nationalities than among the majority Han. Exceptions include the Koreans of Yanbian in Jilin province, whose literacy rate is actually higher than that of the Han.

Another inequality is that between males and females. As of 1990, 70 per cent of China's illiterates were female, this proportion having hardly changed at all over the last decade. Among rural communities, the belief remains strong that girls do not really need much schooling and are better off staying at home and looking after the children or carrying out other such domestic work. In primary schools, the proportion of female students was 44.8 per cent in 1985, rising to 45.6 per cent in 1988 and 45.9 per cent in 1989. The main reason why these figures are substantially below half is because so many girls withdraw after only one or two years at school. Moreover, the higher the level, the lower the proportion of female students. In ordinary secondary schools, girls made up 40.2 per cent of the total in 1985, 41 per cent in 1988 and 41.4 per cent in 1989. The corresponding figures in the three years at tertiary level were 30 per cent, 33.3 per cent and 33.7 per cent.[17] However, the remaining inequalities should not detract from the fact that female education has made enormous progress from 'virtual complete illiteracy' in the 1940s to reasonably good levels, with the rises occurring mainly in the 1950s (to 1958) and from the late 1960s to the mid-1970s.[18] The fact that the proportions have risen slightly in all cases in the late 1980s also suggests that authorities are still giving some attention to keeping girls at school longer.

Between 1978 and the beginning of 1988, the number of Chinese students who had gone abroad to study, including publicly or privately funded students, was approximately 50 000. The United States was by far the largest recipient, but students went to some 70 countries altogether. By the beginning of 1988, only about 20 000 had returned to China, mostly belonging to the older category of 'visiting scholars'. Hardly any of the 10 000 privately funded students had returned to China.[19] From the point of view of the Chinese authorities, these figures have certainly worsened since then. At the time of the massacre, there were about 20 000 Chinese students in Australia alone, among whom the great majority took up the Australian government's offer to remain for four years. As in other Third World countries, virtually all tertiary education institutions in China have lost most (or many) of their best postgraduate students and young staff to the advanced industrialised countries.

To cope with these problems, the Chinese government has introduced an array of measures to try to persuade qualified intellectuals to return to China. These include the imposition of a heavy bond, which is given back on return but otherwise surrendered. However, in the early 1990s it remained fashionable among Chinese intellectuals to go abroad if they could and some universities were complaining that not only their young staff, but even those of middle age were abandoning them.

Conclusion

The record for education in the period of reform, like so many other fields, is very mixed. China is doing a good job in giving at least minimal education to the great majority of its people and literacy and numeracy rates are still increasing. Courses are reasonably well related to the types of work which people are to undertake. Both the number of people attending higher education and the range of courses have improved substantially. There is far more attention given to research than was ever the case from the 1950s to the 1970s.

However, serious problems remain. The quality of teachers has, if anything, fallen, because the best people see more advantage to themselves and their families in other callings. The most glaring failure, measured against Deng Xiaoping's stated aims, is that the Chinese education system does not appear to have convinced the youth of the superiority of the socialist system. The strength of the student movement in 1989 is the prime evidence of this. Many university students in the early 1990s make no pretence at belief in Marxism–Leninism. Those at lower levels may well subscribe to the more important ideology of patriotism and love of the people, but the drive for material wealth can only militate against such noble ideals. The basic tensions between equality and quality, and between the rising expectations of youth and modernisation on the one hand and loyalty to the state and its ideologies on the other are not even nearly resolved, and may become even more severe in the 1990s than they were in the 1980s.

Notes

[1] See Colin Mackerras, with the assistance of Robert Chan, *Modern China, A Chronology from 1842 to the Present*, Thames and Hudson, London, 1982, pp. 541, 573.

[2] See Peter J. Seybolt, *Revolutionary Education in China, Documents and Commentary*, International Arts and Sciences Press, White Plains, NY, 1973, p. 63.

[3] Mackerras, *Modern China*, p. 599.

[4] Deng Xiaoping, *Selected Works of Deng Xiaoping (1975–1982)*, Foreign Languages Press, Beijing, 1984, p. 120.

[5] Marianne Bastid, 'Chinese Educational Policies in the 1980s and Economic Development', *China Quarterly*, no. 98, June 1984, p. 189.

[6] See also Keith Lewin, 'Educational Reforms: Quality, Access and Equity', in Robert Benewick and Paul Wingrove (eds), *Reforming the Revolution, China in Transition*, Macmillan, Basingstoke and London, 1988, pp. 181–82.

[7] See *Beijing Review*, vol. 33, nos 5–6, 29 January–11 February 1990, p. 5.

[8] Suzanne Pepper, *China's Education Reform in the 1980s, Policies, Issues, and Historical Perspectives*, Institute of East Asian Studies, University of California, Berkeley, 1990, p. 193.

[9] *Guangming Daily*, 13 April 1988, as cited in 'Quarterly Chronicle and Documentation', *China Quarterly*, no. 115, September 1988, p. 513.

[10] See Pepper, *China's Education Reform in the 1980s*, p. 190.

[11] See John Cleverley, *The Schooling of China, Tradition and Modernity in Chinese Education*, George Allen & Unwin, Sydney, London, Boston, 1985, pp. 233–34.

[12] Suzanne Pepper, 'Chinese Education After Mao: Two Steps Forward, Two Steps Back and Begin Again?', *The China Quarterly*, no. 81, March 1980, p. 7.

[13] See Pepper, 'Chinese Education after Mao', p. 12.

[14] *Zhongguo tongji nianjian 1990* (*Chinese Statistical Yearbook 1990*), Chinese Statistical Press, Beijing, 1990, p. 721.

[15] See *Beijing Review*, vol. 33, no. 46, 12–18 November 1991, p. 19.

[16] Cui Lili, in *Beijing Review*, vol. 33, no. 37, 10–16 September 1990, p. 22.

[17] *Zhongguo tongji nianjian 1990*, p. 723.

[18] See William Lavely, Xiao Zhenyu, Li Bohua and Ronald Freedman, 'The Rise in Female Education in China: National and Regional Patterns', *China Quarterly*, no. 121, March 1990, p. 61.

[19] See, for instance, Pepper, 'Chinese Education after Mao', pp. 167–68.

14 Health Delivery and Social Welfare

THE provision of social welfare and health delivery to the population at large is central to any socialist experiment. The years since 1978 have witnessed substantial changes in the fields of health delivery and social welfare in terms of policy, nature and scope. At the same time, the changes have been somewhat less drastic in this area than in most others considered in this book.

Health and social welfare before 1978

Very early in its period of government, the CCP began to adopt measures to provide such items as health delivery, labour insurance, housing and pensions. The National Health Conference of 1950 not only declared the aim of providing access to health care for all, but also adopted such principles as prevention before cure and the integration of traditional medicine into an overall national system. Measures were quickly taken to cope with epidemics and to improve immunisation. 'Patriotic health campaigns' were carried out to improve environmental sanitation. Maternal and child health centres were quickly set up: from a low base of only nine at the time the CCP took over in 1949, the number of these had grown to 2795 by the eve of the Cultural Revolution in 1965.[1]

From the first days of the PRC, the trade unions had welfare departments, concerned with such things as labour protection and workers' housing and living standards. One of the earliest pieces of legislation to be adopted by the new PRC government was the Labour Insurance Regulations which, promulgated on 26 February 1951, were designed 'to protect the health of workers and staff members and alleviate difficulties in their livelihood'. Among many other provisions, the regulations provided women workers and staff members with a total of 56 days' leave on full pay before and after confinement.

Both the social welfare and health systems applied far more to the cities than the countryside. Although the Great Leap Forward and commune system hoped to move towards solving the problem, in fact the divisions grew even wider with the passage of time. In June 1965, Mao Zedong issued a directive on public health in which he castigated the Ministry of Public Health for ignoring the countryside: 'The broad masses of peasants are not provided with medical care; they are denied doctors and medical supplies.' His solution was to send most of the doctors to the countryside and to move the centre of gravity of medical and health work there.[2]

Mao was right to draw attention to the gulf between the cities and the countryside in social welfare matters, and in particular in health delivery. Among the results of the Cultural Revolution were the introduction of medical insurance programs in the countryside and of the system of 'barefoot doctors'. These were ideologically inspired paramedics, who were in theory keen to serve the peasants, but had received only very basic medical training. By 1973, there were about two 'barefoot doctors' for every production brigade — a subdivision of a commune — and a co-operative medical system in about 70 per cent of them.[3]

Policy under the Cultural Revolution was naturally in favour of improved social welfare since it was radically socialist in its thrust. The Constitution of 1975 included part of an article on the subject stating that 'working people have the right to rest and the right to material assistance in old age and in case of illness or disability'.[4] Unfortunately, the policies followed during the decade 1966 to 1976 also had the effect of bringing about the virtually total destruction of the trade unions, with a consequent serious effect on the social welfare system in the cities. The 1975 Constitution was notable for its sparseness of detail in all respects, not merely as it applied to social welfare. The Chinese state in Mao's later years laid very little emphasis on the application of the Constitution in any case.

Health delivery in the period of reform

In 1984 the then Minister of Public Health, Cui Yueli, declared that the principle of state monopoly had produced a detrimental effect on public health services and added that it was necessary 'to discard this principle and fully arouse the people's enthusiasm for building hospitals'.[5] The resultant changes have been most marked in the countryside, where the new system has been much more geared to the private individual than the previous one. The evident trend towards privatisation has been accompanied by some important continuities in policy. One of these is a preference for preventive medicine over curative, even though the reality of privatisation often points in precisely the opposite direction, with a marked admiration for high-technology medicine. Another policy continuity is even laid down in Article 21 of the 1982 Constitution: a simultaneous emphasis on both modern and traditional styles of medicine.

The overall effects of these changes and continuities have been mixed. One important indicator of the effectiveness of a health system is the crude death rate. In China this was 18 per thousand in 1950. It had fallen sharply to 6.21 by 1979, but was actually up again to 6.67 in 1990.[6] On the other hand, the 1980s were significantly lower than any previous decade, with a mean of 6.61 per thousand as against 7.08 in the 1970s.[7]

Other indicators show a consistent improvement throughout the PRC period. For instance, the number of both hospital beds and full-time health workers indicated a rise every single year over the preceding one. There were 2.624 million hospital beds in 1990 and 2.689 in 1991 as against 1.982 million in 1980; the number of full-time health workers rose from 2.798 million to 3.985 million — that is, by 42.4 per cent — from 1980 to 1991, among whom there were 1.153 million doctors in 1980 and 1.78 million in 1991.[8] It is also significant that the relative gain in hospital beds was greater in the countryside than it was in the cities, at least between 1978 and 1986.[9] The number of persons per hospital bed in 1991 was 434.78 and per doctor 649.35, both figures being substantially better than other countries of comparable economic development. For instance, in India and Indonesia in 1991, the numbers of persons per hospital bed were respectively 1300 and 1484, while per doctor they were 2522 and 6742.[10]

The number of maternal and child health centres, having fallen as low as 1005 in 1971 and 1972, then began to rise consistently every year, reaching 2796 in 1989. This number was almost exactly the same as in 1965, although the population had risen substantially.[11] So although the 1980s were undoubtedly an improvement on the 1970s, maternity care was not receiving as much priority either as it had done in the 1950s and early 1960s or as other aspects of health delivery. It is possible that the policy of restraining population growth was one reason for this (see Chapter 15).

One of the main results of the trend to privatisation in health delivery has been the disintegration of the 'barefoot doctor' and rural collective insurance systems spawned by the Cultural Revolution. There is still a widespread insurance scheme by which parents pay money to the local hospital for each child, the money then being used mainly to compensate rural doctors who offer childcare services at regular intervals. However, universal free health is no longer conceived as even a desirable aim in the rural areas, and is implemented only in a few specific places, most notably Tibet. At the same time, the system which prevailed during the 1960s, by which it was necessary to go through commune clinics to particular referred hospitals in county towns or cities, has been changed in such a way that those who can afford it may patronise whichever hospital they choose. They also have access to the growth in medical technology which has characterised the period of reform. The effect has been to free up the system and improve health care for those at the upper end of the economic scale. The losers are the poorer rural families. It is still quite common in the less prosperous villages to be forced to rely on prayer to the gods to cure illnesses. One of the effects of privatisaton has been the increase in drug-resistant bacteria due to over-prescription, rural doctors being able to make large profits on selling drugs.

In the cities, state cadres and workers in large state enterprises continue to receive medical cover. However, since October 1986, new employees in urban enterprises have been employed on fixed contracts. These workers contribute to a medical scheme which pays most, but not all, their medical fees.

The policy of preferring prevention to cure has resulted in a large-scale series of immunisation programs, especially of children, ever since the 1950s, which has persisted (with foreign assistance) into the 1980s and 1990s. Infectious diseases showed a marked decrease during the 1980s and by the end of 1990 there were 36 179 inoculation centres, 687 more than in 1980.[12] In March and April 1991 an investigation carried out by government-sponsored teams, including foreign experts, and led by the Minister of Public Health, Chen Minzhang, concluded that the inoculation rate of children throughout the whole of China had reached over 85 per cent. The diseases mainly targeted were tuberculosis, tetanus, poliomyelitis, measles, diphtheria, encephalitis B and whooping cough. As of the early 1990s, most of these diseases have been nearly or fully wiped out in China. The main exception is poliomyelitis, of which there was an epidemic in 1989 and 1990 with 4633 cases reported in 1989. Following the total elimination worldwide of smallpox in the 1970s, the 41st World Health Conference decided in 1988 to aim for the eradication of poliomyelitis everywhere by the end of the century. The Chinese Ministry of Public Health responded to this with its own plan to wipe out the disease by 1995, but although success should not be ruled out, the epidemic of 1989–90 was not a positive start.[13]

Other disease prevention methods include better nutrition and diet, improvements in sanitation and a healthy lifestyle, including the taking of exercise. In terms of daily calories per person, China does quite well among Asian countries. The United Nations Food and Agriculture Organisation estimates that a minimum of 2285 calories per day is necessary to maintain adequate nutrition. The figures for the late 1980s or early 1990s showed Japan at 2864, Singapore at 2840, Malaysia at 2730, China at 2630, Indonesia at 2579, Thailand at 2331, Pakistan at 2315 and India at 2238.[14]

Such Chinese successes are to some extent offset by very serious remaining problems in the field of disease prevention. The positive overall figures on calorie intake have not prevented even an official publication from conceding that 'diseases related to poor nutrition, such as anemia (which has a rather high incidence in some places), rickets, malnutrition, and obesity still have not been effectively controlled'.[15] Despite some positive efforts to improve sanitation, it remains very bad indeed, especially in the countryside, where running water is still rare.

In the mid-1980s there were some 330 million tobacco smokers in China, the largest number of any country in the world, including the great majority of adult males. Any anti-smoking campaigns have been half-hearted and ineffective because the state monopoly of cigarette production accounts for some 8 per cent of national income, a gigantic proportion.[16] The drinking of alcoholic beverages is on the rise, especially among men, and is encouraged by the new system of private enterprise. In a small township square visited in Guizhou, it was found that the owners and workers at a private winery were making on average nearly 20 times as much every month as the doctors in the clinic opposite.

In the large cities, breastfeeding of babies has declined sharply in the period of reform. For instance, in Beijing and its environs, an average of 88 per cent of babies were breastfed in the 1950s, but a late-1980s survey revealed that the proportion had declined to only 41 per cent. The same survey, which applied to most of China, found that about half of all babies in the cities and about three-quarters in the countryside were breastfed.[17] A reason for the decline may be that, under the PRC, many women prefer to wean babies at a very young age and hand them over to grandmother or a crèche so that they can return to work. One sign of a turnabout in this attitude was a consensus reached in a world conference held in China by the Ministry of Public Health in July 1992 'that efforts should be made to reverse the decreasing tendency of breast feeding and to protect, promote and support breast feeding',[18] but as of the end of 1992 it is too early to know to what extent such aspirations will be translated into reality.

In line with the constitutionally specified policy of giving emphasis both to modern and traditional forms of medicine, the government has established a State Traditional Chinese Medicine Administration Bureau under the State Council. Chinese traditional medical services cover treatments such as acupuncture and moxibustion, as well as a large range of pharmaceuticals. In addition, several of the minorities, such as the Tibetans, Mongolians and Uygurs, have their own traditional medicines which are still actively maintained and supported. Of the 1.78 million doctors in China in 1991, 363 000, or 20.4 per cent, were practitioners of traditional Chinese medicines,[19] while many others had mastered both traditional and modern forms. In the late 1980s and 1990s, the practice of *qigong*, a traditional system of health and mind control involving deep breathing and other exercises, has undergone a revival so enthusiastic that to describe it as religious would hardly be an exaggeration. Traditional Chinese medicine is claimed as 'unique in its preventative and curative effects on non-epidemic chronic diseases and acute epidemic diseases, such as cardio-vascular and cerebro vascular diseases, and influenza, hepatitis and dysentery'.[20]

Social welfare since 1978

Social welfare is considered to be separate from public health, and is handled by the Ministry of Civil Affairs. In the term 'social welfare', the Chinese include items of direct assistance, especially pensions and emergency relief, enabling assistance such as burial services and marriage registration, and preventive services such as public education, aimed at avoiding or mitigating disaster.

The aim of social welfare in China is to alleviate or avoid hardships due to such causes as old age, sickness, disability or natural disaster. In the period of reform it is conceived as productive, not merely a question of state handouts. Consequently, 'the main thrust is to rely mostly on the collective efforts of people in promoting production rather than in relief'.[21] Certainly the Chinese view of social welfare does not extend to unemployment benefits, which would be seen as paying able-bodied people to do nothing. Unemployed people should either get their families to look after them or find something productive to do in the burgeoning private sector of the economy.

In 1985 the Ministry of Civil Affairs authorised the province-level administrative areas to take over responsibility for welfare policies and programs which had previously been the preserve of the central government. In 1986 the government decided to allow relief funds to be used for investment, and not merely direct aid. As far as possible, the poor would receive tax relief in preference to outright grants, with emigration being the preferred cure for destitution in the most depressed areas.[22] This was in line with the principle of making relief funds productive, but it signalled a substantial change in the rural social welfare system in the direction of forcing self-reliance among the peasants.

As in the field of health, there have been aspects of social welfare since 1978 which can better be described as developments or continuities rather than outright change. These included two regulations adopted in June 1978: one was The Provisional Measures of Workers' Retirement and Leaving of Jobs, the other The Provisional Measures for the Treatment of the Old, Weak, Sick and Disabled. Among other advances on previous regulations in the same area, these raised pensions and established a basic level for them.

The Constitution of 1982 was much more forthcoming on the subject of welfare than its predecessor of 1975 had been, but what it laid down was not too different from practice in the earlier stages of the PRC.

> ARTICLE 44: The state prescribes by law the system of retirement for workers and staff in enterprises and undertakings and for functionaries of organs of state. The livelihood of retired personnel is ensured by the state and society.
>
> ARTICLE 45: Citizens of the People's Republic of China have the right to material assistance from the state and society when they are old, ill or disabled. The state develops the social insurance, social relief and medical and health services that are required to enable citizens to enjoy this right . . . The state and society help make arrangements for the work, livelihood and education of the blind, deaf-mute and other handicapped citizens.[23]

Those working in the state system are much better covered from the point of view of social welfare than anybody else. This category includes state cadres, workers in state enterprises, factories, commercial ventures, educational institutions, hospitals and so on. Article 44 specifically covers only those working in state organisations. On the other hand, such people are also more subject to state rules. They are regularly allocated to their jobs and it was only since the beginning of 1986 that husbands and wives could choose to work in the same place. Apart from a few special cases, workers in state enterprises continue to receive three-quarters of their last monthly salary until they die.

The number of welfare institutions has grown enormously in the period of reform. In 1989 there were 39 743 in all, which was some five times the number in 1980, looking after 568 800 persons. By far the largest component was homes for the aged in the countryside, of which there were 29 625, with 345 607 inmates, but others included sanatoria and homes for disabled servicemen.[24] In addition, private entrepreneurs or groups have begun founding welfare institutions in recent years. The principle in China is that people should look after the elderly of their own family and go only to public homes if there is absolutely no alternative, but even so supply falls well short of demand. Moreover, considering that age expectancy is rising everywhere and young people are no longer so keen to look after their aged parents, the problem could easily worsen in the coming years, rather than moving towards solution.

One of the major types of welfare on a nationwide basis is relief against natural disaster or poverty. Funds are allocated to alleviate the effects of floods, fires, droughts and the numerous other natural catastrophes which have occurred in China since time immemorial and of which there has been no shortage in the 1980s and 1990s. To take one example, when 20 million hectares of farmland were struck by natural disasters in 1987, affecting over 100 million people, the government quickly allocated relief funds to 43 million victims.[25]

Another type of social welfare, dating from before the Cultural Revolution, is the system of 'five guarantees' *(wubao)* for elderly people with no children to support them, orphans, the disabled and others. The 'five guarantees' are food, clothing, medical care and housing, plus burial expenses for the old or education for orphans. In 1984 the number of people in 'five guarantees' families in the countryside was 2.96 million, but this figure had dropped to 2.5 million by 1988, remaining constant the following year.[26] While some of the fall may indicate a measure of success in reducing the scale of poverty, there could be other explanations casting less favourable light, one of them being the shift in the method of dispensing the 'five guarantees' towards tax relief rather than outright grants. There is no doubt that poverty remains serious in many parts of China, especially the countryside. Those involved in poverty alleviation have reported on the extreme difficulties in getting the poor peasants of China to use initiative to help themselves.

Another of the most significant aspects of welfare, at least in the cities, is pensions for the old or those forced to withdraw from labour early because of accident, illness or some other cause. With the ageing of the population (see Chapter 15), China's pension bill has increased steeply. In 1978 there were 3.14 million retired people in China, of whom 2.84 million had been attached to state enterprises and 300 000 to urban collective units. But in 1989 the total number of retirees had risen to 22.01 million — a more than seven-fold increase — the categories including not only 16.29 million from the state enterprises and 5.62 million from the urban collectives, but also 100 000 from private enterprise. The private sector was first shown with 40 000 persons in 1984 and had thus more than doubled in five years. In 1978 the proportion of those in employment to those who had retired or left their jobs was 80.3:1, but had fallen drastically by 1989 to 6.2:1. In 1978 the total national expenditure on pensions was 1.73 billion *yuan*, but had grown to 38.26 billion yuan by 1989.The organisations themselves paid the vast bulk of this latter sum, with the Ministry of Civil Affairs adding a supplement.[27] On 21 March 1990, Finance Minister Wang Bingqian told the National People's Congress that total state revenues in 1989 had come to 291.92 billion *yuan*, which means that pensions were 13.1 per cent of national income for that year.[28]

Despite the size of the bill, there are still serious weaknesses in the present pension system in China. One of these is that the urban enterprises to which it applies are unevenly prosperous and consequently offer different sums in their pensions. This makes for greater inequality among the various enterprises.

More seriously, the pension system covers only urban enterprises. Most rural people need to find their own means of old-age security, which traditionally implies the duty imposed on younger people to look after their parents in their old age. This attitude, in turn, brings about serious problems for any country trying to reduce its population growth rate (see Chapter 15), because to have children becomes similar to taking out an insurance policy. The homes for the old in the countryside offer one substitute for pensions, but it is not a satisfactory alternative. To establish a pension system in the countryside would multiply the already escalating pension bill to an extent so enormous that the government is likely to balk from it for the foreseeable future.

Even without including the countryside, the pension bill is likely to go on rising in China, and probably even faster than up to the early 1990s. Despite the recent falls in the population growth rates, there are already very large cohorts of people born in the 1960s and 1970s who will probably live longer than their parents, which means that more will reach retirement age. China's pension bill could grow completely unmanageable in the early decades of the twenty-first century, unless some very concrete solutions are found quickly.

One way to reduce the proportion of those on pensions would be to raise retirement age, currently very low at 60 for men and 55 for women. In many organisations, old people continue working after formal retirement, a problem exacerbated by the sparsity of properly qualified people in their thirties and forties — itself the result of the hiatus in training during the Cultural Revolution. There are cogent reasons for increasing the retirement age, as well as making it the same for both men and women. On the other hand, this would intensify pressure on employment opportunities for younger people.[29]

Conclusion

The more complicated society of the reform years since 1978, by comparison with the preceding years, has led people to expect far more in the way of social welfare and health delivery than they did before. At the same time, this was a period in which rapidly improving technology in many parts of the world made health and social welfare provisions far better than they had ever been before, although accessibility for ordinary people did not automatically follow.

In China, where the policy of the open door increased foreign influences, there were two main trends in social welfare and health during the 1980s and into the 1990s. One was that the government allocated increasingly larger amounts of money than in the preceding period, in general reaching far more people. The other was a substantial degree of privatisation — the growth of the collective and even private sector in welfare matters — relieving the state of much of its responsibility. Both these trends were in accordance with developments throughout society and followed directly from the policies pursued by Deng Xiaoping and his supporters.

One observer has written that the medical system has been less seriously affected by rising inequalities than several other areas of social services — most notably education — because, among other reasons, 'medicine is easier to commodify', medical procedures and pharmaceuticals being better able to produce profits.[30] Yet the inequalities are serious enough. On 12 August 1992, the *Farmer's Daily* reported that the infant mortality rate China-wide was 34.3 per thousand, but in nearly 300 poor counties it was 68.01 — almost double.

A more unequal distribution of the benefits of the various kinds of social welfare appears to be a major consequence of the privatisation of the 1980s and 1990s. The underclass that is emerging may not be nearly as great as those groups of people doing well from reform, but it is certainly too large to be ignored. Although the countryside has done well from reform in general, the vast bulk of this underclass appears to be rural, the *Farmer's Daily* conceding that 'it is quite common for farmers of average or even well-to-do means to become poor due to illness'.[31] The fact that the underclass is mainly rural may not be surprising, but considering how much the peasants contributed to the success of the CCP's revolution in the first place, it is ironic to find them bearing the brunt of the disadvantages of reform in the 1980s.

Notes

1 The year-by-year figures for the maternal and child health centres from 1949 on, given in *Zhongguo tongji nianjian 1983 (Chinese Statistical Yearbook 1983)*, Chinese Statistical Press, Beijing, 1983, p. 541, show a sharp growth to 4046 in 1953 and a peak of 4599 in 1957 with fluctuations, but mainly falls after that until 1971.

2 See AnElissa Lucas, *Chinese Medical Modernization, Comparative Policy Continuities, 1930s–1980s*, Praeger, New York, 1982, p. 123.

3 Sheila Hillier, 'Health and Medicine in the 1980s', in Robert Benewick and Paul Wingrove (eds), *Reforming the Revolution, China in Transition*, Macmillan, Houndmills and London, 1988, p. 150.

4 Part of Article 26. See *Beijing Review*, vol. 18, no. 4, 24 January 1975, p. 17.

5 Quoted from *Guangming ribao*, 25 October 1984 in Hillier 'Health and Medicine in the 1980s', p. 153.

6 See the 'Statistical Communique of the State Statistical Bureau of the People's Republic of China on National Economic and Social Development in 1990', *Beijing Review*, vol. 34, no. 10, 11–17 March 1991, p. VIII.

7 See the figures for 1949–89 in *Zhongguo tongji nianjian 1990 (Chinese Statistical Yearbook 1990)*, Chinese Statistical Press, Beijing, 1990, p. 90.

[8] See 'Statistical Communique of . . . 1990', p. vii and *Zhongguo tongji zhaiyao 1992 (A Statistical Survey of China, 1992)*, Chinese Statistical Press, Beijing, 1992, pp. 113–14.

[9] See Deborah Davis, 'Chinese Social Welfare: Policies and Outcomes', *China Quarterly*, no. 119, September 1989, p. 586.

[10] *Asia Yearbook 1992, Far Eastern Economic Review*, Hong Kong, 1992, p. 6.

[11] See the figures in *Zhongguo tongji nianjian 1983*, p. 541 and *Zhongguo tongji nianjian 1990*, p. 799.

[12] See F.P. Lisowski, 'Health Care Developments in China During the 1980s', *Australia–China Review*, no. 45, November 1991, p. 10.

[13] See Cui Lili, 'Immunization Campaign Targets Children', *Beijing Review*, vol. 34, no. 22, 3–9 June 1991, pp. 20–24.

[14] *Asiaweek*, vol. 16, no. 12, 23 March 1990, p. 13.

[15] Wang Jian, 'China's Medical and Health Services', *Beijing Review*, vol. 31, no. 29, 18–24 July 1988, pp. 17–18.

[16] Hillier, 'Health and Medicine in the 1980s', p. 158. According to an officially sponsored survey, the number of smokers in China as of late 1992 was 280 million. Even if it is true that the number has fallen in the seven or so years between the mid-1980s and 1992, the China source giving that figure concedes that in 1991 the tobacco trade 'turned over levies of 27 billion yuan to the state' and represented 'a large slice of state revenue'. See *Beijing Review*, vol. 35, no. 51, 21–27 December 1992, p. 6.

[17] Wang, 'China's Medical and Health Services', p. 17.

[18] *Beijing Review*, vol. 35, no. 38, 21–27 September 1992, p. 32.

[19] *Zhongguo tongji zhaiyao 1992*, p. 114.

[20] Wang, 'China's Medical and Health Services', p. 15.

[21] Eva B.C. Li and Yeung, Wai-tsang, 'China's Social Welfare in the 1980s', in Joseph Y.S.Cheng (ed.), *China, Modernization in the 1980s*, The Chinese University Press, Hong Kong, Allen & Unwin, Sydney, 1989, p. 598.

[22] See Davis, 'Chinese Social Welfare', p. 592.

[23] See *Beijing Review*, vol. 25, no. 52, 27 December 1982, p. 17.

[24] *Zhongguo tongji nianjian 1990*, p. 809.

[25] *Beijing Review*, vol. 31, no. 26, 27 June–3 July 1988, p. 23.

[26] *Zhongguo tongji nianjian 1990*, pp. 810, 817; *Zhongguo tongji nianjian 1986 (Chinese Statistical Yearbook 1986)*, Chinese Statistical Press, Beijing, 1986, p. 799.

[27] See the figures in *Zhongguo tongji nianjian 1990*, p. 816.

[28] *Beijing Review*, vol. 33, no. 14, 2–8 April 1990, p. 5.

[29] See also Rong Zhigang and Cheng Liankong, 'Population Aging and Social Security', in Wang Jiye and Hull, Terence H. (eds), *Population and Development Planning in China*, Allen & Unwin, Sydney, 1991, pp. 283–97.

[30] Davis, 'Chinese Social Welfare', p. 590

[31] Quoted from an abstract of an article in *Farmer's Daily (Nongmin ribao)*, 12 August 1992, in *Beijing Review*, vol. 35, no. 44, 2-8 November 1992, p. 27.

15 Population

THERE has been a very widespread belief in China in the 1980s and 1990s that the country's most serious problem is its excessively large population. The argument in favour of this view is that a rapidly growing population consumes much of whatever economic growth occurs, making real economic expansion very difficult. China cannot modernise effectively unless it can control the growth of its population.

Such arguments are persuasive. For centuries, China's large population has made it extremely difficult to govern — this is one of the reasons for the authoritarian nature of Chinese government. And the larger the population, the more difficult it becomes to institute such prerequisites of a modernised economy and society as universal education and effective and very widely available health care.

Background history

For most of recorded history the Chinese government has controlled more people than any other on earth. In the eighteenth century, one in three members of the human species lived in China, a considerably higher proportion than today.

The Chinese Communist Party (CCP) has not been consistent in its policies towards population control. In 1950 China's population was about 550 million. In the mid-1950s, the government was in favour of family planning, not so much because China could not support or did not want a large population, but because of the effect of large families on women, who were striving, with strong CCP support, to raise their very low social status. The CCP also wanted women to participate in the workforce and believed large families would create an unfavourable impact on public labour. Mao Zedong and his government brimmed over with enthusiasm for China's ability under the socialist system to support a much higher population than it had up until that stage.

In the late 1950s, Mao's view came under serious challenge from a Beijing University academic called Ma Yinchu. He took up a very pessimistic Malthusian view, arguing that China could not support a bigger population and would need to institute serious family planning policies if it were to advance economically and in other ways. Mao had Ma Yinchu subjected to criticism, especially during the Anti-Rightist Movement of 1957. It was a campaign which was very characteristic of Mao's style, and of course it succeeded in ruining Ma Yinchu's career for about two decades. However, Ma Yinchu did enjoy the final victory. He died in 1982 at the age of 101, having outlived Mao by nearly six years and having seen his main ideas not only vindicated but actually instituted as official policy.

During the Cultural Revolution, Mao and his government withdrew to some extent from the policy of rapid population growth, and advocated a moderate increase in accordance with planned economic and social growth. They continued to denounce the idea that overpopulation was the fundamental cause of poverty, arguing that the real culprits were the 'policies of aggression, plunder and war pushed by imperialism, colonialism and neocolonialism, and in particular by the superpowers'.[1]

Despite the rhetoric, the Chinese government was in fact taking considerable action to implement family planning. In 1969 it established a Birth Planning Leading Group and the 1970s saw a very significant decline in fertility rates, which one Western authority describes as 'dramatic'. The birth rate fell from 33.6 per thousand in 1970 to 17.9 per thousand in 1979, and was most pronounced in the rural areas. The authority added that 'No other large developing country has achieved such a decline so rapidly'.[2] Probably the main reason for the success was 'the determined government effort to reduce fertility through its family planning program'.[3]

Population policy in the period of reform

A new and more definite policy of population growth control emerged at the end of the 1970s. At the First Session of the Fifth National People's Congress (NPC) in 1978, Premier Hua Guofeng called for the population growth rate to fall to 1 per cent within three years, an absolutely impossible target, but nevertheless one which showed that the government was very serious about population growth control. At the Third Session of the same National People's Congress in 1980, the target of one child per couple was formally approved for the dominant and incomparably most numerous Han people. The minority nationalities were still generally allowed two children, but with major exemptions for very sparsely populated areas such as Tibet.

In his Report on the Sixth Five-Year Plan given in 1982, Premier Zhao Ziyang stated: 'We must take effective measures and encourage late marriage, advocate one child for each couple, strictly control second births and resolutely prevent additional births.' He also strongly condemned the 'criminal activities of female infanticide and maltreatment of the mothers' which had apparently come back again or increased in the Chinese countryside, and emphasised the need to keep the annual natural population growth rate under thirteen per thousand.[4]

From 1984, the Chinese government began allowing more exceptions to the birth control policy, especially in the countryside. One of the main reasons for this was the re-emergence of female infanticide to which Zhao Ziyang had referred. A major factor in allowing a second child was the first one being a girl. The peasants continued to demand a son, and in some cases were prepared to follow ancient custom and kill the first child if it was a girl so that they could try again for a son.

By the beginning of the 1990s, and in particular when the results of the 1990 census were announced at the end of October 1990, it was very clear that the population policy had been considerably less successful than the government had hoped. In response to this situation, the government signalled its intention to tighten policy. On 12 May 1991, the State Council and CCP Central Committee issued a joint 'decision on strengthening family planning work and strictly controlling population growth'.[5]

The government attempts to implement its family planning policies through a range of methods. Quotas are imposed and people are encouraged to sign pledges that they will not exceed the limit. Special committees and people are appointed to keep watch, ensuring that the quotas are followed and applying persuasion to those reluctant to comply. There are reports suggesting that this 'persuasion' can become tantamount to compulsion: relevant officials have been known to so heavily 'persuade' women to get an abortion that their actions cross the border into forced abortion. Economic and social penalties are imposed on those who exceed the limit, and promotion is barred to some of those who fail to obey the rule. Education is also used, with many schools having programs pushing the advantages of family planning and the disadvantages of uncontrolled population growth. However, such courses are still extracurricular and, in national terms, not nearly as widespread as they could be. The May 1991 'decision' made reference to increasing family planning content in the education system, including at the secondary level, in an attempt to overcome this problem. It also called for the allocation of more funds for population growth control, and more efforts to control the floating population, prevent illegal or under-age marriages, and improve social security in the countryside with a view to reducing the incentives for peasants to have more children.[6]

Policy on the minority nationalities tended to tighten during the 1980s. By the early 1990s, most were allowed two children in rural areas, although in the cities more and more couples were expected to restrict themselves to one. China's most populous minority, the Zhuang of Guangxi, were allowed only one child, but those living in the countryside could have a second if the first was a girl. The only part of China where no restrictions at all applied was the Tibetan countryside. Among all China's nationalities, the one which the 1990 census showed with the smallest increase since 1982 was not the Han but the Koreans.[7] With a population increase of 8.73 per cent since 1982, they were the only nationality to grow by less than one-tenth.

Censuses

There have been four censuses in the history of the PRC. All of them refer to the midnight separating 30 June from 1 July and to those areas of China under the control of the government of the PRC — in other words, not including Taiwan, Hong Kong or Macao. The 1953 census revealed a population of 582.6 million, and that of 1964 showed 694 581 759 people. By the time of the 1982 census, China had become the world's first billionaire in terms of population, with 1 008 175 288 people.[8] The 1990 census showed the population of the PRC areas of China to be 1 133 682 501.[9]

The growth rate of the total population from the middle of 1981 to the middle of 1982, according to the 1982 census, was 14.55 per thousand — in other words, higher than the maximum figure of thirteen per thousand which Zhao Ziyang was demanding in his report on the Sixth Five-Year Plan given at about the same time as the census. In reality the growth rates, as announced by the State Statistical Bureau, tended to fluctuate over the remainder of the 1980s. Several years did indeed show growth rates lower than twelve per thousand, with 1984 being the lowest of all at 10.8 per thousand. Unfortunately, however, most years were over fourteen per thousand.[10] The 1990 census confirmed this trend by showing a growth rate in the population over the year preceding 1 July 1990 as 14.70 per thousand. Being a little higher than the corresponding rate as indicated in the 1982 census, this result does not augur well for a major slowdown in the rate of China's population growth.

An average annual growth rate of 20 per thousand will double a population in 35 years. This is approximately what happened in China over the first 35 years after 1949. The annual average growth rate from 1953 to 1981 was given as 1.9 per cent, or nineteen per thousand.[11] Incidentally, the population of the planet as a whole also approximately doubled in the 35 years following the end of World War II. Although there are numerous reasons for China's fairly rapid population growth in the years after the CCP came to power, part of the blame can undoubtedly be allocated to the over-optimistic population policies of Mao Zedong's government. It takes a very long time to correct such policies because a baby boom produces a marriage boom with a lag of not much more than 20 years; unless strong action is taken, this tends to result in yet another baby boom. It is under these circumstances that the Chinese authorities are trying to bring down the population growth rate.

According to the 1982 census, the sex ratio of the Chinese population was 106.3 — in other words, there were 106.3 males for every hundred females. In percentages, this means that 51.52 per cent of Chinese people were male, while the remaining 48.48 per cent were female. The 1990 census put the sex ratio at 106.6, meaning that the male-to-female ratio was 51.6 to 48.4. Thus the imbalance had increased slightly since the 1982 census. Naturally it takes a very long time to change sex ratios in any population. It is, however, worth mentioning that in the 1930s the Chinese population was claimed as about 54 per cent male and 46 per cent female,[12] while in 1950 it was 51.94 per cent male and

48.06 per cent female. In other words, the proportion moved in favour of females over the half-century and more from the 1930s to 1990. Although accurate statistics are difficult to obtain without a full census, the figures issued by the State Statistical Bureau suggest that in fact this movement was not particularly steady from 1950 to 1990. There are no years over those four decades with a male proportion higher than 51.94 per cent or lower than 51.1 per cent, but there are quite a few years before 1982 showing male percentages lower than 51.52 and also few after 1982 with the percentage of males at higher than 51.52 per cent of the total population.[13] Figures for the end of 1991 show males made up 51.34 per cent of the total population and females 48.66 per cent, meaning that the balance had shifted slightly in favour of females since the 1990 census.[14]

The 1982 census claimed that 79.4 per cent of the total population was rural, and the remaining 20.6 per cent urban. Over the following years there was a rapid rise in the urban rate, with a fall in the absolute numbers of rural Chinese every year from 1983 to 1989. The figures given in the 1990 census were 73.77 per cent living in the countryside and 26.23 per cent in the cities. The main reason for this substantial change is the rise of the new towns. One of the results of the reform policies has been an enormous increase in the service sector and in commerce and small-scale industry in the villages. This has meant the growth of some villages into towns and a drift towards towns by peasants. In the short term, this urbanisation may result in economic and social problems because of the outdated rural ideas of most of the population of the new towns, and may impede modernisation. However, in the long term, urban life and the more sophisticated conditions will probably influence the mentality of the people towards a more forward-looking approach, just as has happened in numerous other countries of the world.

The censuses also produced figures for the minority nationalities. These showed not only fairly rapid rises in the absolute numbers of the minority nationalities, but also an overall growth in their proportion of the total Chinese population. The absolute figures and proportions of the total population as shown in the four censuses are given in Table 15.1.[15]

The absolute figures show a fairly consistent and large rise. The proportions show a slight fall between 1953 and 1964, but the growth after that is substantial. In particular, the rise over the eight years from 1982 to 1990 is large enough to require explanation.

Table 15.1 Census figures

Census year	*Population of minorities*	*Proportion of China's population*
1953	35 320 360	6.06
1964	39 993 046	5.76
1982	67 233 254	6.70
1990	91 200 314	8.04

There are two main reasons. The first and more obvious is the exemption which almost all the minority nationalities enjoyed from the one-child-per-couple policy. But the second reason, namely reregistration, is probably the more important. What this means is that groups of people formerly registered as Han simply had themselves reregistered as members of one of the minorities. According to Chen Xin, a Deputy Minister in the State Nationalities Affairs Commission, 'at least 5 million Chinese people have asked to have their nationality identity changed'.[16] Reregistration was practicable, especially in the case of nationalities which were very well integrated with the Han and not too different from them. One very good illustrative example is the Manchus, whose population between 1982 and 1990 rose by 128.18 per cent, the largest rise of all the main nationalities. Several sources maintained that the main reason why Han people might have wished to reregister as a minority was in order to have another child. Still, the fact that numbers of people substantial enough to be reflected demographically wished to become members of minority nationalities was a positive reflection on the government's policy towards the minorities.

Some ramifications of population policy since 1978

Although China's is still a relatively young population by comparison with the West or Japan, it has begun the process of ageing which tends to accompany modernisation. The proportion of those in the age group 14 or less fell from 33.6 per cent to 28.76 per cent between 1982 and 1987, while those in high age groups rose both in number and proportion of the total population.[17] Chinese demographers expect that the proportion of people over the age of 64 will reach 7 per cent by the year 2000, 'marking the entry of China into an aged society'.[18] This will bring its own problems because, as the number of non-productive dependants decreases among the lower age group, it will rise among the old, imposing pressures on production and consumption, and of course on the welfare system (see Chapter 14).[19]

One of the ramifications of the ageing of the population is that life expectancy has gone up substantially. Official figures claim 68.92 years for 1988, with men about 68 and women about 70, as against an overall life expectancy of about 35 in China before the CCP came to power in 1949.[20] A non-Chinese source referring to 1991 puts China ahead of most other Asian countries, including some with better developed economies: China 69; Japan 79; Thailand 65; Indonesia 61; and India 57.[21]

While the rise in life expectancy shows one aspect of incipient modernisation, other issues reflect a return to traditional values. One of concern is the question of having a son, which has loomed large in the period of reform. Tradition demands that all couples produce a son in order to carry on the family line. No less a person than the philosopher Mencius (c. 372 BC–c. 289 BC), the famous disciple of Confucius, propounded that the most unfilial and therefore wicked act that anybody could perform was to fail to produce a son.

There are also economic reasons why sons are preferable to daughters. A son is a better labour unit because he is muscularly stronger. But more important is the fact that, in Chinese practice, it is the wife who joins her husband's family when she marries, not the other way around. A child of either sex requires a great deal of money and effort to bring up, but a son will remain in the family and even attract another labour unit in the form of a wife, whereas another family will reap the benefit of investment in a daughter. To some extent there is compensation for this imbalance in the fact that the man's family pays the wife's dowry. But the compensation is partial enough that economics, like tradition, points decisively in favour of a son as against a daughter.

Chinese sources suggest that the tradition of preferring sons, although still strong, is beginning to break down. A report in China's English-language newspaper acknowledged the bad effect which traditional values were having on the family planning program in rural areas, especially the desire 'to have more children, particularly sons'. However, it went on to claim that this way of thinking was changing among peasants 'as their standard of living improves, better health care is made available for the mothers and children, and social welfare institutions such as old-age homes and child-care centres are established'.[22] However, this may be an exaggeration of the actual change in mentality that has occurred, and may even be an excessively rosy view of the rise in the standard of living, undoubtedly impressive though that may be. Certainly the kind of thinking which encourages the desire for sons rather than daughters is unlikely to decline rapidly or to disappear for a very long time indeed.

One of the results of this preference for boys is that female births are generally not welcome in the countryside if the family is to be restricted to one child only. The Chinese State Statistical Bureau has released sample figures for the sex ratio of births in 1989. These show that there are 112.12 male births in China for every 100 female births.[23] A normal sex ratio at birth is of the order of 105 or 106. There are several possible explanations for this clearly abnormal figure, of which three stand out. One is that female infanticide has reached significant proportions. The Chinese government has, at the highest levels, acknowledged the existence of female infanticide, as for instance in Zhao Ziyang's 1982 report on the Sixth Five-Year Plan. On the other hand, when the 1982 census produced some similarly abnormal figures from the province of Anhui, Chinese sources were at pains to deny that infanticide was the primary reason for the abnormality — a view that won at least some support from responsible foreign observers.[24]

Another explanation is different levels of abortion between male and female foetuses. As with the first explanation, there is no doubt a degree of validity here. On the other hand, neither the process of amniocentesis nor ultrasound equipment, either of which enables the sex of the baby to be known before birth, is widespread in China, especially in the rural areas where the most serious problems lie. It follows that differential abortion is also probably rare.

The third and most important explanation is under-registration. In other words, many peasants simply do not register the birth of a daughter, because that would prevent their getting permission to try for a son. The number of unregistered births appears to be very substantial, and a survey carried out by the State Statistical Bureau applying to new births between January 1987 and October 1988 found that 16.75 per cent of babies born were not registered.[25] There are also peasant families which, in order to have a child outside the quotas, migrate to border areas where they believe the one-child policy will be more lax in implementation and then move elsewhere. The problem of these 'non-children' (i.e. unregistered babies) is a serious one and may have an impact on the reliability of the population estimates released by the Chinese government. Even the census figures may be affected, except perhaps those of the 1990 census. The reason for the exception is that by 1990 the authorities had become far more aware of the under-registration and migration problems than during any of the previous censuses. At a news conference given just after the first results of the census were announced, Zhang Sai, President of the State Statistical Bureau, emphasised that the census workers had been at pains to take account of potential inaccuracies caused by such phenomena as under-reporting of births and the existence of transients.[26]

One of the implications of all of these explanations is that the status of women has fallen in the countryside during the era of Deng Xiaoping. The old family values have been allowed to reassert themselves and the population policy has had the effect of encouraging this trend. The situation is better in the cities, where women have, for example, joined in the race to make money with great enthusiasm. Indeed, women in economic business actually outnumbered men in the late 1980s, female representation being 38.92 per cent in 1982 and 50.75 per cent in 1987.[27] Few are suggesting real equality between the sexes, either in the cities or the countryside, but since the rural areas still contain the great majority of the population, the general picture is probably even less equality between the sexes in the period of reform than during the Cultural Revolution.

Conclusion

Although most Chinese may concede the necessity of the population program, very few are enthusiastic about implementing it. There is a strong tendency for people to expect that, while others should limit offspring to one child, they themselves should be free to have as many as they want. In the cities, where educational levels are now reasonably high, people will go along with the policy and make the most of the benefits which it brings. The desire for sons is no longer a major factor in the cities, where traditional thinking has weakened greatly in the last few decades and economic pragmatism does not point towards the preference of one sex over the other. But in the countryside the problems are very much greater, and people will go to great lengths to avoid implementing the policy if they can. Moreover, the rise in the standard of prosperity there in the period of reform means that more and more people can afford to pay the fines which may be imposed on those who opt for more than one child. Higher life expectancy and lower infantile mortality rates are both clearly desirable, but nevertheless contribute to a high population. The initial target of keeping the population of China below the 1.2 billion level by the year 2000 remains official policy,[28] but in effect is recognised as unachievable. A 'less ambitious goal of between 1.25 billion and 1.28 billion'[29] is sometimes cited and more feasible, but even that may prove unduly optimistic.

On the other hand, although the population policy of the Chinese government has been very much less effective than the authorities hoped when they introduced it, neither has it been a total failure by any means. But for the attempts to control population growth, the population would have been considerably higher by 1990 than it in fact was. At a news conference given just after the first results of the 1990 census were released, Zhang Sai commented that without the family planning program there would have been an additional 200 million babies born over the decade preceding the middle of 1990.[30] Moreover, if one compares China's performance in attempts to control population explosion with that of other countries of a similar economic level, China does not come off too badly. It is possible that, as educational and economic levels rise, the obsession of the Chinese peasantry with large families and with sons may weaken. It is even likely that in the twenty-first century China may relinquish the dubious honour of being the world's most populous country.

Notes

1 Speech of the Chinese Delegation to the 29th Session of the United Nations Economic Commission for Asia and the Far East, in *Peking Review*, vol. 16, no. 17, 27 April 1973, p. 16.

2 Penny Kane, *The Second Billion*, Penguin, Ringwood, 1987, p. 169.

3 Judith Bannister, *China's Changing Population*, Stanford University Press, Stanford, 1987, p. 121.

4 *Beijing Review*, vol. 25, no. 51, 20 December 1982, pp. 18–19.

5 See Li Chengzhi et al. (eds), *Renkou yu jihua shengyu shiyong daquan (Pracctical Compendium of Population and Family Planning)*, Anhui People's Press, Hefei, 1992, pp. 36-37.

6 ibid., pp. 37–38.

7 The overall figures on the nationalities, comparing the 1990 and 1982 censuses, were published, among other places, in *Guizhou ribao (Guizhou Daily)*, 14 November 1990, p. 3. For more detailed figures from the 1990 census, showing the populations of every nationality in every province or province-level area, see *Zhongguo renkou tongji nianjian 1990 (China Population Statistics Yearbook 1990)*, Science and Technology Documents Press, Beijing, 1991, pp. 78–86.

8 See the figures for the 1953, 1964 and 1982 censuses in Colin Mackerras and Amanda Yorke, *The Cambridge Handbook of Contemporary China*, Cambridge University Press, Cambridge, 1990, p. 175. See also *Zhongguo renkou tongji nianjian 1990*, pp. 26–27, 32–33 and 38–40.

[9] The results of the 1990 census were published, among many other places, in *Renmin ribao (People's Daily)*, 31 October 1990, pp. 1, 4. For very detailed figures, see *Zhongguo renkou tongji nianjian 1990*, pp. 62–239.

[10] See these figures in *Zhongguo tongji zhaiyao 1990 (A Statistical Survey of China 1990)*, Chinese Statistical Press, Beijing, 1990, p. 14.

[11] *Beijing Review*, vol. 25, no. 48, 29 November 1982, p. 19.

[12] *The Chinese Year Book 1937*, Kraus Reprint, Nendeln, Liechtenstein, 1968, p. 45 puts the sex ratio in China at 118.7, but the figure may not be reliable.

[13] See the figures in Mackerras and Yorke, *The Cambridge Handbook of Contemporary China*, p. 171.

[14] See the figures in *Zhongguo tongji zhaiyao 1992 (A Statistical Survey of China, 1992)*, Chinese Statistical Press, Beijing, 1992, p. 15.

[15] See the figures of the first three censuses in Mackerras and Yorke, *The Cambridge Handbook*, p. 205, and for the 1990 census see *Zhongguo renkou tongji nianjian 1990*, p. 3. For total breakdowns of pop-ulation by nationality for all four censuses, see *Zhongguo tongji nianjian 1992 (Chinese Statistical Yearbook 1992)*, Chinese Statistical Press, Beijing, 1992, pp. 83–84.

[16] See *China Daily*, 15 November 1990, p. 1.

[17] *Beijing Review*, vol. 31, no. 49, 5–11 December 1988, p. 27.

[18] See *Beijing Review*, vol. 33, no. 44, 29 October–5 November 1990, p. 27.

[19] See also Rong Zhigang and Cheng Liankong, 'Population Aging and Social Security', in Wang Jiye and Terence H. Hull (eds), *Population and Development Planning in China*, Allen & Unwin, Sydney, 1991, pp. 277–97.

[20] See Mackerras and Yorke, *The Cambridge Handbook of Contemporary China*, pp. 180–81.

[21] *Asia Yearbook 1992, Far Eastern Economic Review*, Hong Kong, 1992, pp. 6–7.

[22] Zhu Baoxia, in *China Daily*, 27 September 1990, p. 4.

[23] *Zhongguo renkou tongji nianjian 1990*, p. 340.

[24] See the comments of Li Chengrui, Director of the State Statistical Bureau in *Beijing Review*, vol. 26, no. 18, 2 May 1983, pp. 9, 13. A major international conference on the 1982 census was held in Beijing late in March 1984, at which Sweden's Director General of Statistics, Sten Johansson, addressed the problem of abnormal sex ratios in China. He drew detailed comparisons with very reliable Swedish data and rejected the suggestion, prevalent at the time, that the imbalances in China could be explained primarily by female infanticide. See Sten Johansson, 'A Swedish Perspective on Sex Ratios and Other Intriguing Aspects of China's Demography', in Li Chengrui et al. (eds), *A Census of One Billion People, Papers for International Seminar on China's 1982 Population Census*, Economic Information & Agency, Hong Kong, 1987, pp. 410–34, especially pp. 412–15.

[25] See Ellen Salem, in *Far Eastern Economic Review*, vol. 143, no. 9, 2 March 1989, p. 63.

[26] See *China Daily*, 1 November 1990, p. 1.

[27] *Beijing Review*, vol. 31, no. 49, 5–11 December 1988, p. 28.

[28] See Li Chengzhi et al. (eds), *Renkou yu jihua shengyu shiyong daquan*, p. 35.

[29] See Patrice de Beer in *Le Monde*, English section, in *The Guardian Weekly, The Washington Post, Le Monde*, vol. 139, no. 19, week beginning 6 November 1988, p. 14.

[30] See *People's Daily*, 1 November 1990, p. 1.

16 FOREIGN RELATIONS I
The Superpowers

THE decade or so from the beginning of the period of reform was one of spectacular swings in China's foreign relations. At the beginning of the period, China's relations with the Soviet Union were at an ebb as low as any in the entire history of Sino-Soviet relations. On the other hand, China had just established full diplomatic relations with the United States and Deng Xiaoping, to enormous fanfare, made a visit there which probably marked the high point of Sino-American relations since 1949.

In 1989, however, China 'normalised' relations with the Soviet Union and the two countries entered a brief period when their relations, if not nearly as close or warm as at the high point of the 1950s, were at least friendly and reasonably constructive. China maintained a 'correct' policy towards the successor states of the Soviet Union after its collapse at the end of 1991. At the same time, the Beijing massacre of June 1989 and its aftermath had done enormous damage to China's relations with the Western countries in general and the United States in particular.

In many extremely important ways, the whole international context surrounding China's relations with the Soviet Union and the United States had changed. Whereas in 1980 these two countries were quite clearly the world's superpowers, by early 1992 the Soviet Union no longer existed. There was only one superpower, the United States, and among runners-up, the Soviet Union's main successor state, Russia, ranked at best only third after a just-reunited Germany and Japan, and at worst even below China itself.

The United States and the Soviet Union were on incomparably better terms with each other in 1990 than they had been in 1980. The cold war between them, which had been the essential fact underlying the formation of international relations ever since 1945, was over. By 1993, Russia and many of the various other independent republics which had once formed the Soviet Union stood towards the United States in a relationship rather like that of aid beggars. But in the meantime, China's two relationships with the United States and the Soviet Union had contributed substantially to the international environment itself. Although many of the implications of Sino-Soviet and Sino-American relations were regional, focusing specifically on the Asian–Pacific area, the triangular relationship was so important that it affected much more than any single part of the world.

According to its own official statements, China's basic foreign policy — particularly towards the United States and the Soviet Union — was independence. Discussing the first half of the 1980s, the CCP's official journal stated that China's policy towards the two superpowers was that it would not form any strategic relations with any great power involving an alliance: 'This is a new development in China's independent and peaceful foreign policy'.[1] Certainly China formed no alliances with great powers, but for most of the period China definitely leaned more towards the United States than it did towards the Soviet Union.

China's relations with some of the regional powers will be considered in the next chapter. This chapter will explore China's relations with the United States from 1978 to 1992 and with the Soviet Union from 1978 to 1991. It will also be necessary to consider very briefly the background history of the PRC's relations with the superpowers as well as China's reaction to the collapse of communist power in Eastern and Central Europe from 1989 to 1991.

Background

In the few years after 1949, China's relations with the two superpowers were determined in large part by the cold war between the Soviet Union and the United States. The Soviet Union agreed to assist China in its socialist construction, while the United States adopted a uniformly hostile stance towards the emergence of CCP power. In the late 1950s, serious strains emerged in the Sino-Soviet relationship and in 1960 the Soviet Union withdrew all its experts and assistance from China at a time when the Chinese economy was in dire straits anyway, one of the causes of a major famine and economic crisis in China in the early 1960s.

The Cultural Revolution placed even further strains on Sino-Soviet relations because the whole movement was aimed against revisionism, the very evil of which Mao was accusing the Soviet Union so vociferously. From 1965 the United States was involved in a full-scale war in Vietnam, China's neighbour, while China supported the enemies of the Americans there. Even so, by 1969 China was experiencing border clashes with the Soviet Union and had come to regard it as a more vicious and aggressive imperialist power even than the United States.

In July 1971, United States President Richard Nixon's National Security Advisor Henry Kissinger made a secret and totally unexpected visit to Beijing, securing an invitation for the President himself to visit China, which he did in February 1972. This extraordinary event represented a major improvement in Sino-American relations, and had major repercussions throughout the world. Even though the United States' withdrawal from Vietnam was well underway by that time, it was nowhere near complete, and Nixon had in no way conceded defeat.

As relations with the United States improved, those with the Soviet Union worsened. For a brief period after Mao's death in 1976 there seemed a slight possibility of a mild thaw, but by late 1977 relations were worse than ever. The Chinese government gave fulsome praise to a theory Mao had developed in 1974, according to which all countries could be divided into 'three worlds': the first world being the two superpowers; the second Europe, Canada and some other middle-level powers; and the third China and other poor countries of Asia, Africa and Latin America. But a major commentary of late 1977, while glorifying this theory as a major contribution to Marxism–Leninism, stressed that 'of the two imperialist superpowers, the Soviet Union is the more ferocious, the more reckless, the more treacherous, and the most dangerous source of world war'.[2] The Chinese press regularly described the Soviet Union as a 'social-imperialist power' and even likened it to Hitler's Germany. By 1978 China's relations with the superpowers were almost diametrically opposite to what they had been in 1949: reasonably friendly with the United States, but violently hostile to the Soviet Union.

Sino-American relations

Only a couple of days before the Third Plenum of the Eleventh Central Committee began on 18 December 1978, simultaneous announcements were made in Beijing and Washington that China and the United States had decided to establish full diplomatic relations at ambassadorial level as from 1 January 1979. The joint communiqué stated that the United States 'recognises the Government of the People's Republic of China as the sole legal Government of China'. Although the United States thus withdrew recognition from the government of Taiwan, the communiqué noted that 'the people of the United States will maintain cultural, commercial, and other unofficial relations with the people of Taiwan'. In addition, the United States 'acknowledges the Chinese position that there is but one China and Taiwan is part of China'.[3]

For many years the question of whether to recognise the Republic of China (ROC) on Taiwan or the People's Republic of China (PRC) on the Chinese mainland as the legitimate government of China had been a sticking point in China's relations with many countries. In the 1970s a whole series of countries, including most of those of the West, had signalled their recognition of the PRC government as 'the sole legal government of China' and, among a number of diplomatic formulae, acknowledged or noted that Taiwan was part of China. For the United States to adopt the same stance and to promise specifically to restrict relations with Taiwan to a people-to-people and unofficial level was a considerable victory for China. In one sense it marked a beginning of the period of reform in the foreign affairs sphere in the way that the Third Plenum did in the domestic sphere. There was probably some connection between the two events, since 'opening to the outside world', and to the West in particular, was to be an extremely significant component of China's policies during the Deng Xiaoping years.

From the Chinese side, Deng had clearly been the driving force behind the move to establish full diplomatic relations with the United States. In any case, it was he who reaped the immediate benefit in the form of a visit to the United States. While there he was feted like a hero. He visited the Boeing Corporation near Seattle and made arrangements for the Chinese purchase of Boeing aircraft. He also made threatening statements condemning Vietnam for its recent invasion of Cambodia (or Kampuchea, discussed in Chapter 17) and while visiting Japan on the way home suggested that Vietnam should be 'taught a lesson' for its immoral behaviour.

Sino-American relations developed very favourably over the next few years. By classifying China as a 'friendly non-allied country', the United States government liberalised regulations on technology transfer to China. Trade between the two countries grew substantially, being valued both ways at $5.5 billion in 1981 and $10 billion in 1988.[4] Joint ventures and American investment in China burgeoned. In 1987, private American investment in China accounted for 13.3 per cent of all direct investment undertaken by private businesspeople — the largest proportion of any country.[5] In addition, cultural and educational exchanges blossomed. Between 1979 and 1986, 35 000 Chinese students went to study in the United States, while 6600 American students went to China. Between 1979 and 1986, 4000 Americans went to teach in China.[6] Exchanges in the arts grew to an extent unprecedented since 1949.

These various exchanges were not necessarily trouble-free or equal. The Chinese expressed extreme displeasure at the range of legal impediments to Sino-United States trade and its protectionist policies, especially regarding textiles.[7] The numbers of students going either way reflected the greater attraction of the United States for the Chinese students than vice versa. The Americans who taught in China were often more than willing to impart to their Chinese students not only their expertise, but their own values. Despite some enthusiasm for China on the part of many Americans, the rich and powerful country was the teacher, while the poor and backward one remained the willing pupil.

In the first few years of the reform period, the shared interests of the two seemed far greater than any differences which might divide them. The most important shared interest was hostility to the Soviet Union, especially after the latter's invasion of Afghanistan at the end of 1979. By far the most important point of division still concerned the status of Taiwan.

In April 1979 the United States Congress adopted the Taiwan Relations Act by an overwhelming majority which President Jimmy Carter signed into law the following month. On the basis of the Act the United States continued to sell arms to Taiwan, including advanced jet fighters and other modern weaponry. China protested vociferously, arguing that such sales went far beyond the unofficial people-to-people relations allowed for in the joint communiqué by which diplomatic relations had been established. The Chinese authorities considered that these sales were tantamount to 'treating Taiwan as an independent political entity'.[8]

In August 1982, the two parties signed yet another communiqué in an attempt to solve the problem of the arms sales to Taiwan. The United States promised to reduce and eventually cease the sales, but no timetable was laid down and the wording of just how and when the reductions were to be made was deliberately left vague. In fact, the communiqué did not really solve the problem. The arms sales continued at high levels. The Americans could always argue that they were not contravening the agreement because they were careful to ensure that the levels did not actually rise. The Chinese, on their part, elected not to continue making a fuss about the issue. Clearly they saw the technological and economic advantages of good relations with the United States as outweighing the losses they might suffer from the continued sales to Taiwan. The communiqué had enabled them to save face, and that was probably enough for their purposes.

Late in 1992, United States President George Bush announced the sale of 150 F-16 fighter jets to Taiwan. This was part of a desperate — but as it turned out, unsuccessful — move to gain reelection as President by increasing the number of jobs in the industry and hence reducing unemployment. The announcement was in direct contravention of the 1982 agreement, which contained no sunset clause. The Chinese government reacted furiously with statements of anguish and outrage against the American government not seen for many years. American spokespeople justified Bush's stand by pointing to increased Chinese arms purchases from Russia and elsewhere in the former Soviet Union, but, in contrast to the United States sale of fighter jets to Taiwan, the PRC was not obligated by any international agreements to abstain from updating its arsenal.

China took its own steps to move towards reunification with Taiwan, and these began to be reciprocated as the 1980s progressed. By the early 1990s, relations between the PRC and Taiwan were better than at any time since 1949. People visited the mainland from Taiwan in substantial numbers and the government of Taiwan was comparatively conciliatory in its reaction to the Beijing massacre. Although reunification did not appear imminent and Taiwan remained a serious issue in China's foreign relations, as made obvious from its reaction to the announcement of the sale of the F-16 fighter jets, it did not bulk nearly as large as a divisive issue between China and the United States in the early 1990s as it had done in the early 1980s.

Meanwhile, two other issues arose which revolved essentially around human rights and produced a deleterious effect on Sino-American relations. These were Tibet and the crisis of 1989, in particular the Beijing massacre.

The Dalai Lama had actually appeared before two United States Congressional bodies on 21 September 1987, a few days before the first of a series of riots took place in the Tibetan capital Lhasa (see Chapter 4). Western, and especially American, backpackers had swarmed into Tibet following its opening in 1985, the great majority favouring independence for Tibet. The Chinese had some grounds for laying some of the responsibility for disturbances on the Americans.

For the United States government, and above all for the Congress, Tibet represented a human rights issue. The United States administration recognised that Tibet was part of China, but it was bitterly hostile to Chinese actions in Tibet, believing them to contravene the human rights of the Tibetans. The Congress not only gave the Dalai Lama a substantial and sympathetic hearing, but issued a series of resolutions condemning the Chinese for violations of human rights in Tibet, the first being a unanimous Senate vote on 6 October 1987.

When martial law was declared in March 1989, the American Senate passed a resolution on 16 March 1989 condemning the Chinese again for human rights violations in Tibet. The Chinese reacted furiously with a statement of their own, issued on 19 March, which charged the American Senate with total misunderstanding of the riots: 'The recent incident in Lhasa was not an ethnic or religious question, even less a human rights issue. Rather, it was a violent incident premeditated and deliberately staged by a few separatists attempting to split China.'[9] There seemed no possibility of agreement over this issue. Even though it was the Congress, rather than the administration, which took the initiative in condemning China, the Tibet question undoubtedly did considerable harm to Sino-American relations.

The other issue of human rights was actually considerably more serious: the Beijing massacre. The American government had taken a fairly low profile during the student demonstrations of April–June 1989, although United States President Bush did make it clear that he was on the side of freedom and democracy, which the students were claiming to represent. On the other hand, individual Americans, and especially reporters, were very active indeed in supporting the students. Many of them regarded the demonstrations as a dream come true. Here were millions of students and others demonstrating for a cause which they had traditionally taken for granted as the acme of human achievement. Some American reporters marched alongside the students in support of their cause.

The massacre came as a gigantic shock to most Americans. People from all walks of life and political colours came out in condemnation of what the Chinese government had done. President Bush immediately declared a series of sanctions against the Chinese, including a temporary ban on the visit of high-level delegations to and from China and a freeze on military sales, but not including major trade restrictions. A few days after the massacre, Fang Lizhi, a major leader of the student movement in 1986, took refuge in the American embassy in Beijing, with the Americans promising to shield him from the Chinese authorities. Shortly afterwards, the World Bank deferred several large loans to China and the Group of Seven most industrialised capitalist countries (the United States, Japan, West Germany, Great Britain, France, Italy and Canada) condemned the Chinese authorities again, although they did not add greatly to the sanctions. In their public statements, Western governments — and indeed most others — ignored or dismissed the Chinese claim to have quelled a counter-revolutionary rebellion.

Naturally enough, the Chinese government reacted very sharply against all these measures. The essence of their response was that the student demonstrations were an internal affair. The Americans, and others, ought not to meddle in Chinese affairs, but should mind their own business. The Chinese authorities were insistent that a counter-revolutionary rebellion had taken place which needed to be suppressed. They even insisted that other countries would have responded in the same way under similar circumstances, a claim which turned out to be mainly invalid in country after country of Eastern and Central Europe from late 1989 to the end of 1991.

Later in 1989, President Bush tried to mend fences slightly with the Chinese by sending his National Security Affairs Adviser, Brent Scowcroft, to China. Congress reacted negatively, with the Democrat Stephen Solarz charging that Bush would 'look like a wimp in Peking and a hypocrite in Washington'.[10] A battle developed in which Congress wanted to take a harsher line in condemning China than the Bush administration appeared willing to agree to. Meanwhile, China released many of the dissidents it had imprisoned at the time of the crackdown, and in the middle of 1990 Fang Lizhi was allowed to go to Britain for what the Chinese authorities described as 'health' reasons.

On 2 August 1990, Iraq invaded Kuwait. The effect of this action was to instantaneously make Iraq the world's prime international pariah. Both the Soviet Union and China supported the United States and the Western powers in condemning Iraq. International, and in particular American, ire moved away from China and towards Iraq. On 22 October 1990, the foreign ministers of the European Community agreed to lift sanctions against China, one of the main reasons being China's support for the United Nations campaign to try to force Iraq out of Kuwait. Although the United States was not involved in the decision, it clearly had implications for China's relations with all Western countries, not only those of Europe.

Late in 1990, China's Foreign Minister, Qian Qichen, visited the United States. Apart from holding talks with Bush, he attended the United Nations Security Council meeting which resolved to authorise all member states to 'use all necessary means' to force Iraq out of Kuwait. China abstained from the 29 November vote, which imposed a deadline of 15 January 1991 for Iraq to withdraw from Kuwait or face war. Qian argued that China opposed both Iraq's aggression and any violent means of solving the crisis.[11] The real reason for its decision, when by vetoing the resolution it could materially have altered the chances of war, was almost certainly to protect itself from American anger. The United States duly responded by abstaining from a World Bank vote on 4 December 1990 and thus allowing, through a loan worth US$114.3 million, for development of rural industrial technology in China.

The Bush administration appeared to want a recovery in relations with China. However, the quick victory of the United States and its allies in the Gulf War of early 1991 took away the impetus towards any immediate improvements. Moreover, the attention of the United States and the West in general was transferred away from China and East Asia and towards Eastern Europe and the rapidly disintegrating Soviet Union.

It had been the Democrat United States President Jimmy Carter who had actually bitten the bullet to establish full diplomatic relations with the PRC. Yet the reaction of the Democrat-dominated Congress to the Beijing massacre was rather harder than that of the Republican Bush administration. In 1990 a strong lobby led by the Democrats attempted, against opposition from the Bush administration, to have the most-favoured-nation treatment to the Chinese in trade discontinued, largely on the grounds of China's human rights record. What most-favoured-nation treatment meant was that the American government set tariffs on trade with China at the same level as that with non-communist countries instead of the higher and less favourable rate demanded of the Soviet Union and other communist countries — in other words, there is nothing particularly favourable about most-favoured-nation treatment, but not having it is highly *un*favourable. Bush prevailed by a rather narrow margin in 1990, but the next year the same lobby in Congress made an even stronger, though again unsuccessful, attempt to reverse the most-favoured-nation treatment. This time a range of other issues was added to that of human rights, including criticism of China's alleged violation of United States intellectual property rights. In January 1992, the United States and China reached an agreement by which China promised to join the international Berne Convention on copyright, bringing the two countries nearer to a normal trading relationship. A threatened trade war was narrowly averted when the Chinese agreed to the main American demands on tariff cuts, publication of trade laws and regulations and other matters in October 1992, just a week after the United States Senate upheld yet another veto by President Bush in favour of most-favoured-nation treatment. However, there was absolutely no guarantee that the problems between the two countries over trade had been solved permanently, and they could easily intensify under an administration led by Democrat Bill Clinton, who became United States President in January 1993. China's application to join the General Agreement on Tariffs and Trade (GATT) was aimed, among other things, at reducing the risks posed by the annual hearings in Washington over most-favoured-nation treatment, but as of April 1993, the United States remained opposed to China's admission to membership.

Moreover, the human rights issue showed no signs of disappearing. The Americans continued to denounce Chinese human rights abuses, with the Chinese reacting with some of their own accusations. For instance, the *People's Daily* of 26 November 1991 declared that, in the United States, 'there are millions of people who do not have enough food or clothing or personal security'. This was a contravention of the most basic of all human rights, which the Chinese government repeatedly stressed to be that of subsistence. When serious ethnic rioting and looting broke out in Los Angeles at the end of April 1992, killing over 50 people, the Chinese media carried out 'a paroxysm of America-bashing' focused on accusations of human rights abuses and racial discimination, including the claim that China was actually superior to the United States in many forms of human rights.[12]

Despite the recovery in relations in late 1989 and 1990, the massacre and its aftermath were a disaster in terms of Sino-American relations. It is doubtful whether the shared interests between the United States and China were ever really as numerous or strong as they appeared, and a decline after the honeymoon period was inevitable. But the particular combination of events which happened could have been avoided.

The reality is that in the new world order which has followed the Gulf War of early 1991 and the collapse of the Soviet Union, China does not matter to the United States nearly as much as it did during the 1980s. It can no longer be played off against a powerful Soviet Union in a kind of triangular strategic balance. The fact that so many countries of the former Soviet Union have become recognised as sovereign states separate from Russia has added greater conviction to the beliefs of many in the United States and other Western countries that Tibet could and should split off from China to become independent also. Although trade and economic relations with China still matter to the United States, Japan is incomparably more important. A trade deficit with China pales into insignificance in the American psyche beside one with Japan. The overall implication is that no United States administration of either main political party is likely to place a high priority on restoring the excellent relations with China which existed from 1978 to the eruption of the Tibet issue in 1987. As of early 1993 it remained unclear whether the newly inaugurated Democrat American President Bill Clinton, with a Democrat-dominated Congress, would lead to an even harder line on human rights and most-favoured-nation treatment than that of George Bush, but such a course would follow from Clinton's policy statements up to that time and from his appointment of anti-China former United States Ambassador in Beijing Winston Lord as Under Secretary of State for Far Eastern Affairs. What did appear extremely likely, however, was that China would continue to occupy a much lower priority in American foreign relations than had been the case during the Cold War.

Sino-Soviet relations

While the Cold War lasted (i.e. until the end of the 1980s), one of the main determining factors in relations between the United States and China was the state of Sino-Soviet relations. The trend here was gradual, but cumulatively there was substantial improvement from a low point in the early 1980s. The improvement began before the accession of Mikhail Gorbachev to power in March 1985. Although Soviet-American and Sino-Soviet relations moved roughly in the same direction in the 1980s, China had its own reasons for what it did, and there was not nearly as much harmony between the United States and China in their relations with the Soviet Union as there might have been.

One major common interest binding the United States and China in the early 1980s was the Soviet invasion of Afghanistan at the end of 1979. China reacted with enormous fury to this event, believing its own borders to be threatened. China felt justified in its view that the Soviet Union was the greatest danger to its own security as well as to world peace. Both China and the United States boycotted the summer Olympic Games held in Moscow in 1980 because of the invasion of Afghanistan.

China and the United States also held similar — although by no means identical — views on the Cambodia (Kampuchea) issue, examined at greater length in Chapter 17. What is important for this chapter, however, is that China and the United States both shared an anti-Soviet position, because it was Soviet-supported Vietnam which had invaded Cambodia and installed a pro-Vietnamese government there in 1979.

In March 1982, the Soviet leader, Leonid Brezhnev, made a speech in Tashkent in which he called for better relations with China, promising that the Soviet Union would not interfere in China's internal affairs, as the United States was doing through its continuing sales of arms to Taiwan. China reacted very slowly but positively to the call and, when Brezhnev died later the same year, China was even mildly laudatory about the man who had been its arch-enemy for so long.

In the meantime, the Chinese government articulated 'three obstacles' to the normalisation of relations between China and the Soviet Union. An early expression of these obstacles came during the Twelfth Congress of the CCP in September 1982:

> For the past 20 years, the Soviet Union has stationed massive armed forces along the Sino-Soviet and Sino-Mongolian borders. It has supported Viet Nam in the latter's invasion and occupation of Kampuchea . . . Moreover, it has invaded and occupied Afghanistan, a neighbour of China, by force of arms.[13]

These three obstacles were to play an enormous role in Sino-Soviet relations until 1989, at least from the Chinese point of view.

Mikhail Gorbachev continued and accelerated the thaw which had got underway at the end of the Brezhnev era. In particular, he made a crucially important speech on 28 July 1986 in Vladivostok, in which he paid respect to the CCP and called for China and the Soviet Union to support each other: 'The Soviet people respond with understanding and respect to the objective advanced by the Communist Party of China — to modernise the country and build in the future a socialist society worthy of a great people . . . Why not support each other?' Gorbachev also said he would withdraw some troops from Mongolia, thus going some way towards resolving the first 'obstacle' to normalisation, and announced that he had suggested co-operation with China in space research.[14]

The 'obstacle' to normalisation of Sino-Soviet relations posed by Soviet troops in Afghanistan was resolved in February 1989, when the last troops were withdrawn. It is true that the regime which the Soviet Union was protecting did not fall until April 1992. However, what mattered was not the regime in place in Kabul, but whether China was being threatened. That matter was resolved by the total withdrawal of the troops.

China officially regarded Soviet support for the Vietnamese occupation of Cambodia as the most important of the three obstacles to normalisation of their relations. In the event, it proved possible to 'normalise' relations without the removal of this obstacle.

Deng Xiaoping had for some time declared his wish to visit the Soviet Union for the normalisation of relations. As it happened, it was Gorbachev who went to China, visiting Beijing and Shanghai from 15–18 May 1989. There were the usual banquets and other marks of such a successful and important state visit. Both sides had intended that there would be enormous fanfare throughout the world over the normalisation of their relations, and a ceremony was planned to take place in Tiananmen Square in the centre of Beijing. Reporters had swarmed into Beijing from all over the world to cover the Gorbachev visit. However, on 13 May, two days before Gorbachev was due to arrive, student demonstrators occupied the square and announced that they would remain there indefinitely until their demands, including those for freedom and democracy, were met (see Chapter 5). They completely upstaged Gorbachev, especially from the point of view of the Western reporters. Hundreds of thousands of students occupying a major square in the centre of a major city, many willing to give interviews in English, are far more interesting television than any state leaders, even Gorbachev and Deng Xiaoping, with their talks, their banquets and their joint communiqués. The banquet was covered on world television, of course, but the main shot of Deng Xiaoping showed him dropping his food, with the commentary explaining the symbolism: Deng Xiaoping was losing control of the situation, just as he was becoming unable to eat properly. In terms of the public relations exercise which was supposed to be the crowning achievement of Deng Xiaoping's long career, Gorbachev's visit was a dismal failure.

A Sino-Soviet joint communiqué was issued on 18 May, covering a variety of issues. Naturally enough, the main one was the long-awaited normalisation of bilateral relations:

> The two sides agreed that the Sino-Soviet high level meeting symbolized the normalization of relations between the two countries. This is in conformity with the interests and aspirations of the Chinese and Soviet peoples and contributes to the maintenance of world peace and stability.[15]

Naturally enough, Cambodia was among the topics addressed by the communiqué. This was, after all, the main outstanding issue of difference between the two countries. On this topic, the two sides found some points of agreement. They did not want a civil war in Cambodia after the Vietnamese withdrawal was completed, and favoured national reconciliation with all Cambodian political factions participating. In particular, they agreed that, 'with the withdrawal of Vietnamese troops from Kampuchea, the countries concerned should gradually reduce and eventually stop all their military aid to any of the parties in Kampuchea'.[16] They also disagreed on some matters, with neither side withdrawing from their basic earlier positions of support for the pro-Vietnamese Hun Sen regime on the part of the Soviet Union and for a four-party coalition dominated by Norodom Sihanouk and the Khmer Rouge on China's part.

For China, it was a considerable compromise to normalise relations without having fully resolved this 'obstacles' of Soviet support for the Vietnamese occupation of Kampuchea. Vietnam had announced that it would complete its withdrawal by the end of September 1989, but it had not yet done so and China was still refusing to accept Vietnam's claims of the extent of the withdrawals so far. Indeed, China continued to refuse to accept that the Vietnamese had actually fully withdrawn, even after September 1989. The wording of the phrase about withdrawing military aid from their respective sides suggested that China should begin to suspend aid to the Khmer Rouge quite soon. This was a considerable concession on its part, considering how fervently it had been supplying the Khmer Rouge with military and other support for so long. As it happened, the aid continued for much longer than the joint communiqué might have suggested. By the time a settlement was actually reached on Cambodia in October 1991, the Soviet Union was itself on the point of disintegration and no longer cared greatly what happened there.

Meanwhile, there had been a major expansion of both trade and cultural relations between China and the Soviet Union in the five or six years before the normalisation of relations. Soviet experts again began to appear in China. Tourism began to pick up. Trade expanded rapidly to again make the Soviet Union one of China's main trading partners; bilateral trade reached US$3.3 billion in 1988.[17] The first China Fair for Economic Relations and Trade with the USSR and East European Countries, held in June 1990 in Harbin, presaged further significant expansion in trade and economic relations. From the beginning of 1991, barter trade across China's northern and western borders, which had dominated economic dealings between China and the Soviet Union, was replaced by spot exchange trade using hard currency. However, despite the expansion, China's bilateral trade with the Soviet Union remained far below the level of that with Japan, the United States or the European Economic Community. It was clear that China did not regard the Soviet Union as being in any sense as important as the main Western countries or Japan from the point of view of assisting its modernisation program.

While in China, Gorbachev had likened the students to the many 'hotheads' he himself had to face in the Soviet Union — people who were demanding change far more rapidly than was either feasible or desirable. When the Beijing massacre occurred, the Soviet Union's reaction was extremely low key by comparison with that of the Western countries. The Soviet Union did express regret at what had happened, but there was none of the fierce condemnation meted out by the United States and other Western countries. Naturally the Soviet response pleased the Chinese authorities, who were greatly taken aback by the strength of the Western reaction.

In April 1990, Chinese Premier Li Peng went to the Soviet Union, repaying Gorbachev's visit of the preceding year. On the surface, the visit was a total success, but there were a few issues of underlying disagreement which were given no public coverage in the

Soviet or Chinese press. One of the main ones was the recent development of serious independence movements in the Soviet Union, which posed a major threat to the unity of the Soviet Union. For the Chinese, the most worrying movement was that taking place in Tajikistan, an Islamic republic bordering one of the Muslim areas of China. Certainly the Chinese leaders believed that Gorbachev was being somewhat too tolerant of independence movements, even though he had recently sent troops to Azerbaijan to suppress rioting and racial clashes between the Azeris and Armenians. The Chinese were very concerned about separatism in Tibet, as previously explained. Moreover, the fighting for independence in the Muslim area of Tajikistan had just spilled over into Xinjiang, where the Chinese had suppressed an 'armed counter-revolutionary rebellion' by Muslims earlier the same month.

The collapse of communist power

In April 1990, Gorbachev and the Communist Party of the Soviet Union appeared to be in serious trouble. Soviet troops had been forced to withdraw from Afghanistan and nationalist rebellions appeared to be pulling the Soviet Union itself apart. A third issue of central importance which had supervened since the middle of 1989 was the collapse of communist power in most of the countries of Eastern and Central Europe. Together with factors such as the decline of the Soviet economy, these three in combination implied that, as the 1990s dawned, the Soviet Union hardly counted as a superpower any longer. In August 1991, a faction within the Soviet leadership launched a *coup d'état* against Gorbachev in an attempt to halt the disintegration of the Soviet Union. The coup backfired, largely owing to the intervention of the Russian President, Boris Yeltsin. Gorbachev returned to his position as President of the Soviet Union, although he was completely under Yeltsin's thumb. By the end of 1991, the Soviet Communist Party had been overthrown, Gorbachev had resigned and the collapse of the Soviet Union was complete. Most of those countries which had formerly belonged to the Soviet Union formed themselves into a very loose Commonwealth of Independent States.

The Chinese government was deeply distressed over these developments. Its relations with Eastern European countries had improved during the 1980s much more quickly than those with the Soviet Union. A succession of communist leaders of East and Central Europe had visited China, and Chinese leaders had paid their respects in East European capitals. For instance, the Polish and East German leaders, Wojcieck Jaruzelski and Erich Honecker respectively, had visited China as recently as the northern autumn of 1986. China's distaste for Poland's Solidarity, which was now winning certain victory against the communists, has already been mentioned (see Chapter 5). Zhao Ziyang had undertaken a major tour of Eastern Europe in mid-1987, including Poland, East Germany, Czechoslovakia, Hungary and Bulgaria. Admittedly, Zhao Ziyang was a fallen leader as the 1990s dawned, but that aspect of his activities was certainly much approved by the Soviet-trained Li Peng and his supporters.

At first the Chinese authorities mentioned the dramatic events in Europe only in very broad terms in their public statements. Three themes emerged. One was that the events proved that China had indeed been right to quell the 'counter-revolutionary rebellion' in Beijing itself. Without this action, would not China's Communist Party have been overthrown, as the Eastern European parties were later the same year? What these events seemed to prove to China's leaders was that, contrary to what the vast majority of Western commentators were saying, the survival of the CCP itself had indeed been under threat.

A second, and closely related, theme was the central position of the Communist Party in a socialist state. It was crucial to Leninism that the Communist Party was the vanguard of the proletariat and must under all circumstances retain its monopoly of power. Yet not only had many of the Communist Parties collapsed in Eastern and Central Europe, but even in the Soviet Union Gorbachev seemed willing to countenance that the Soviet Communist Party might forego its monopoly of power. The CCP was absolutely resolute that it would not follow this example if it could conceivably avoid doing so.

The other point was that the events in Eastern Europe would be a factor for instability. China's Foreign Minister Qian Qichen, commenting on the world situation at the beginning of 1990, denied that the improvement in Soviet-American relations would mean greater world stability. His view was that hegemonism and interference in the affairs of others by major powers were still common. He went on:

> There has been much concern over the recent drastic changes in Eastern Europe that have accumulated new elements of instability in East–West relations and will produce a far-reaching impact on the European situation as well as the over-all pattern of international relations.[18]

His wording suggests strongly that Qian was displeased over what had happened. In view of the situation in 1990, this is not surprising, although China might have reacted differently had the same events happened a few years earlier.

Of the chain of events in Europe in 1989, the incident which upset the Chinese authorities most was the overthrow and execution of Nicolae Ceausescu in Romania in December 1989. It is true that he had been a friend of China's, but the main point is that the Chinese leaders may have wondered if their own position might not be seen to be rather similar to that of the Romanian leader.

However, in terms of its impact on Europe and the world, the 1989 event they recognised as most important was the fall of the Berlin Wall in November. A reunited Germany would to some degree replace the Soviet Union, and to a lesser extent even the United States, as a focus of power in Europe. When Germany was formally reunited on 3 October 1990, China welcomed the event and called for a strengthening of friendly bilateral relations. At the same time, through expressing its hope that the unification would be 'conducive to peace, stability and development in Europe and the whole world',[19] China confirmed that it was in fact still nervous that the rise of Germany would produce precisely the opposite effect — in other words, militate *against* peace and stability. On many occasions, China had noted its concern about the dominant role a resurgent Germany could play in Europe and the world.

But even worse was to follow in 1991 for communist power. Early in the year, Gorbachev made a last-ditch but unsuccessful attempt to prevent the independence of the three Baltic states — Lithuania, Estonia and Latvia — from the Soviet Union. China immediately accepted the inevitable and established diplomatic relations with all three, but was in fact deeply nervous about the implications for the rest of the Soviet Union. China stayed silent during the attempted coup against Gorbachev of August 1991, but actually it hoped that Gorbachev's pro-communist enemies would win. The Chinese leaders had much earlier reached the conclusion that Gorbachev's policies were inimical to their own interests, because they could lead only to a further disintegration of communist power. If they distrusted Gorbachev, they were even more hostile to the role Boris Yeltsin was playing. Although they said nothing publicly, his emergence as the real victor and powerholder in August 1991 filled them with dismay.

At the end of 1991 their worst fears were realised, when the Soviet Union collapsed altogether. Again they accepted the inevitable, by recognising the independence of the republics which had made up the Soviet Union and establishing diplomatic relations with them. But for the Chinese leaders the fate of the Soviet Union was a lesson by negative example. The two biggest nightmares for them remained the overthrow of the Party and the disintegration of the country's unity, both of which had happened in the world's first long-lasting socialist state. Despite remaining outwardly confident that such disasters would not befall China, they could not help worrying that the Soviet malaise would prove infectious and that pressures would now mount for the independence of Tibet and even Xinjiang, which borders several of the newly independent republics of Islamic peoples. In particular, there are over a million Kazaks in northern Xinjiang in an area bordering Kazakhstan, a newly independent and large republic dominated by their co-nationals.

There is a very old tradition in China that the worst fate that can befall any nation is chaos (*luan*). According to the Chinese leaders, that is precisely what had befallen the former Soviet Union. It is quite likely that a substantial majority of the Chinese people shared their view on this particular matter.

Another implication of the Soviet collapse was that it gave Taiwan the opportunity to compete with the PRC for influence in the new states. Since Taiwan has much more money to give these newly independent countries than the PRC does, and since they are anyway better disposed to the capitalist system than to the socialist one which they have just overthrown, they are likely to be quite receptive to approaches from Taiwan. In February 1992, the Taiwan Foreign Minister actually visited several of the newly independent states, signalling rivalry between the PRC and Taiwan over influence there. The PRC responded with strong, and mainly successful, efforts to retain good diplomatic relations with the former Soviet states.

By the end of 1992, however, China appeared not only to have accepted the collapse of the Soviet Union — though it certainly did not change its mind about the need to avoid 'chaos' or to maintain the leadership of the Party — but even to have turned the new developments to its own advantage. One highly ironical aspect was China's moving in to purchase cheap arms from the former Soviet Union to update its arsenal. In a context in which Russia's trade with most other countries was declining, that with China continued to expand healthily. In December 1992, Boris Yeltsin crowned the newly emerging relationship with a visit to Beijing. This was carried out with considerable fanfare, even though he was not granted an interview with the ageing leader Deng Xiaoping.

Late in 1992, China's Foreign Minister Chen Qichen visited four of the newly independent countries of the former Soviet Union: Uzbekistan, Kighizstan, Kazakhstan and Russia. At a news conference given in Moscow on 26 November 1992 he said that his chief impression of all four countries was 'that they wish to develop relations with China'.[20] All of these four but Russia are states with strongly Muslim populations, two of them, Kazakhstan and Kirghizstan, having common borders with China. The Chinese government's thirst for stability can only be assisted by coming to terms with the independent Muslim Central Asian states.

Conclusion

The major fact behind the unexpected improvement in China's relations with Russia and the Central Asian states was that Russia no longer constituted a threat to China. Not only did the Western section of China's boundaries with what had been the Soviet Union now border its weak but apparently friendly Central Asian successor states, but Russia itself was still in serious decline economically and in no position to threaten China. If anything, the potential for threat lay the other way round. The new threat to China in the form of ethnic tensions and Islamic revival in the newly independent Central Asian states could hardly be serious for some time to come in view of the political divisions still afflicting those countries and their willingness to be friendly to China, and at the same time both Russia and China had a strong interest in trying to prevent such tensions from getting out of hand or spreading to either country.

For China during the 1980s and 1990s, 'openness to the ouside world' has been part and parcel of reform, and of 'socialism with Chinese characteristics'. The overwhelming aim of China's foreign relations has been to assist its domestic modernisation program. It believed that friendly relations with the United States, other major Western countries and Japan were the principal key to this end. It also wanted stability both in its own region and in the world at large. The thaw and then normalisation with the Soviet Union and other countries of Eastern Europe could assist in bringing about stability, which could only be beneficial for its own modernisation program. The fear that the collapse of communist power in Eastern and Central Europe would bring about a less stable world situation was one of the central reasons for China's worries about developments there. In the days of Mao Zedong, China may have been happy to compete with the Soviet Union for the premiership of the communist world, but that was hardly a position actively sought by China's leaders in the new age of the 1990s.

Yet China continued to be deeply concerned about its status as a world power and its reputation abroad. In 1986 it could claim that its 'prestige and position had risen' in the first half of the 1980s, which had been 'the most beneficial and active' since 1949, as well as 'the one when most initiatives were taken'.[21] The second half of the 1980s was not nearly so successful. In particular, China was certainly very much more worried about being branded again as an international pariah because of the Beijing massacre than it was prepared to admit. China had had experience of this status during the 1960s and was not keen for a repetition. Moreover, by the 1990s its economy was based on the assumption that outside countries, and especially the rich countries of the West and Japan, were willing to assist it economically and in other ways and invest in its future. That is why the reaction of the Western powers and Japan to the Beijing massacre was such a disaster for China.

In the 1990s, China may be less important for the United States and the West than it used to be. However, it is simply no longer possible, or in anybody's interests, for an important segment of the world to again turn its back completely on this most populous of all nations. Moreover, though the early 1990s have seen considerable problems in China's relations with the countries of the West, particularly the United States, it has so far done quite well as far as it own region is concerned. This will become clearer in the course of the next chapter.

Notes

1 Xue Mouhong, 'Woguo waijiao de xin jumian' ('The New Appearance of Our Country's Foreign Diplomacy'), *Hong qi zazhi (Red Flag Magazine)*, no. 6, 16 March 1986, p. 19. The journal was renamed *Qiu shi (Seeking Truth from Facts)* in July 1988.

2 The enormously long article, of over 35 000 characters, was entitled 'Chairman Mao's Theory of the Differentiation of the Three Worlds Is a Major Contribution to Marxism-Leninism' and appeared first in *People's Daily* on 1 November 1977. The above quotation comes from a translation in *Peking Review*, vol. 20, no. 45, 4 November 1977, p. 22.

3 See the text of the communiqué, among many other places, in *Peking Review*, vol. 21, no. 51, 22 December 1978, p. 8.

4 See Paul H. Kreisberg, 'The United States and Asia in 1984', *Asian Survey*, vol. xxv, no. 1, January 1985, p. 8 for the 1981 figure; and Colin Mackerras and Amanda Yorke, *The Cambridge Handbook of Contemporary China*, Cambridge University Press, Cambridge, 1990, p. 167 for the 1988 figure.

5 See 'Quarterly Chronicle and Documentation', *The China Quarterly*, no. 117, March 1989, p. 207.

6 On US–China educational exchanges in general, see Linda A. Reed, *Education in the People's Republic of China and U.S.–China Educational Exchanges*, National Association for Foreign Student Affairs, Washington, DC, 1988, pp. 89–160. For the figures given on education in this and following paragraphs in particular, see p. 100.

7 For example, see Kreisberg, 'The United States and Asia in 1984', pp. 9–10, for a discussion of economic problems between the United States and China in 1984.

8 Hu Yaobang's report of 1 September 1982 to the 12th CCP National Congress, in *Beijing Review*, vol. 25, no. 37, 13 September 1982, p. 30.

9 *Beijing Review*, vol. 32, no. 13, 27 March–2 April 1989, p. 8.

10 *Asiaweek*, vol. 16, no. 1, 5 January 1990, p. 19.

11 *Beijing Review*, vol. 33, no. 50, 10–16 December 1990, p. 4.

12 See Lincoln Kaye, in *Far Eastern Economic Review*, vol. 155, no. 20, 21 May 1992, p. 26.

13 Hu Yaobang's report of 1 September 1982 to the Twelfth CCP National Congress, in *Beijing Review*, vol. 25, no. 37, 13 September 1982, p. 31.

14 *Speech by Mikhail Gorbachev in Vladivostok, July 28, 1986*, Novosti Press Agency Publishing House, Moscow, 1986, pp. 29–30.

15 *Beijing Review*, vol. 32, no. 22, 29 May-4 June 1989, p. 11.

16 ibid., p. 12.

17 See Mackerras and Yorke, *The Cambridge Handbook of Contemporary China*, p. 167.

18 *Beijing Review*, vol. 33, no. 3, 15–21 January 1990, p. 10.

19 Chu Qimen, in *Beijing Review*, vol. 33, no. 43, 22–28 October 1990, p. 9.

20 *Beijing Review*, vol.35, no. 50, 14-20 December 1992, p. 9.

21 Xue Mouhong, 'Woguo waijiao de xin jumian', p. 19.

17

FOREIGN RELATIONS II
The Neighbours

SINCE the late 1970s, China's relations with most of its neighbours have improved markedly, and until 1991 the only exception to this trend was Vietnam, with which China fought a brief but costly and unsuccessful war in 1979. But the collapse of communist governments in Eastern Europe and the disintegration of the Soviet Union have forced both China and Vietnam to make peace with each other. Even though the post-Mao leadership has repeatedly emphasised its support for independent paths of development for all countries, socialist or not, it is hard not to see the normalisation of Sino-Vietnamese relations as part of a common front to defend their respective Communist Parties against the onslaught of democracy and human rights movements. While ideology may have been an important factor behind China's decision to patch up its differences with Vietnam, economic pragmatism was the driving force behind its rapidly growing ties with the avowedly anti-communist member states of the Association of South East Asian Nations (ASEAN) and behind the development of closer ties with Japan. Economic ties with South Korea have also grown over the last few years, and the two states actually established dipomatic relations with each other in August 1992. Relations with the other Asian giant, India, have improved considerably, although the long-standing border dispute between the two has not been resolved. Normally friendly relations with Pakistan and Nepal have remained so in spite of the establishment of democratic governments in those countries.

China enjoys a unique place in the Asia–Pacific region. While it is economically a Third World nation, China's military achievements, including its arsenal of nuclear weapons, have been a source of fear and apprehension among its neighbours. Its material and moral support for left-wing movements in Southeast Asia at one time contributed to tensions in the region. America's paranoia about the spread of communism led it to provide military cover against the threat of communism to its allies in Asia, where it continues to maintain military bases. However, since the normalisation of Sino-American relations, especially since Deng Xiaoping's rise to power, China has repeatedly assured its neighbours that it does not provide any kind of support to left-wing parties or movements in other countries.

China's preoccupation with economic and technological modernisation under Deng has caused it to seek friendly ties with its neighbours. It now sees Southeast Asia and Japan as major sources of technology and investments to aid its four modernisations program. Its pursuit of economic prosperity, rather than military or ideological domination of the region, sits nicely with its neighbours' objectives. China's readiness to use the language of economics in international relations is understood better by its neighbours than the ideological rhetoric it used in the past to define its stand on regional and global issues. This change of priorities, of course, does not mean that other factors do not figure in China's foreign policy calculations. China is beyond doubt the most important military power in the region and it seeks to play a role commensurate with its status. It is the only Asian country to hold a permanent seat on the United Nations Security Council, where it plays an important part in making decisions of global importance.

In contrast with strong emotive Western reactions to the Beijing massacre of June 1989, China's Asian neighbours were restrained in their comments, choosing to keep any 'interference' in China's internal affairs to an absolute minimum. While striving to clean up their image in the West, Chinese leaders shifted their attention to Third World nations to create the impression of business as usual on the international front in the eyes of the Chinese people. President Yang Shangkun, Premier Li Peng and other senior leaders visited several developing countries, while Western governments, under pressure from their peoples, were hesitant to welcome them.

Southeast Asia and China

Since the founding of the PRC in October 1949, its relations with Southeast Asian countries have been shaped largely by developments outside the region. Its regional policy under Mao was heavily dependent upon its global policy *vis-à-vis* the superpowers. Until the early 1970s, when the United States was regarded as the number one enemy, China sought to thwart American attempts to create a ring of containment against the spread of communism. When the Americans launched their military offensive against North Korea and towards the Manchurian border in 1950, the fledgling PRC decided to take on the mighty superpower with all its strength. Later, in the 1960s, it supported the government of North Vietnam in its fight against the Americans in the South.

China's relations with Southeast Asia have also been moulded by historical and ethnic factors. The states and peoples of this region have had a long and complex historical association with China, in which China was always the dominant partner. The bilateral ties between China and individual Southeast Asian states have also been complicated by the presence of large numbers of overseas Chinese. Historically, the Chinese people in Southeast Asia have been treated with suspicion by the governments of the region. Following the communist victory, thousands of ethnic Chinese in the region expressed their support for the new regime, either by returning to China or by sending their children to study there. Moreover, China's support for left-wing parties in the region further contributed to distrust between China and the non-communist Southeast Asian states. Unable to cope with the growing revolutionary movements, the ASEAN states supported the presence of American forces in the region as a bulwark against communism. Until the early 1970s, when it began to talk directly with the Americans, China was bitterly opposed to this and ridiculed the governments of the five member states of ASEAN as 'lackeys of American imperialism'.

Since the implementation of the open-door policy, however, there has been a radical change in China's relations with the ASEAN states, although it must be said that the process of normalisation had begun while Mao was still alive. Malaysia was the first ASEAN country to establish diplomatic relations with China in 1974, followed by the Philippines and Thailand in 1975. Indonesia, which had enjoyed friendly relations with China prior to 1965, resumed diplomatic ties in 1990. Singapore established diplomatic relations with the PRC for the first time in October the same year. The cornerstone of China's relations with the ASEAN states in the 1980s was their mutual opposition to the Vietnamese invasion of Cambodia and the installation of a pro-Vietnamese government there.

China has never accepted the idea of Vietnamese domination of Indo-China, which it sees as being within its own sphere of influence. Thus there is a clear divergence in the strategic imperatives of China and Vietnam, which was evident as early as 1975. But the actual character of the Sino-Vietnamese conflict did not become public until 1978.[1] Because of their need for economic and technical aid, Vietnamese leaders leaned towards the Soviet Union after the reunification of the country, much to the chagrin of China. In any case, China was then unable to afford the cost of buying influence in Vietnam through economic and military aid in excess of what the Soviet Union was already offering. Emboldened by its growing military and economic ties with the Soviet Union, Vietnam invaded Cambodia (Kampuchea) on 25 December 1978, and overthrew the Chinese-backed Khmer Rouge government led by Pol Pot. China retaliated by launching a punitive attack on Vietnam on 17 February 1979, which ended on 5 March when China began pulling out its troops after having captured Lang Son, a major town close to the border. But the Chinese mission to 'teach Vietnam a lesson' had clearly backfired when Chinese troops were held off by the battle-hardened Vietnamese forces. Moreover, most of Cambodia continued to be ruled by the Vietnamese-sponsored government in Phnom Penh, while various Cambodian factions, aided by China, Singapore and many Western countries, waged a struggle to overthrow the Phnom Penh government.

The search for a solution to the Cambodia problem helped China maintain a regular dialogue with the ASEAN states, which also had a spin-off effect for China's bilateral relations with them. China was the main backer of the murderous Khmer Rouge faction of the anti-Vietnamese coalition led by Prince Norodom Sihanouk. Because of this, China's support was crucial for any formula to resolve the crisis. Throughout the 1980s, China was unwilling to agree to any proposal for the resolution of this problem that did not include its client, the Khmer Rouge, whereas Vietnam insisted that the Khmer Rouge leaders should not be allowed to participate in any future government of Cambodia. Western governments, too, were unsympathetic towards the idea of giving the genocidal Khmer Rouge another chance to rule over Cambodia. In 1986, however,

China had softened its stand on the make-up of a future Cambodian government by agreeing to the participation of the Phnom Penh government of Prime Minister Hun Sen in a future government.[2]

One of the 'three obstacles' that China had earlier listed to the normalisation of Sino-Soviet relations was the Soviet support for the Vietnamese invasion of Cambodia and the continued presence of Vietnamese troops there (see Chapter 16). With the Soviet government under Mikhail Gorbachev attempting to develop closer ties with the West and China, the Soviets tried to persuade the Vietnamese to withdraw all troops from Cambodia to pave the way for the normalisation of Sino-Soviet relations. Once the Vietnamese troops had left, by September 1989, the way became clear for the Cambodian factions to try to resolve the Cambodian crisis with the support of international community.

A settlement of the Cambodian problem was finally reached, but not without China's consent. Under a United Nations-brokered peace pact signed in Paris in October 1991, all three Cambodian resistance factions, including the Khmer Rouge and the Vietnam-installed government of Prime Minister Hun Sen, are represented on a twelve-member body known as the Supreme National Council. The Chairman of the Supreme National Council is Prince Norodom Sihanouk, who returned to Phnom Penh in November 1991 aboard a Chinese airliner after nearly thirteen years in exile, most of which was spent in Beijing. The peace plan called for all Cambodian parties to the agreement, including the Hun Sen government, to cut their troops by 70 per cent and put them under United Nations supervision until elections are held in 1993. The United Nations set up a Transitional Authority in Cambodia to supervise the takeover by an elected government, the elections taking place in May 1993. China's continuing support for the United Nations Peace Plan was crucial to its implementation.

Since the signing of the Cambodian peace plan, relations between China and Vietnam have also been 'normalised' after more than a decade of hostilities. Following a series of clandestine meetings between the top-level officials of the two countries, the leader of the Vietnamese Communist Party, Do Muoi, and Prime Minister Vo Van Kiet paid an official visit to China in November 1991. As indicated at the outset of this chapter, the fact that China and Vietnam are the two most populous communist countries left in the world may have played an important part in the normalisation of relations. But, apart from underlining the ideological challenges that the two Communist Parties face, the visit also emphasised the economic realities that have forced both China and Vietnam to adopt distinctly unsocialist economic policies. One of the agreements signed was a border trade agreement which has enhanced economic co-operation. Since the unofficial reopening of the border in 1989, the cross-border trade has been growing rapidly, totalling about US$5000 a day across the narrow Bac Luan River which separates the Chinese town of Dong Hung from Mong Cai in Vietnam.[3]

Despite the normalisation of relations, it is unlikely that the ties between the two countries will return to the 'lips and teeth' level of closeness which prevailed from the 1950s to the late 1970s. One reason for this is that there are still unresolved issues between them, which include Vietnam's debt to China, the status of ethnic Chinese refugees from Vietnam who were forced to flee to China in the late 1970s, and the ownership of the Spratly and Paracel Islands over which several Southeast Asian countries lay their claims.[4] In February 1992, the Chinese passed a law through their National People's Congress restating in legal terms their often made claim to all the Spratly Islands. In May they actually signed a deal with the United States-based Crestone Energy Corporation to drill for oil in one of the Spratly Islands and sent a ship to occupy one of the uninhabited islands with the aim of implementing the agreement. These actions aroused considerable annoyance and anxiety, not only with Vietnam but with the ASEAN countries as well.

The second reason why relations between China and Vietnam are unlikely to return to the warmth of the 1950s and 1960s is that their strategic imperatives about Indo-China continue to clash. But the leaders in both countries realise that they need stability to improve the economies of their nations, which could be the key to their retaining power a while longer. Both China and Vietnam have charted a similar course to economic modernisation in the 1980s, seeking foreign capital and technology to boost their economies.

Other Southeast Asian countries have taken advantage of the pragmatic economic policies being pursued by both China and Vietnam by expanding their economic relations with the two countries. China has been the main destination of Southeast Asian capital in the last ten years. Economic relations between China and the ASEAN member states have grown steadily in spite of the slow pace of developments in other areas. For example, in the case of both Indonesia and Singapore, trade and economic relations with China developed far in advance of formal diplomatic ties. After many years of indirect trading, Indonesia decided in 1985 to restore direct trade relations with China. Singapore, too, has maintained close economic relations with China and, in addition to direct trade, many Singapore firms have invested in manufacturing and service sectors there.

The improvement of China's relations with Southeast Asian countries is integral to its strategy of creating a peaceful regional climate to facilitate its economic development. Moreover, the current Chinese leadership does not lay much emphasis — if any at all — on the ideological soundness of its relations with other countries. Today its national interests are better defined, and its foreign policy is more resilient, than in the heady days of the Cultural Revolution. As Li Peng said during his visit to Indonesia in August 1990, 'international practice has proved that state-to-state relations are not determined by similarities and divergences in social system[s] and ideology'.[5]

Sino-Japanese relations

Among its neighbours, aside from the former Soviet Union, no other country has figured so prominently in China's foreign policy considerations as Japan. There are two reasons for this: firstly, the past history of Japanese militarism in China; and secondly, the economic and technological advances that Japan has made in the postwar period. In spite of the bitterness and mistrust that the Chinese leaders harbour towards Japan for its cruel treatment of China in the past, they are nonetheless impressed and awed by its spectacular economic successes. Such mixed feelings are also reflected in China's relations with Japan. During the 1950s and 1960s, the presence of American bases in Asia and United States military association with Japan were perceived by the Chinese as the main sources of threat to China's national security. At the same time, however, China kept trying to develop trade ties with Japan.

The thaw in Sino-American relations in 1972 also marked a major turning point in Sino-Japanese relations. Late in September the same year, China and Japan established diplomatic relations, following which their bilateral trade grew rapidly. The improvement in Sino-Japanese and Sino-American relations also coincided with, and contributed to, further deterioration in Sino-Soviet relations. Chinese attempts to draw Japan into a common anti-Soviet nexus of relations, however, met with rejection from Japan. Unwilling to take sides and restrained by its postwar constitution and public opinion from adopting aggressive postures against another country,

Japan was content with having improved political and economic relations with its neighbour without being dragged into a conflict situation.

In August 1978, China and Japan signed the 'Treaty of Peace and Friendship' which, at China's insistence, included an 'anti-hegemony' clause aimed against the Soviet Union. Since the signing of the treaty, Sino-Japanese relations have had their ups and downs. Many of the setbacks in the relationship between the two countries have been caused by events which have their origins in Japan's militaristic past. In 1982, for instance, China strongly objected to the use of the term 'advance' to describe the Japanese invasion of China in history books for Japanese school students. A few years later, another controversy erupted when the Japanese Prime Minister, Yasuhiro Nakasone, visited Yasukuni Shrine, a symbol of Japanese militarism. However, there have also been other sources of friction between the two countries. Within months of the signing of the peace treaty, China cancelled billions of dollars worth of contracts with Japanese firms and put on hold several major Japanese investment projects, including the construction of the Baoshan Steel Complex in Shanghai. Some of these projects, including Baoshan, were later resumed, but only after they had been scaled down.

Another low-level irritation in Sino-Japanese relations was the so-called Kokaryo case, in which a Japanese high court in 1987 rejected China's claim to a student dormitory in Kyoto, instead awarding it to Taiwan. This matter was raised each time senior officials and ministers from the two countries met during 1987, but in subsequent years it did not figure prominently in their bilateral relations. In August 1988, Prime Minister Noboru Takeshita visited China to mark the tenth anniversary of the Peace and Friendship Treaty. During his visit, Takeshita also witnessed the signing of an agreement to protect Japanese direct investments in China. That year also marked the first time in five years that China ran a trade surplus with Japan. In April 1992, Jiang Zemin visited Japan and even met with the Emperor.

Although at the time the Emperor declined Jiang's invitation for a return visit, in fact he did visit China in October 1992 to mark the twentieth anniversary of the establishment of diplomatic relations. Being the first such visit of a Japanese Emperor to China in history, and given the nature of Imperial Japan's relations with China, the event gave rise to some controversy, both in China and Japan itself. As expected, the Emperor forebore actually to apologise for Japan's crimes in China, especially the 'rape of Nanjing' in December 1937 when Japanese occupying troops massacred many thousands of Chinese. However, he did 'deeply deplore' the 'unfortunate period' in history when Japan had invaded China. The Chinese government did everything it could to prevent any public signs of protest against the Emperor, and none took place, even though a survey suggested that the great majority of Chinese believed that the Emperor should formally apologise on behalf of Japan, and that his country should pay war reparations.[6] What most interested the Chinese government was the likelihood that the visit would lead on to closer Sino-Japanese economic and political ties.

Overall, therefore, the development of China's relations with Japan has proceeded rather smoothly. The Beijing massacre of June 1989 posed a low-level threat to Sino-Japanese relations. After the incident, the Japanese government suspended US$5.5 billion in loans to China, but such measures were short-lived. In August 1991, Japanese Prime Minister Toshiki Kaifu became the first leader of an industrialised country to visit China since the massacre. Although the economic sanctions had already been lifted several months prior to that, Kaifu's visit to China was a great moral victory for China's hardline leadership. During his visit, the Japanese leader told his Chinese hosts that, in his meetings with Western leaders, he has often stressed that in the developing countries of Asia, political stability can only be achieved through economic development, thus echoing the well-publicised views of his hosts.[7] Such comments are meant to indicate to the Chinese leadership that Japan understands China's problems and is prepared to help China in solving them through greater economic co-operation. In 1990, China was the only Asian country to enjoy a healthy trade surplus with Japan, which totalled US$5.9 billion.

Sino-Australian relations

In the words of one Australian scholar, since the establishment of diplomatic relations between the People's Republic of China and Australia in 1972, 'their bilateral relationship has expanded into one of complex diversity'.[8] The relationship is certainly more complex today than it was before the Beijing massacre, when by all official accounts there were no major differences between the two countries, although they did hold divergent views on some international issues. The relationship is also diverse in the range of areas in which China and Australia have established official and unofficial links.

Prior to the establishment of formal diplomatic relations, the contacts between the two countries were limited to wool and wheat trade — more precisely, to Australian exports of these commodities to China. Politically, however, there was little desire on either side to develop any meaningful relationship. Indeed, in the eyes of Australia's conservative government, 'the downward thrust of Chinese communism' posed the major threat to Australia's national security. China, on the other hand, saw Australia as a minor pro-American power inconsequential to China's interests, except perhaps as a source of some agricultural commodities.

In the 20 years since 1972, the governments of China and Australia have developed a sound relationship based on a greater understanding of each other's history, culture and national interests, both economic and strategic. The improved relations are a result of substantive changes in each country's domestic and foreign policies. China welcomed the support Australia was able to give to its modernisation program, while Australia, recognising its political and economic interdependence with Asia, was very willing to expand and upgrade relations with its largest northern neighbour.

Although many important Chinese leaders, including the late Hu Yaobang, Zhao Ziyang and Li Peng, visited Australia on separate occasions, relations with Australia never ranked as highly in China's foreign policy as vice versa. All Australia's prime ministers from 1972 to 1989, Gough Whitlam, Malcolm Fraser and Bob Hawke, paid official visits to China, and many ministers of the Hawke government also made regular trips there. According to a former Australian ambassador to China, 'China became a symbol of the need for change in Australia's foreign policy'.[9] The imbalance in official attention paid to the relationship notwithstanding, China's relations with Australia have matured to the extent that they are able to grow even in the face of dramatic international, regional and domestic changes. China and Australia have established mutually beneficial links in economic, scientific, educational, cultural and other fields. Over the last 20 years, the two governments have created an institutional framework to promote co-operation in various areas. The two-way trade between the two countries has grown from about A$78 million in 1972 to A$2.6 billion in 1990. There are over 160 representative and branch offices set up in Australia by Chinese provinces, ministries or business enterprises.[10]

A major setback to Sino-Australian relations was caused by the brutal suppression of protests by the Chinese military in June 1989 and Australia's reaction to this. Reflecting popular opinion in the country, the Australian government widely condemned the 'use of violence and force' by the Chinese government against 'innocent people peacefully exercising their rights'. Australia also imposed economic and political sanctions against China, including the cancellation of the Prime Minister's planned visit to China later in the year. The Australian government, however, soon began to take a more pragmatic approach to economic sanctions, realising that international pressure was unlikely to have any significant impact on China's domestic political situation in the short term. Moreover, economic sanctions cut both ways. While they would make life difficult for the Chinese, they would also harm Australia's own economic interests. Probably following this logic and the examples of other Western governments, Australia began to lift sanctions only months after they were introduced. All remaining economic and political restrictions on relations with China were lifted in February 1991.

The Beijing massacre and subsequent developments in Sino-Australian relations have changed the character of this relationship somewhat. It is more balanced, rational and free of any illusions in the minds of either side. On Australia's side there is a far greater weight placed on human rights. China is willing to hold 'dialogue' on this issue and even allowed a human rights delegation to visit China, including Tibet, in the middle of 1991, but it is also aware of its own strategic and economic importance to Australia. Such a reassessment of Sino-Australian relations as has taken place in Australia has produced positive results for that country. Australia appears to have gained a new kind of confidence in its relations with China, especially in relation to its ties with Taiwan. Although Australia continues to recognise the government of the PRC as the legitimate government of China, and acknowledges that Taiwan is a part of China, it is now more frank about its growing commercial relations with the island. As a manifestation of this, direct air links between Australia and Taiwan were established at the end of 1991.

Although it will be some time before Sino-Australian relations fully recover from the damage caused by the Beijing massacre, the conditions have improved enough to facilitate the conduct of diplomatic and economic business between the two countries. The Australian Minister for Foreign Affairs and Trade, Senator Evans, visited China in April 1991, and in February 1992, Chinese Vice Premier Zhu Rongji became the most senior Chinese official to visit Australia since June 1989.

Sino-Indian relations

Since the late 1940s, Sino-Indian relations have passed through several phases. The first phase began even before the founding of the PRC, in the form of bilateral relations between the CCP and the Indian National Congress. It was a period of close friendship and lasted until the late 1950s when relations between the two Asian giants began to deteriorate over Tibet and the boundary issue. The second phase, from the late 1950s to the mid-1970s, was a period of conflict and hostility during which they fought a brief war in 1962 and poured scorn on each other. The third and the latest phase began when they resumed ambassadorial-level relations in 1976. Since then their bilateral contacts have grown steadily over the years.

While India has always been a champion of the non-aligned movement, of which it was a founder, in practice it leaned towards the Soviet Union for economic and military aid. It was therefore seen by the Chinese as a close ally of the Soviet Union. China, for its part, developed close political and military ties with India's traditional enemy, Pakistan, and used it as an intermediary to open diplomatic dialogue with the United States. Sino-Indian relations thus became linked to the Sino-Soviet conflict and the Sino-Soviet-American power struggle. Because of this, it is sometimes argued that India's close association with the Soviet Union served to hinder the improvement of Sino-Indian relations.

The Soviet Union was a major factor in Sino-Indian relations, but nevertheless one that can be exaggerated. Sino-Indian relations developed their own momentum which was not entirely due to the normalisation of China's relations with the former Soviet Union. Still, there are several outstanding issues between China and India which cannot be resolved unless the two sides agree to make major concessions. External factors play only a secondary role in these matters. The resolution of the boundary dispute is a key to complete normalisation of Sino-Indian relations.

While the boundary issue remains unresolved, valuable progress has been made in other areas. Since the restoration of direct trade between the two countries in 1977, bilateral trade has increased, although the volume of two-way trade is still miniscule compared with the trade each one carries on with other major countries. Bilateral trade amounted to US$270 million in 1989 despite the signing of a trade agreement between the two countries in 1984, granting most-favoured-nation status to each other. Cultural, educational and scientific exchanges have also increased. In

December 1988, the late Prime Minister Rajiv Gandhi paid an official visit to China, clearing the way for further high-level contacts. His visit, however, failed to produce any breakthrough on the boundary question, on which several rounds of talks had already been held. In December 1991, Premier Li Peng became the first head of Chinese government in 31 years to visit India. Like Gandhi's visit to China three years earlier, Li's state visit to India failed to result in a resolution of the border dispute.

On several other issues, however, China and India seem to have found a common position. In a joint communiqué issued at the end of Li's visit to India, the two countries expressed their disagreement with the Western position on the issue of human rights, instead describing the 'right to subsistence and development' as a basic human right. Given India's pride in its open political system and independent judiciary, it was perhaps surprising to see India allow itself to be seen in the same category as China on the subject of human rights.

Sino-British relations and the Hong Kong issue

Even before Deng Xiaoping's ascendancy in the late 1970s, China had developed substantive economic and political contacts with the countries of Western Europe, including the United Kingdom, which had ruled the Chinese Territory of Hong Kong since 1842. Although China had never allowed Britain to forget that it was the real owner of the territories collectively known as Hong Kong, the question of Hong Kong's future did not become the focal point, or a major cause for irritation, in their bilateral relations until the early 1980s. Before this time, the general feeling in Hong Kong and Britain was that China would not want to take control of Hong Kong even after 1997, when the 99-year lease reached on the New Territories in 1898 expires, because it had thus far expressed no clear intention to this effect. This line of argument was based on the fact that Hong Kong was the largest source of foreign currency for China and that China would not want to destabilise Hong Kong by starting a controversy on its future.

By 1983, however, the question of Hong Kong's future had begun to dominate the Sino-British relationship. During her visit to China in September 1982, Britain's Prime Minister, Margaret Thatcher, was left in no doubt by Deng Xiaoping that China planned to regain sovereignty over Hong Kong come 1997. Flushed with the victory in the Falklands War of 1982, Thatcher found China's plans for Hong Kong unacceptable. Before her visit, it was hoped by the residents of Hong Kong that she would be able to get an assurance from the Chinese that Hong Kong would be allowed to stay out of China's control well beyond 1997. The actual effect of her trip proved to be quite contrary to these expectations. At the end of her visit to China and Hong Kong, there was greater nervousness in the territory than had been the case before her arrival. The Chinese position was firm and clear: Hong Kong would become a Special Administrative Region of China in 1997. The provision for the creation of special administrative regions was incorporated into the Chinese constitution of 1982 under the 'one country, two systems' formula propounded by Deng for the reunification of the country.

The period following Mrs Thatcher's visit to China was characterised by heightened diplomatic activity between the two countries. The two sides began the arduous process of negotiations over Hong Kong's future in July 1983. While in the past China had shown no haste for the resolution of the Hong Kong issue, it now wanted a speedy conclusion to these negotiations. China maintained intense pressure on the government of the United Kingdom as the two countries negotiated. On 30 September, Ji Pengfei, the then head of the Hong Kong and Macao Affairs Office, said that China would make a unilateral statement on the future of Hong Kong by the end of 1984 if no agreement had been reached between the two sides by that time. Although Deng Xiaoping was not directly involved in the talks, it was clear that he was calling the shots. When Ji Pengfei said in 1984 that China would not station troops in Hong Kong, Deng quickly reprimanded him and went on the record saying that the People's Liberation Army troops would be stationed in Hong Kong after 1997.

Finally, on 19 December 1984, an agreement was signed by the prime ministers of China and Britain in Beijing, settling the question of Hong Kong's future. According to the Sino-British Joint Declaration, as this document is officially known, China will regain sovereignty over Hong Kong on 1 July 1997, but the territory will retain its free market economic system for at least another 50 years. Among the promises made by China in the Joint Declaration is one which guarantees financial independence for Hong Kong. Although Hong Kong will be free to maintain and develop economic and cultural relations with states, regions and international organisations under the name of 'Hong Kong, China', the central government in Beijing will be solely responsible for overall foreign policy and external security matters. Both sides stated their view that the Joint

Declaration was the best possible solution to the problem, yet Hong Kong-related issues continue to occupy a prominent place in Sino-British relations.

One major controversy was over a massive international airport in Hong Kong, plans for which were announced in October 1989. China complained that it had not been consulted by the Hong Kong administration over the planned construction of the airport. It demanded a freeze on the entire project and asked that nothing should proceed until the governments of China and Britain had reached an agreement on the issue. In the end, China got what it wanted: a promise that it will have a say in the running of the territory in the period leading up to 1997, albeit not in such explicit terms. A memorandum of understanding on the construction of the new airport was initialled by the representatives of the two governments in Beijing in June 1991. As part of this agreement, a joint 'airport committee' was set up to maintain a regular dialogue on the airport construction. The Bank of China was also given a role in loan syndicates for the airport project. And the airport agreement marked a significant diplomatic victory for China when British Prime Minister John Major travelled to Beijing in September 1991 to sign the agreement, thus becoming the first Western leader to visit China since the incident of 4 June 1989.

In 1992, Chris Patten, a distinguished Conservative Party member who had been defeated in the April 1992 British elections, replaced Sinologist David Wilson as Governor of Hong Kong. His more assertive style against the Chinese, and especially his demand for a greater degree of elective and democratic power for the people of Hong Kong, raised considerable anxiety and even ire in Beijing. Patten visited Beijing in October 1992, gaining only a frosty reception there, with Chinese authorities stating simply that they would reverse Patten's democratic measures after the 1997 transfer. Patten appeared more determined than ever to push ahead with the airport, no matter what the misgivings or objections of the Chinese. While Patten's new policies won initial strong support from the people of Hong Kong and especially from the West, it remains to be seen how effectively they contribute to a smooth transition of power in 1997.

Conclusion

Apart from the countries mentioned above, China's relations with other countries in the region have also undergone radical change.

The last few years have witnessed a shift in China's attitude towards South Korea. Economic relations have been growing substantially for some years, two-way trade amounting to US$3.8 billion in 1990.

China has for some time been active in promoting reconciliation between the two sides of the Korean peninsula. In September 1991, the two sides simultaneously joined the United Nations, and in December the same year, North and South Korea signed a reconciliation and non-aggression pact, with China fully supporting these developments. In November 1991, the Chinese Foreign Minister, Qian Qichen, attended the third ministerial conference of the Asia Pacific Economic Co-operation Forum in Seoul, South Korea. He used this opportunity to meet with South Korean President Roh Tae Woo, senior officials and business leaders. A major breakthrough came in August 1992 with the establishment of full diplomatic relations between the PRC and South Korea. Taiwan reacted furiously, breaking off relations with South Korea. North Korea, by contrast, was not in such a strong position. Although obviously deeply distressed, it retained friendship and relations with China, which since the fall of the communist powers of Europe has been its only major supporter.

In the post-Cold War era, China finds itself moving towards a new role in the world and in its own region. The United States, which has emerged as the only superpower, has no further need for the 'China card', while the Soviet Union no longer exists as a political entity, with the successor states being only too willing to follow the American line. As the United States gradually reduces its presence in the Pacific, smaller and less powerful countries in Asia are beginning to worry about the future power structure of the region. A question to the fore in the minds of their leaders is whether China can or will fill the power vacuum that might be created in the event of a full-scale American pullback, or whether it wants to do so anyway. With the signing of the Cambodian agreement in 1991, the region of Northeast and Southeast Asia is notable for its relative lack of trouble spots. This is in sharp contrast not only to the past few decades, but also to quite a few other parts of the world. As the largest and militarily most powerful player in the region of Eastern Asia, China is especially well placed to contribute to the maintenance of peace and stability there.

Notes

1 Michael Yahuda, *China's Foreign Policy After Mao*, Macmillan, London, 1983, p. 225.

[2] Nayan Chanda, 'National Reconciliation in Kampuchea: The Road Ahead', in Donald H. McMillen (ed.), *Conflict Resolution in Kampuchea*, Centre for the Study of Australia–Asia Relations, Brisbane, 1989, p. 60.

[3] 'A Lesson in Ideology', *Far Eastern Economic Review*, vol. 154, no. 47, 21 November 1991, pp. 10–11.

[4] ibid.

[5] 'A New Era for Sino-Indonesian Relations', *Beijing Review*, vol. 33, no. 34, 20–26 August 1990, p. 8.

[6] The Australian Broadcasting Corporation's Kate Wall reported on 23 October 1992 that *Beijing Review* had carried out a survey attributing such views to 85 per cent of those surveyed, but that the Chinese authorities suppressed the findings in the interests of good Sino-Japanese relations.

[7] Xinhua News Agency report of 10 August 1991, in *Summary of World Broadcasts*, FE/1148, p. A3/1.

[8] Russell Trood, 'From Co-operation to Conflict: Australia and China in 1989', in Colin Mackerras, Kevin Bucknall, and Russell Trood, *The Beijing Tragedy: Implications for China and Australia,* Centre for the Study of Australia–Asia Relations, Griffith University, Brisbane, 1989, p. 57.

[9] Garry Woodard, 'Australia–China: The Broadening Base of Relations', in Dunn, Hugh, and Fung, Edmund (eds), *Sino-Australian Relations: The Record, 1972–1985,* Centre for the Study of Australia–Asia Relations, Griffith University, Brisbane, 1985, p. 30.

[10] 'Australia and China: Looking Back — And Forward', address of 17 April 1991 by the Australian Minister for Foreign Affairs and Trade, Senator Gareth Evans, *Australian Foreign Affairs and Trade, The Monthly Record,* vol. 62, no. 4, April 1991, p. 136.

18 Conclusion

THE various chapters of this book have focused attention on particular aspects of the central themes of modernisation and reform. It is the task of the this final chapter to evaluate China's success in modernisation and reform, and to comment on the situation in the early 1990s as well as the prospects for the future.

Modernisation and reform: An evaluation

It is impossible to make an evaluation of anything without stating criteria. In the present study, the criteria for modernisation and reform are those which Deng Xiaoping and his followers adopted in the late 1970s, and which are discussed in the Introduction. There is in fact an enormous literature on modernisation which it is impossible and unnecessary to treat here. Suffice it to say that the most important strands of 'modernisation' put forward by Western modernisation theorists are in most respects not very different from those advocated by the Deng leadership from 1978 on. China is a long way from being the 'post-modern' society found in the advanced industrialised countries.

Assuming the criteria proposed by the Deng Xiaoping leadership and mentioned in the Introduction, China has indeed achieved quite a few successes in its program of modernisation and reform. Compared with 1978, when the Third Plenum of the Eleventh

Central Committee ushered in the period of reform, the country is indeed much more industrialised, with output far higher than it was then. China has introduced and adopted far more technology, some of it of a level much higher than was found before 1978. Even in remote villages it is quite normal in the early 1990s to see a tractor or some other form of motorised facility. The general standard of living rose enormously all over the country during the 1980s and into the 1990s for the overwhelming majority of people. On the other hand, it is important not to overstate the level of development. There are still quite a few places which are still not served by any electricity grid and survive on their own generators or batteries. Poverty is still widespread.

In terms of the political situation, Deng's modernisation has also met its formal goals, although along a rockier road than expected. There have been several major power struggles, with chosen successors to leadership Hu Yaobang and Zhao Ziyang falling by the wayside under untoward or extremely unfortunate circumstances. Yet as of the early 1990s, the CCP has remained in power — one of the few Marxist–Leninist parties to resist the worldwide trend in favour of their overthrow. The notions of 'socialism with Chinese characteristics' and 'the initial stage of socialism', which appear to owe a great deal to Deng Xiaoping, are still official policy as this book goes to press in 1993.

The law system has changed fundamentally in the 1980s and, despite the disaster of the Beijing massacre, legal reform remains on the agenda. Human rights are very badly served if understood according to the Western notion which emphasises the rights of the individual against the state. On the other hand, China has not done too badly since 1978 if the basic human right is considered as subsistence, as Deng's media have so repeatedly insisted in recent years that it should. Western-style democracy does not appear imminent, but it was never part of Deng Xiaoping's modernisation program to preside over its introduction in the first place. The emergence of the 'civil society', in which citizens can take part in political, administrative and economic mechanisms autonomously from the state, is a notable factor in China since 1978. On the other hand, it remains weak and shows no signs of reaching the stage where it can challenge the leadership of the CCP.

In the sphere of the mind, Deng Xiaoping has been in his own terms of modernisation successful in some respects, but much less so in others. The notion of socialism has undergone radical reinterpretation, but that was precisely what Deng Xiaoping wanted. The education system is much more open than it was and it has been reasonably successful in bringing basic literacy and numeracy to the population, and it may even be producing more 'modern' attitudes in most people. On the other hand, able people are attracted towards the teaching profession less than they were, and the system does not appear to have convinced the youth of the superiority of socialism. Traditional ideas and culture have made a real comeback, including Confucianist values and classical arts. Religious practice is incomparably freer than it was, but Deng probably did not bargain for the very substantial religious revival which his policies have spawned and might not regard some of its manifestations as 'modern'.

One issue which the Deng leadership always saw as crucial to the success of modernisation was that of controlling population growth. In this respect China has implemented a highly controversial and radical policy, the cornerstone of which is to prevent couples from producing more than one child. The results have been mixed. On the one hand the policy has not been nearly as successful in reducing the population growth rate as the government had wished, but on the other, China's population by the early 1990s would have been far higher without the policy than it was. The need to restrict population has assisted the re-strengthening of some traditional values — in particular, the one-child policy has resulted in the promotion of the ancient desire for sons and even the revival of female infanticide.

A balanced evaluation of reform and modernisation from the late 1970s to the early 1990s would generally be positive if the criteria used are the goals which Deng and his cohort set for themselves in the late 1970s. In their terms, China is undoubtedly a more 'modern' country in the early 1990s than it was in 1978. On the other hand, the foregoing account makes clear that the beginnings of the modernisation process have come at a considerable cost. Other than those already mentioned, problems have included ecological degradation, widening inequalities, official corruption and cynicism and disillusionment among the intelligentsia and youth.

As economic development has gathered momentum, so also has damage to the environment. The problem was highlighted on a worldwide basis by the holding of the Earth Summit in Rio de Janeiro in June 1992, but China is affected with particular severity by environmental problems, above all because of its enormous population. Industrial and economic development has traditionally brought with it poisoning of the atmosphere and of water and soil, the cutting down of forests, and noise incompatible with a decent lifestyle. Although China's policy on the environment is reasonably enlightened, the forces fighting for economic development are likely, in case of conflict, to win out against those trying to protect the environment. Up to now, China has by no means been rich enough to give top priority to that kind of clean industry which will develop the economy without damaging the environment. Its insistent demands for funds and technology from the advanced industrialised world to help with its sustainable development have been only partly successful.

To a large extent, inequalities were expected by the Deng leadership as part of the modernisation process — in fact, they were even welcomed. As early as March 1978, Deng Xiaoping himself demanded adherence to the socialist principle of 'distribution according to the quantity and quality of an individual's work',[1] so that reward and income reflect work and ability, not need. The CCP continually lambasted the preceding Maoist leadership for promoting the 'iron rice bowl' which kept people in employment, however incompetent or lazy they were. Yet probably the extent of these still growing inequalities has gone well beyond what the Deng leadership bargained for. The growth of inequalities affects both regions of China and classes of people within particular regions, as well as those between males and females.

The southeast of China, and above all the special economic zones, has gone ahead, and continues to advance very much faster than the rest of the country, while progress in parts of the western regions has been very much more modest. What this means is that, although all parts have progressed economically, the gap between the west and the more prosperous eastern seaboard, especially the south, has actually widened rather than narrowed.

In class terms, the reform policies, including the slogan that 'to get rich is glorious' have given entrepreneurial people their head but have been much less kind to those who had adapted themselves to the socialist and egalitarian ways of thinking which the Cultural Revolution claimed to be promoting. New rich, and even very rich, classes and people have emerged, while the social security safety net for those who cannot cope with the competition has failed to keep pace with need. Huge areas of poverty have been wiped out, but the reform period has failed seriously in its efforts to eradicate poverty on a national scale.

Gender equality of the sort advocated by some schools of Western feminism was never on the agenda for Deng Xiaoping and his followers. At the same time, Article 48 of the 1982 Constitution of the PRC lays down that women 'enjoy equal rights with men in all spheres of life, political, economic, cultural and social, including family life'.[2] The CCP and Deng Xiaoping undoubtedly regard a degree of gender equality as being 'modern'. However, while many women have benefited from the reforms, especially in the cities, the modernisation process has also allowed the strong revival of the patriarchal family in the countryside. This has militated strongly in favour of men and against gender equality. Quite a few women may well have been more equal during the Cultural Revolution than in the period of reform.

One area of failure of reform and modernisation has been in corruption, which, while ever-present in Chinese society at all times, grew rapidly in the 1980s, with cadres and CCP members using their power to make money illicitly or to oppress those subordinate to them. Deng Xiaoping and others in the leadership have frequently expressed alarm at this development — for instance, at a meeting of the Politburo on 10 April 1982, when Deng called for greater struggle against cadres guilty of economic crimes.[3] The fact that the issue of corruption loomed so large in the student demonstrations of 1989 forced the government to clamp down on it much harder after the massacre than it had done before. Yet while there have been quite a few charges laid and punishments carried out, corruption remains a serious problem in the early 1990s and shows no signs of going away.

One obvious failure of reform and modernisation for the Deng leadership is the defection of a substantial part of the intelligentsia from socialism and the CCP. Cynicism and disillusionment about 'socialism with Chinese characteristics' is widespread among this group, while many interpret it simply in terms of their own standard of living. As of the early 1990s, very few people maintained an active interest or belief in Marxism–Leninism. Many young people, especially intellectuals, dreamed only of getting out of China, preferably to the West. Those with an interest in ideological matters were increasingly interested in systems of thought alternative or even hostile to Marxism–Leninism.

The situation in the early 1990s

Although Deng Xiaoping retired from his last major official post, that of Chairman of the State Military Commission, in March 1990, he retained strong influence in important state decisions. His visit to South China early in 1992, amid a renewed blaze of publicity, strengthened his control even more (see Chapter 5). On 22 May 1992 he went to the Capital Iron and Steel Corporation in Beijing, one of the country's major large-scale industrial enterprises, and his visit became the cue for a decision by the State Council to grant it more autonomy in decision-making, especially in regulating its own foreign trade and even setting up its own banking institution. One visit by Deng was enough to contribute to the 'ongoing effort to bring more dynamism to China's large and medium-sized enterprises'.[4]

Behind the scenes, Deng was still planning the shape of the country's leadership. The Fourteenth National Congress of the CCP, held in October 1992, not only showed his political influence at its peak but was the occasion for a cult of personality for Deng greater in extent than at any previous time, although it showed no signs of approaching even remotely the Mao cult of the 1960s and 1970s. The main slogan to emerge from the Congress was the desirability of the 'socialist market economy', with General Secretary Jiang Zemin putting forward the view that the socialist system could operate a market economy more readily than could a capitalist one. The main way of establishing this socialist market economy, according to Jiang, was to 'change the way in which state-owned enterprises operate, especially the large and medium-sized ones, and push them into the market so as to increase their vitality and efficiency',[5] which appeared to foreshadow a high degree of privatisation in the Chinese economy over the following years. The Fourteenth Congress put into place a younger and more reformist Central Committee, with the clear intention that the leadership should advocate Deng's reformist 'socialism with Chinese characteristics' for the indefinite future.

In the early 1990s most people appeared to have accepted, either willingly or reluctantly, that the post-4 June 1989 leadership would stay in power more or less intact at least until after Deng Xiaoping died. The CCP General Secretary Jiang Zemin had come to enjoy some respect, but there was still widespread doubt that he could really fulfil the role of the major leader whom China so badly needed. Despite his acknowledged intelligence, it was not clear that Li Ruihuan could really fulfil such a role either, even though he was retained in the Standing Committee of the Politburo at the First Plenum of the Fourteenth Central Committee in October 1992. To be leader of Tianjin and leader of the whole of China were seen as two quite different matters. As for the fallen General Secretary, Zhao Ziyang, he still commanded a substantial following, especially in Sichuan, where he had been so successful as CCP leader in the late 1970s. The sentencing of Zhao's former adviser Bao Tong in July 1992 provided no evidence or sign that the trial presaged a similar one for the former General Secretary himself, especially with the ending of the examination of his case in October 1992 without any threat of a trial. Bao may well have been merely a scapegoat, and Zhao could easily return to a position of favour. But that is far from suggesting that he has the potential to regain his former top position as CCP General Secretary.

In the early 1990s, Yang Shangkun and Li Peng were still widely hated and despised among the inhabitants of Beijing and the intelligentsia because of their role in the Beijing massacre. At the First Session of the Eighth National People's Congress held in March 1993, Yang Shangkun was replaced as PRC President by Jiang Zemin, who thus achieved the top formal positions in the Party, military and state spheres. Despite the reverses Li Peng suffered at the National People's Congress meeting of March 1992 (see Chapter 5), he succeeded in regaining influence to the extent that he was appointed to a second five-year term as Premier of the State Council at the National People's Congress meeting of March 1993. It was strongly rumoured that, as of 1992, Li Peng and Jiang Zemin enjoyed very good relations. In other words, the friction between them caused by the fact that Jiang Zemin got the top job as General Secretary of the CCP in preference to Li, who has received only hatred for his support of the massacre, appeared to have abated, as had the likelihood of a power struggle between them, such as the one between Zhao Ziyang and Li Peng which poisoned the atmosphere so severely in 1989. One name frequently mentioned as a rising star is Zhu Rongji, the reformist who rose to be a Vice-Premier in April 1991 and to the Standing Committee of the CCP's Politburo just after the Fourteenth Congress in 1992. It was Zhu who had followed Deng's initiative so enthusiastically and taken the lead on making the Capital Iron and Steel Corporation a model for giving great autonomy to the country's biggest economic enterprises. If anyone was in the reformist mould so favoured by Deng, it was he.

Meanwhile, the Chinese economy in the early 1990s was going from strength to strength. The recession caused by the attempt to cool down the overheated economy in the late 1980s came to an end about the middle of 1990 with the pumping back of money. This had the desired effect, making China one of the most rapidly expanding economies in the world by 1992, showing a national growth rate of over 12 per cent, with the southeast provinces, and especially Guangdong and its Shenzhen Special Economic Zone, much faster still. One journalist was prompted to write in August 1992 that 'rapid economic reform this year has opened up the Chinese economy in a fashion previously unheard of. For foreign investors, the so-called "billion consumers" are now real and spending.'[6] On the other hand, there remain problems, among which the danger of a repetition of the overheating of the late 1980s looms large.

This 'previously unheard of' economic reform resulted in accelerating privatisation of the economy and society. More and more entrepreneurs set up private businesses and companies, especially in the southeastern provinces and the Special Economic Zones there, with investors from Hong Kong and Taiwan very willing to help. The state handed over more responsibility for social services to private insurance companies, in which individuals could invest. When the 1992–93 academic year began in August 1992, nearly 15 per cent of all beginning students were self-funding, by far the highest proportion for four decades.

Ordinary people appeared to have lost interest in politics, diverting their energies into making money and, in the case of many young people, getting as much amusement from life as time and means permitted. Peasants, workers and professionals seemed content to get on with the job, doing it as well as possible. As the private sector of the economy grew, so also did private life. As of late 1992 it was still true, as one commentator put it, that 'the intellectuals remain, as a stratum, an artifact of the system they oppose'.[7] Yet they also became more able to create ideas and arts, and even publish, quite independently of the government, provided that their ideas posed no threat to the rule of the CCP. There appeared no likelihood at all of any united front between intellectuals and students, workers and entrepreneurs against the CCP; such a coalition seeming as unlikely in 1993 as it had been unsuccessful in 1989.

The CCP still commanded widespread support, especially among ordinary workers and peasants, but more because it brought stability and a rise in prosperity than because of its overt adherence to Marxism–Leninism–Mao Zedong thought. The overthrow of the Soviet Communist Party in August 1991 and the breakup of the Soviet Union at the end of the same year were signals to the CCP to try to persuade the Chinese people that only continuing Party leadership could prevent the chaos, disintegration and economic misery which had befallen the world's first socialist state. In terms of membership, the CCP grew from about 48 million in August

1989 to 51 million in October 1992,[8] about a million per year. What this suggests is that, whatever their motivation, people have enough confidence in the long-term survival in power of the CCP to think it worth joining, a fact in striking contrast to the Soviet Communist Party during its last years in power.

In its foreign relations, China's successes have been mixed in the early 1990s, being greatest in its own region. Events quite unimaginable at the beginning of the Deng era actually took place when the PRC and South Korea established diplomatic relations in August 1992 and the Japanese Emperor visited China in October the same year. China 'normalised' its relations with Vietnam in November 1991, with overland links being resumed the following year. On the other hand, in 1992 competition flared over oil resources in the Spratlys, with the potential to damage China's relations not only with Vietnam but with other countries of Southeast Asia as well.

Relations with the West have been somewhat rockier than those within the Asian region. The Beijing massacre of 1989 was a source of severe anguish to the Western powers, which continued to criticise China for its abuse of human rights. Governor Chris Patten's proposals for democratic reform in Hong Kong persisted as an irritant in Sino-British relations, with the Western powers, and the United States under President Bill Clinton in particular, expressing strong support for him for his willingness to stand up to Beijing. Meanwhile, what really worried the Chinese authorities most in 1993 about the situation in Hong Kong was that success for Patten could bring about a long-term destabilising effect in China itself or 'peaceful evolution' towards a new order in which the CCP had no role. There were elements in the Clinton administration making no secret of their hope to see the CCP overthrown. All sides saw a movement for democracy based on Hong Kong and assisted from overseas as a potential threat against CCP rule. The Western powers and Clinton's United States might be happy with such an outcome, but there was no doubt that a rising and still CCP-ruled China would resist it strongly, with the CCP even trying to use any such new cold war with the West to persuade the Chinese people to close ranks behind it.

The prospects for the future

Relations with the West were among the bleaker side of a generally rather positive situation for China in early 1993, much better than most people had expected at the time of the 1989 crisis. Yet nobody could avoid asking 'how long could all this last?' What would happen after the death of Deng Xiaoping? How long would the CCP remain in power in China? Even more dramatic: how long would China continue to exist as a state with its present borders? Would China follow the Soviet Union into disintegration and the collapse of Marxism–Leninism and the Marxist–Leninist Communist Party? How long would socialism with or without Chinese characteristics survive?

A non-PRC Chinese leader, former Singapore Prime Minister Lee Kuan Yew, predicted soon after the 1989 crisis that China would not remain backward for long. He foresaw the country choosing its own way towards development and articulated its main problem as 'how to move into a competitive, highly-productive free market economic system but without losing the Chinese Communist Party's dominance and its all-embracing control of Chinese society'.[9] It is true that predicting the future in any country is very hazardous and in China has on many occasions been shown to be notoriously dangerous. Yet Lee's views are an appropriate starting point for some tentative speculation on China's short-term future, based upon how things have developed in recent years. 'Short-term future' means the years to the end of the twentieth century.

China's experience has been very different from that of the Soviet Union in the past few years. The rank and file of the CCP have shown themselves somewhat more malleable and less reluctant to change than their counterparts in the Soviet Communist Party. But it is also important to note that Deng Xiaoping actually required somewhat less drastic changes in the CCP than did Mikhail Gorbachev in the Soviet Communist Party. Gorbachev always gave priority to political rather than economic reform, whereas Deng Xiaoping's policy was just the reverse. In China the CCP encouraged and implemented elections, but they were always local in scope and never national. Certainly they were never of the kind which could bring to power a rival of the supreme leadership, as did in fact happen when Boris Yeltsin was elected Chairman of the Russian Federation's Supreme Soviet in 1990 in spite of Gorbachev's persistent and intense opposition. It is likely that Deng Xiaoping's successors will do everything they can to prevent from attaining a position of great authority any person with the potential to overthrow the CCP, and their chances of success during the twentieth century would appear to be great.

One very major difference between China and the Soviet Union is in the state of the economy. Whereas the Soviet economy was in decline for years before the Party was overthrown in 1991, and resisted all of Gorbachev's attempts to try to improve the situation, that of China has generally been doing very well since the late 1970s, with an impressive rate of growth. It has scored notable success in moving 'into a competitive, highly-productive free market economic system'. It is never possible to predict just how long economic growth will last, but unless civil war breaks out, the chances appear very good that, for the rest of the twentieth century, China will be able to avoid depression on the scale which accompanied and to a large extent brought about the end of the Soviet Union.

One of the principal factors behind the collapse both of the Soviet Union and the Soviet Communist Party was the nationalities question. For several years, the various republics of the Soviet Union had been tugging at the centre with growing insistence. It was less than a year after the Baltic states of Lithuania, Latvia and Estonia actually achieved independence that the Soviet Union itself fell apart. Remembering that not only the Soviet Union but also Yugoslavia and Czechoslovakia fell apart in the early 1990s, the question must be asked whether the same will happen in China, which also has a nationalities problem.

The answer is probably not, at least for the rest of the twentieth century. Several factors lead to this conclusion. The first is that China regards itself as a multinational unitary state, whereas the Soviet Union, Yugoslavia and Czechoslovakia each considered themselves as collections of republics. China has a long history as a united state, although it is certainly true that the PRC placement of its borders is not nearly as long-standing as the notion that there should never be more than one Chinese emperor at any one time. On the other hand, the Soviet Union, Yugoslavia and Czechoslovakia all dated only from World War I.

Secondly, China as a state is far more strongly dominated by a single national group than the Soviet Union, Yugoslavia or Czechoslovakia. Whereas Russians were only 51.6 per cent of the total population of the Soviet Union in 1989, Han Chinese were 92 per cent of the PRC's population at about the same time. Only a few ethnic groups hold territory large enough to make an independent state even approach viability.

Of these the most important are the Tibetans and Uygurs. The 1980s did indeed see attempts at secession by both groups. They were all very easily suppressed. Without very powerful military support from outside, these attempts at secession seem unlikely to grow strong enough to effect the disintegration of China by the end of the twentieth century. Unless there is a total collapse of the central government, it appears most unlikely that even the Tibetans could gain independence from China by that time.

Another factor with the potential for splitting China is the differing degrees of loyalty to the centre of the northern provinces and those of the south. Already Guangdong, Fujian and several other provinces enjoy considerable autonomy in economic matters. However, although ideologically driven decisions by people like Li Peng may rankle with them, it is extremely unlikely that such autonomy could develop into attempts to secede from China. They would need not only totally independent economies, but also military power. It is just not in their interests to take such a step when their economy is doing so well within a stable China.

A question worth asking is whether those countries which have indeed fallen apart really constitute such positive models worthy of emulation. Were the central Chinese government to collapse and various minorities or southern provinces secede, the possibility of large-scale conflict could not be ruled out. Having seen what has actually happened in the early 1990s in the Balkans and parts of what was the Soviet Union until 1991, even the most ardent secessionist would need to think carefully before risking the kind of conflict which could ensue if China fell apart. Even under its capitalist system, Russia does not appear to be doing anything like as well as China. The history of China from ancient to modern times suggests that disintegration would be most unlikely to be peaceful.

Two factors which played a very important role in the dramatic shifts of power in the countries which used to make up the Soviet Union were the masses of Moscow and the army. In China, both were central to the events of 1989. In contrast to Moscow during the attempted *coup d'état* against Gorbachev in August 1991, the Chinese People's Liberation Army (PLA) sided firmly with the Communist Party. Although dormant as of 1993, the student movement could easily reassert itself in the future, especially some time after the death of Deng Xiaoping. If the past is any guide, however, the PLA is more likely to be a crucial player in determining which group or party comes to power than student or other demonstrators. The history of the PLA would make it unlikely to support any party but the CCP, although which faction it would favour in the wake of Deng's death is uncertain.

Even if the PRC survives the twentieth century within its present borders and controlled by the CCP, there is no guarantee that capitalism will not tend to replace socialism. Already the private market economy has grown enormously at the expense of the planned centralised economy. Capitalist phenomena such as private hiring and firing of labour, private investment and private ownership of the means of production have tended to increase. While the commanding heights of the economy are still very much in the hands of the state sector, this could change in the coming years, even with the CCP remaining in power. Capitalist phenomena such as stock exchanges are already beginning in China and are highly likely to grow in the coming period. Perhaps most important of all, the prevailing ethos of wishing to get rich as quickly as possible is likely to undermine socialist patterns of thinking. Chinese people appear more interested in accumulating money and capital and in improving their standard of living than in pushing for a more equal society or preventing what socialists regard as economic exploitation. The Singapore model, a centrally controlled system with free-ranging capitalism, appears to have great appeal in China.

It is thus quite likely that the CCP will see in the twenty-first century still in power in China, still controlling roughly — or, apart from the addition of Hong Kong and Macao, even exactly — those territories it administers as of early 1993. Perhaps Hong Kong will influence the mainland of China just as much as, or more than, the other way around. 'Socialism with Chinese characteristics' may blend into and turn out rather similar to 'capitalism with Chinese characteristics'.

Notes

1 Deng Xiaoping, 'Adhere to the Principle "To Each According to His Work"', *Selected Works of Deng Xiaoping (1975–1982)*, Foreign Languages Press, Beijing, 1984, p. 117.

2 See *Beijing Review*, vol. 25, no. 52, 27 December 1982, p. 17.

3 'Combat Economic Crime', *Selected Works of Deng Xiaoping*, p. 380.

4 *Beijing Review*, vol. 35, no. 33, 17–23 April 1992, p. 4.

5 *Beijing Review*, vol. 35, no. 42, 19–25 October 1992, p. 6.

6 Florence Chong, in *The Australian*, 26 August 1992, p. 25.

7 David Kelly, 'Chinese Intellectuals in the 1989 Democracy Movement', in George Hicks (ed.), *The Broken Mirror: China After Tiananmen*, Longman, Essex, 1990, pp. 46–47.

8 See these figures in Colin Mackerras and Amanda Yorke, *The Cambridge Handbook of Contemporary China*, Cambridge University Press, Cambridge, 1990, p. 63 and *Beijing Review*, vol. 35, no. 38, 21–27 September 1992, p. 8.

9 'China Will Not Remain Backward', interview in Hong Kong on 9 January 1990, in *Lee Kuan Yew on China and Hongkong after Tiananmen*, Lianhe Zaobao, Singapore,1991, p. 26.

Select Bibliography

THIS bibliography is not intended to be complete. Rather, it is meant to provide a brief selection of useful books relevant to this subject and to be helpful to anyone seeking further reading. Most of the books listed were recent at the time the script was completed, meaning that they were published after 1985. Only books in the English language are included. For a further recent, annotated bibliography of China with the focus on the period of reform from 1978 onwards, see Colin Mackerras and Amanda Yorke, *The Cambridge Handbook of Contemporary China*, Cambridge University Press, Cambridge, 1991, pp. 120–45.

Books relevant to several chapters

Benewick, Robert, and Wingrove, Paul (eds), *Reforming the Revolution, China in Transition*, Macmillan, Houndmills and London, 1988. The focus here is on the decade or so after the death of Mao Zedong, that is, from 1976 to 1986. The coverage includes politics, the political structure, political participation, economics, the countryside, technology, health, the household, education, literature and foreign relations.

Bonavia, David, *Deng*, Longman, Hong Kong, 1989. This biography of Deng Xiaoping traces his career from childhood to the mid-1980s, and also covers particular aspects of this multi-faceted leader, such as 'the reformer', 'the statesman', 'the commander-in-chief' and 'the thoughts of Deng'. The author, a very distinguished journalist, died shortly after finishing this work in May 1988, so it takes no account of the crucial events of 1989.

Cheng, Joseph Y.S. (ed.), *China, Modernization in the 1980s*, The Chinese University Press, Hong Kong; Allen & Unwin Australia, Sydney, 1989. This large and fairly comprehensive volume contains chapters by various authorities on Party and civil service reforms, ideology, price reform, education, science and technology, agriculture, banking and other topics.

Dietrich, Craig, *People's China, A Brief History*, Oxford University Press, New York, 1986. This is a chronological and analytical history of the PRC from 1949 to 1985. It is scholarly and informative, but written in an accessible style.

Gittings, John, *China Changes Face, The Road from Revolution 1949–1989*, Oxford University Press, Oxford, 1990. First published in 1989, the new edition contains a thoughtful chapter on the Beijing massacre and its aftermath. The book traces the history of the PRC from its beginnings and argues that the revolution has failed and that the Chinese Communist Party has lost its mandate. One of the main questions for the 1990s is who will take the place of the Chinese Communist Party (p. 291).

Goodman, David and Segal, Gerald (eds), *China at Forty, Mid-Life Crisis?*, Clarendon Paperbacks, Oxford, 1989. In nine chapters, this book takes up ideological, political, social, economic and foreign policy issues. While it has coverage on the whole period of the PRC, the focus is on the 1980s, especially the second half of the decade. An excellent introduction by Gerald Segal presents a sober but not altogether bleak balance sheet of China's problems, achievements and future prospects. This book, heavily revised and updated to focus more on the late 1980s and 1990, was reissued by the same publisher under the title *China in the Nineties, Crisis Management and Beyond.*

Harding, Harry, *China's Second Revolution: Reform After Mao*, The Brookings Institution, Washington, 1987. There are three parts to this book, on the origins of post-Mao reforms, the reform policies themselves, and the future of reform. Economic reform is discussed within the political context, including both the main political cleavages and conflicts and the efforts at political reform. Harding considers the period of reform to be a second revolution, but acknowledges the possibility of a conservative backlash against it.

Hinton, William, *The Great Reversal, The Privatization of China, 1978–1989*, Monthly Review Press, New York, 1990. Hinton's focus is on agriculture in the period from 1978 to 1989. He strongly attacks the reform policies and argues that privatisation 'all but guarantees agricultural stagnation' (p. 173).

Mackerras, Colin and Yorke, Amanda, *The Cambridge Handbook of Contemporary China*, Cambridge University Press, Cambridge, 1991. The coverage here is factual, with many facts and figures, rather than interpretative. Included are a chronology, and chapters on politics, eminent figures, population, the minority nationalities and the economy.

Townsend, James R. and Womack, Brantly, *Politics in China*, Little, Brown and Co., Boston, Toronto, 3rd edn, 1986. This focuses on the Chinese political culture and system. It covers such topics as the origins of the communist political system, the institutional framework, ideology and change, political interests and the government process. This edition takes account of both the period down to 1976 and the few years following.

Chapter 2

Brugger, Bill, *China: Liberation and Transformation 1942–1962*, and *China: Radicalism to Revisionism 1962–1979*, 2 vols, Croom Helm, London, 1981. This is an excellent general history of China, taking the story just past the beginning of the reform period. It is thorough and thoughtful.

Dittmer, Lowell, *China's Continuous Revolution: The Post-Liberation Epoch, 1949–1981*, University of California Press, Berkeley and Los Angeles, 1987. This scholarly work is based on a wide variety of sources. It examines contemporary Chinese politics as a case study of continuous revolution and finds that China began to approach the status of a post-revolutionary phase from the early 1980s.

Gao Yuan, *Born Red: A Chronicle of the Cultural Revolution*, Stanford University Press, Stanford, 1987. This is among a number of books denouncing the Cultural Revolution, written by people who actually took part in it. The author tells of the disasters which he brought both on himself and others through his revolutionary activities from 1966 to 1969.

MacFarquhar, Roderick, *The Origins of the Cultural Revolution, 1: Contradictions among the People 1956–1957*, Columbia University Press, 1974, 1987; and *The Origins of the Cultural Revolution, 2: The Great Leap Forward 1958–1960*, Columbia University Press, New York, 1983, 1987. These two volumes are a pathbreaking study of Chinese politics in the years leading up to the Cultural Revolution. Their aim is to explain the Cultural Revolution.

MacFarquar, Roderick and Fairbank, John K. (eds), *The Cambridge History of China, Volume 14: The People's Republic, Part 1: The Emergence of Revolutionary China, 1949–1965*, Cambridge University Press, Cambridge, 1987. This is among the last of the many volumes of the *Cambridge History of China* and the first on the PRC. The authors discuss politics, economics, culture, education and foreign relations.

White, Lynn T. III, *Policies of Chaos, The Organizational Causes of Violence in China's Cultural Revolution*, Princeton University Press, Princeton, New Jersey, 1989. Covering the history of the PRC down to 1968, this book focuses on the causes of the Cultural Revolution, and draws implications for the theory of revolution. 'Official status groups, tight patronage, and policies of fear were the main causes of the Cultural Revolution as trauma.' (p. 310) The author is optimistic about China's future, believing no repetition of the Cultural Revolution is likely.

Yue Daiyun and Wakeman, Carolyn, *To the Storm: The Odyssey of a Revolutionary Chinese Woman*, University of California Press, Berkeley, 1985. This book describes the life and times of literature specialist Yue Daiyun from the late 1950s until the late 1970s. Denounced as a rightist, she underwent severe hardships and humiliations, particularly during the Cultural Revolution.

Chapters 3, 4 and 5

Barmé, Geremie, and Jaivin, Linda (eds), *New Ghosts, Old Dreams, Chinese Rebel Voices*, Times Books, Random House, New York, 1992. This book offers several different categories of first-hand anti-government items written by Chinese people. The great majority are very contemporary, coming from the 1980s or 1990s. The first section, entitled 'The Cry', concerns the protest movement of 1989.

Burns, John P. and Rosen, S. (eds), *Policy Conflicts in Post-Mao China, A Documentary Survey, with Analyses*, M.E. Sharpe, Armonk and London, 1986. A general introduction surveys Chinese politics since 1976 and discusses the use of primary sources. The documents themselves are categorised according to 'structure and process' (e.g. ideology, political participation and bureaucracy) and 'policy arenas', such as industry, agriculture, education and population.

Derbyshire, Ian, *Politics in China, from Mao to Deng*, Chambers, Edinburgh, 1987. The main focus of this brief survey of Chinese history under the PRC is on the late 1970s and 1980s. There are chapters on political organisation and philosophy, economic and social developments, and defence and foreign policies.

Feigon, Lee, *China Rising: The Meaning of Tiananmen*, Ivan R. Dee, Chicago, 1990. One of quite a few substantial studies of the crisis and crackdown of 1989. The main feature is the historical parallels drawn, especially with the Cultural Revolution.

Hicks, George (ed.), *The Broken Mirror: China After Tiananmen*, Longman, Essex, 1990. A fine collection of essays by many leading specialists on China, revolving around the background and aftermath of the Beijing massacre. There are five sections, including the history of what happened, the 'broken mirror' (i.e. the change in Western images of and policy towards China) and 'whither China?' There are short sections of documents and biographies.

Mackerras, Colin, Bucknall, Kevin and Trood, Russell, *The Beijing Tragedy: Implications for China and Australia*, Centre for the Study of Australia–Asia Relations, Brisbane, 1989. This is a study of the lead-up to the Beijing massacre, the 'tragedy' itself and its immediate aftermath. The three authors consider, respectively, the political and economic dimensions, and the implications for China's relations with Australia.

Moody, Peter R. Jr, *Chinese Politics after Mao, Development and Liberalization 1976 to 1983*, Praeger, New York, 1983. The book concerns the main aspects of China's political culture after Mao. The author summarises the changes as evolution within totalitarianism but not a departure from it.

Nathan, Andrew, *China's Crisis*, Columbia University Press, New York, 1990. Although the focus of this book is the crisis of 1989, it in fact includes essays on a range of subjects which Nathan has written earlier. Nathan's view is that it is only through democracy that China can become stable and strong.

Ogden, Suzanne, Hartford, Kathleen, Sullivan, Lawrence and Zweig, David (eds), *China's Search for Democracy: The Student and the Mass Movement of 1989*, M.E. Sharpe, Armonk and London, 1992. This book collects documents on the pro-democracy activities about the time of the 1989 movement. It explicitly includes no documents from the CCP leadership. There are six parts in chronological order, each with a theme and commentary by one of the authors.

Unger, Jonathan (ed.), *The Pro-Democracy Protests in China, Reports from the Provinces*, M.E. Sharpe, Armonk and London; Allen & Unwin, Sydney, 1991. The main feature of this book is that, while not ignoring Beijing, it deals mainly with the provinces. The majority of accounts are based on personal experience. In the introduction, Jonathan Unger discusses the different forms the movement took in various parts of China and suggests that those places near Hong Kong or Taiwan were less severely affected than those inland because they had more to lose from the failure of reform (p. 3).

Woodruff, John (ed.), *China in Search of its Future: Years of Great Reform, 1982–87*, University of Washington Press, Seattle and London, 1989. A journalist's view of China in the mid-1980s, this book is divided topically and includes chapters on the élite, rural reform and the demonstrations of late 1986. He depicts these years as bringing about very great change, including improvements in the standard of living and extent of freedom.

Chapters 6, 7 and 8

Chow, Gregory C., *The Chinese Economy*, Harper and Row, New York, London, 1985; World Scientific Publishing Company, Teaneck, NJ, 1987. This book is designed as a textbook for courses in Chinese economy for tertiary students. It attempts to apply the theories and concepts of modern economics to the Chinese economy. The economic organisation and performance of several sectors are discussed.

Crane, George T., *The Political Economy of China's Special Economic Zones*, M.E. Sharpe, Armonk, New York, 1990. This book uses the special economic zones as examples of economic policy decision-making in China. The author has adopted a 'political structuralist' approach to the study of China's special economic zones and takes the view that many of their problems and failures can be explained by looking at the nature of the Chinese state.

Jao, Y.C. and Leung, C.K. (eds), *China's Special Economic Zones: Policies, Problems and Prospects*, Oxford University Press, Hong Kong, 1986. This is a fairly comprehensive study of China's special economic zones, written mostly by Hong Kong scholars. It is divided into three parts: the physical environment; the political and legal framework; and economic and management perspectives. The data are a bit outdated now, but this is still a good work for the study of early special economic zone policies.

Journal of Comparative Economics, 'Chinese Economic Reform: How Far, How Fast', vol. 11, no. 3, September 1987. This issue is entirely devoted to a study of the Chinese economy. Its seventeen articles are edited versions of the papers presented at a conference organised in October 1986 in New York under the auspices of the Association for Comparative Economic Systems. Some articles include comparisons with other countries.

Lardy, Nicholas R., *Agriculture in China's Modern Economic Development*, Cambridge University Press, Cambridge, 1983. This book traces the development of Chinese agriculture since 1949. By examining such crucial issues as the role of agriculture, planning and allocative efficiency, prices, etc., the author is able to highlight the factors that impinge upon the performance of agriculture in China.

Longworth, John W., *China's Rural Development Miracle*, University of Queensland Press, St Lucia, 1989. This is a collection of papers presented at an international symposium organised by the International Association of Agricultural Economists in Beijing in October 1987. The book is divided into seven sections, including one solely devoted to international experience in the field of agriculture. There are also a few chapters comparing China's experience with that of other countries such as India and Canada.

Luo, Hanxian, *Economic Changes in Rural China*, New World Press, Beijing, 1985. Written by a prominent Chinese scholar, this book looks at the developments in Chinese agriculture since 1978 against a background of fundamental changes introduced since 1949. It is informative but not very analytical. A major feature of this book is the 30-odd pages of agricultural statistics for the period 1949–82.

Oborne, Michael, *China's Special Economic Zones*, The Organisation for Economic Co-operation and Development, Paris, 1986. This OECD study is devoted exclusively to the study of the economies of China's special economic zones and does not dwell on their politics. It also contains a bibliography of works on the special economic zones.

Riskin, Carl, *China's Political Economy: The Quest for Development Since 1949*, Oxford University Press, Oxford, 1987. This is a major comprehensive survey of China's economy for the period 1949–85. Written in a descriptive but scholarly style, it provides an insightful account of developments in all sectors of Chinese economy. Statistics on China's economy are also plentiful.

Chapters 9 and 10

Dirlik, Arif and Meisner, Maurice (eds), *Marxism and the Chinese Experience: Issues in Contemporary Chinese Socialism*, M.E. Sharpe, Armonk, New York, 1989. With contributions from scholars in diverse fields, this work examines contemporary Chinese Marxism, the interpretation of 'socialism', the principal dimensions of Chinese political economy and the significance of recent general trends in society and politics.

McCormick, Barrett L., *Political Reform in Post-Mao China, Democracy and Bureaucracy in a Leninist State*, University of California Press, Berkeley, Los Angeles, Oxford, 1990. Containing a chapter on law, this book focuses on political change as a whole. It concludes that the contra-diction between socialism in China and Party leadership on the one hand and 'the autonomous efficiency of liberal markets' on the other 'will remain at the center of Chinese politics for some time to come' (p. 201).

Ogden, S., *China's Unresolved Issues: Politics, Development, and Culture*, Prentice-Hall, Englewood Cliffs, NJ, 1989. This work provides useful perspectives for the understanding of Chinese politics in terms of 'traditional Chinese cultural, developmental, and socialist variables'.

Stavis, Benedict, *China's Political Reforms: An Interim Report*, Praeger, New York, 1988. The main focus of this work is the Chinese discussion of political reform, especially in 1986. Although much of the framework for change was altered by the disturbances and repression of 1987 and 1989, this analysis remains useful in revealing some of the key issues and dilemmas of political reform.

Wang, J.F.C., *Contemporary Chinese Politics: An Introduction*, 3rd edn, Prentice-Hall, Englewood Cliffs, NJ, 1989. As a straightforward introductory text, this work contains much useful information on many areas of Chinese politics.

Chapter 11

Bonavia, David, *Verdict in Peking, The Trial of the Gang of Four*, Burnett Books, London, 1984. This book contains extensive excerpts from the transcripts of the trial of Jiang Qing and various others which proceeded from November 1980 to January 1981. There is also related commentary on the Chinese political and legal system.

Brady, James P., *Justice and Politics in China: Legal Order or Continuing Revolution*, Academic Press, London, 1982. There are two parts, the first on historical background and current issues in the development of Chinese justice and society, and the second on the dialectical path of justice in the PRC. Only Chapter 9, the last one, deals with the post-Mao period.

Du Xichuan and Zhang Lingyuan, *China's Legal System: A General Survey*, New World Press, Beijing, 1990. This covers various aspects of the Chinese legal system in the 1980s, with some historical background. There are fifteen chapters, including those on the legislative system, the judicial system, the notary and attorney systems, and mediation. It is a thorough coverage, but presented very much from the official Chinese point of view.

Oldham, John R. (ed.), *China's Legal Development*, M.E. Sharpe, Armonk and London, 1986. The May 1983 issue of the *Columbia Journal of Transnational Law* was devoted to China, and most of the articles collected here derive from it. There is also a comprehensive bibliography of English-language sources on modern Chinese law. Among the topics covered are economic law and legislation, the teaching of international law in China, Western scholarship on Chinese law and international legal issues.

Chapter 12

Cannon, T. and Jenkins, A. (eds), *The Geography of Contemporary China: The Impact of Deng Xiaoping's Decade*, Routledge, London and New York, 1990. There are several chapters in this edited volume which are of relevance to the study of environmental issues in China. Chapter 4 by Derbyshire and Chapter 10 by Glaeser are particularly useful.

Glaeser, Bernhard (ed.), *Learning from China? Development and Environment in Third World Countries*, Allen & Unwin, London, 1987. This book discusses Chinese environmental policy in the context of planning in agriculture, industry, energy production and human settlements. Positive examples of environmental policies and developmental planning from China are discussed and their usefulness for other developing countries is underlined.

He Bochuan, *China on the Edge, The Crisis of Ecology and Environment*, China Books and Periodicals, San Francisco, 1991. This book was first published in Chinese in 1988. He paints an exceedingly bleak view of environmental and other policy and reality in China, warning that China is 'on the edge' of a unprecedented ecological devastation, but is less forthcoming in terms of realistic solutions.

Smil, Vaclav, *The Bad Earth: Environmental Degradation in China*, M.E. Sharpe Inc., Armonk, New York, 1984. Based on a report the author prepared for the World Bank, this book is one of the first Western studies of environmental issues in China. It contains a critical evaluation of China's environmental situation and paints a rather grim picture of it.

Chapter 13

Cleverley, John, *The Schooling of China, Tradition and Modernity in Chinese Education*, George Allen & Unwin, Sydney, London, Boston, 1985; 1991. Three of the fifteen chapters of this book cover the period since the fall of the gang of four. It treats all levels of the education system, and looks at theory as well as practice. The updated edition of 1991 includes analysis of the repercussions of the 1989 crisis.

Epstein, Irving (ed.), *Chinese Education, Problems, Policies, and Prospects*, Garland Pulbishing Inc., 1991. This is a very large and broad-ranging book, with the focus on the period of reform. Chapters include an account of the post-Mao reforms by Suzanne Pepper and also deal with early childhood, secondary and tertiary schooling, adult education, teachers and political education.

Hayhoe, Ruth, *China's Universities and the Open Door*, M.E. Sharpe, Armonk and London, 1989. The early part discusses the history of Chinese higher education and the reforms of the 1980s. Later sections have a great deal to say about China's 'knowledge relations' (p. 6) with six industrialised countries and other matters concerning China's international relations in the field of higher education.

Hayhoe, Ruth (ed.), *Contemporary Chinese Education*, M.E. Sharpe, Armonk, Croom Helm, London and Sydney, 1984. This book covers all levels of the Chinese education system, its structure and such special factors as teacher training and adult education. There are analyses of the relationship between the Chinese education system and the remainder of the community.

Pepper, Suzanne, *China's Education Reform in the 1980s, Policies, Issues, and Historical Perspectives,* China Research Monograph 36, Institute of East Asian Studies, University of California, Berkeley, 1990. This is the best available study of Chinese education in the 1980s. The study is fairly comprehensive and includes not only some historical background, but also some commentary on the aftermath of the 1989 crisis.

Chapter 14

Henderson, Gail E. and Cohen, Myron S., *The Chinese Hospital: A Socialist Work Unit*, Yale University Press, New Haven and London, 1984. This work concerns a single hospital in Wuhan, capital of Hubei, where the authors lived with their daughter for five months during 1978–80. Henderson is a sociologist and Cohen a specialist in infectious disease, the range of expertise enabling them to present a detailed picture of a single unit from a various points of view.

Jamison, Dean T. et al., *China, The Health Sector*, World Bank, Washington DC, 1984. Based on information gathered by six members of the World Bank during a visit to China in 1982, this book presents a dominantly positive but also critical view of China's achievements and problems in the field of health. It documents the serious urban bias, including in health expenditure.

Lucas, AnElissa, *Chinese Medical Modernization, Comparative Policy Continuities, 1930s–1980s*, Praeger, New York, 1982. The thrust of this highly scholarly book is to see medical modernisation in China on the basis of a framework first outlined in the 1930s. While acknowledging adjustments in policy, the author's emphasis is on continuity between the Republican period from the 1930s on and the PRC.

Chapter 15

Banister, Judith, *China's Changing Population,* Stanford University Press, Stanford, 1987. This very scholarly book covers the whole period of the PRC, but with most attention given to the post-Mao period. It covers such matters as fertility decline, mortality, late marriage and birth planning.

Croll, Elisabeth, Davin, Delia and Kane, Penny (eds), *China's One-Child Family Policy*, Macmillan, London, 1985. This covers various aspects of the one-child policy, including the policy in the cities and countryside and birth-control methods. It derives from a workshop in 1983. While recognising the problems in the one-child family policy, the authors tend to be defensive about it.

Kane, Penny, *The Second Billion, Population and Family Planning in China*, Penguin Books, Ringwood, Victoria, 1987. This book, which is considerably smaller than Banister's, traces the development of the PRC's population policies in great detail, and also covers family planning in both urban and rural areas. At the time she wrote it, the author was of the view that China's family-planning program had been 'successful on a scale not previously seen anywhere' (p. 2).

Wang Jiye and Hull, Terence H. (eds), *Population and Development Planning in China*, Allen & Unwin, Sydney, 1991. This book takes up some very difficult issues connected with China's population policies, especially in the 1980s. The emphasis is on various aspects of development, including the relationship between population on the one hand, and employment, the labour force, consumption, urbanisation, the environment, social security and so on on the other. The overall tone is decidedly sympathetic to China's population policy.

Chapter 16

Harding, Harry (ed.), *China's Foreign Relations in the 1980s,* Yale University Press, New Haven and London, 1984. Designed to get Americans to take a more balanced view of China, these valuable essays cover such topics as the relationship between domestic politics and foreign policy, China in the international economy and the PRC as a regional power.

Hsiao, Gene T. and Witunski, Michael (eds), *Sino-American Normalization and its Policy Implications*, Praeger, New York, 1983. This large book covers the history of Sino-American relations in the 1970s and 1980s, as well as commentary on the Taiwan issue, educational exchange and strategic implications. There are numerous useful appendices.

Jacobsen, C.G., *Sino-Soviet Relations Since Mao: The Chairman's Legacy*, Praeger, New York, 1981. The author examines the causes of tension and conflict between China and the Soviet Union, the function of Sino-Soviet relations in China's domestic politics, the Sino-Vietnamese war and other factors. He quite rightly expected that the dominance of Deng Xiaoping over an extended period would lead to improved Sino-Soviet relations.

Kim, Samuel S. (ed.), *China and the World: New Directions in Chinese Foreign Relations*, 2nd rev. edn, Westview, Boulder, Col., and London, 1989. This work includes three essays on theoretical issues, four on China's relations with the United States, the Soviet Union and the countries of the Second and Third Worlds, and four others on specific issues like defence.

Short, Philip, *The Dragon and the Bear: China and Russia in the Eighties*, William Morrow, New York, 1982. This large study traces Sino-Soviet relations through the PRC down to 1981. Along with analysis of Sino-Soviet relations is extensive commentary on Chinese and Soviet society and politics.

Stuart, Douglas T., and Tow, William T. (eds), *China. The Soviet Union, and the West, Strategic and Political Dimensions in the 1980s*, Westview Press, Boulder, Col., 1982. This highly scholarly collective work is based on a conference held in West Germany in 1980. It contains four parts, 'determinants of Chinese and Soviet foreign policy behavior', the military dimension, 'regional competition between Beijing and Moscow' and 'policy considerations for the West'.

Chapter 17

Andrews, E.M., *Australia and China, the Ambiguous Relationship*, Melbourne University Press, Melbourne, 1985. This book provides an excellent account of the history of Sino-Australian relations up to the Fraser years. There are two chapters on the China policy of the Liberal Party.

Hoffmann, Steven A., *India and the China Crisis*, University of California Press, Berkeley, London, 1990. This book looks at the Sino-Indian dispute through a detailed study of foreign policy and defence decision-making in India during the period 1959–63. It challenges some of Neville Maxwell's (the author of *India's China War*) assumptions concerning the origins of Sino-Indian border war of 1962.

Ross, Robert S., *The Indochina Tangle: China's Vietnam Policy 1975–79*, Columbia University Press, New York, 1988. This book uses a chronological approach to study the Indo-China problems, especially China's involvement in them. There is extensive use of primary sources from China, Vietnam, the United States and the Soviet Union.

Yahuda, Michael, *Towards the End of Isolationism: China's Foreign Policy After Mao*, The Macmillan Press Ltd, London, 1983. Although relatively out of date, this book provides an analytical account of developments in China's foreign policy. The coverage of China's relations with its neighbours is brief but incisive. It attempts to distinguish between the geopolitical and societal dimensions of China's foreign relations.

Index